Perspectives on the Politics of Abortion

Edited by **TED G. JELEN**

PRAEGER

Westport, Connecticut
London

Library of Congress Cataloging-in-Publication Data

Perspectives on the politics of abortion / edited by Ted G. Jelen.
p. cm.
Includes bibliographical references and index.
ISBN 0–275–95225–8 (alk. paper)
1. Abortion—United States. 2. Abortion—Government policy—United States. 3. Abortion—Law and legislation—United States. 4. Abortion—Religious aspects. I. Jelen, Ted. G.
HQ767.5.U5P48 1995
363.4'6—dc20 95–6937

British Library Cataloguing in Publication Data is available.

Library of Congress Catalog Card Number: 95–6937
ISBN: 0–275–95225–8

First published in 1995

Praeger Publishers, 88 Post Road West, Westport, CT 06881
An imprint of Greenwood Publishing Group, Inc.

Printed in the United States of America

The paper used in this book complies with the Permanent Paper Standard issued by the National Information Standards Organization (Z39.48–1984).

10 9 8 7 6 5 4 3 2 1

Contents

Acknowledgements

This volume had its beginnings at a conference on the politics of abortion, held at Illinois Benedictine College (IBC) in 1993, that was funded by a generous grant from the Abbey Endowment Fund at Illinois Benedictine.

In addition to the contributors to this volume and the Abbey Endowment Fund, I would like to thank Richard C. Becker, Abbot RP Rev. Hugh R. Anderson, Robert Preston, Phyllis Kittel, Robert Tenczar, Karen Gleason, David Dibblee, Diana Spiller, Sara Scheiner, and Lisa Jossey-Junco for their valuable assistance.

I would also extend my deepest appreciation to the members of the IBC community as a whole, who have provided the sort of environment in which this type of scholarship can flourish and prosper.

Ted G. Jelen
June, 1995

1

Introduction: Beyond Polemics and Toward Healing

Carol J. C. Maxwell

One Thursday evening in 1993 I settled down to read "Who Killed the Innocent--Michael Griffin or Dr. David Gunn?" in that August's edition of *Life Advocate*, a magazine that is popular among pro-life direct activists.[1] I had not encountered so blatant an advocacy of violence in four years of research among these activists. After citing many incidents in which biblical characters did "whatever was necessary to protect innocent life," the author argued that the zealous and deadly act of an individual can "turn God's wrath away from the people," that a person who kills guilty individuals will spare the people as a whole from "destruction."[2] The author quoted Biblical precedents and injunctions that justified his position and cited constraining moral qualifications for such actions. He went on to praise civil disobedients (people who sat-in to obstruct abortion patients), then suggested that they "should also consider the justice of taking all action necessary to protect innocent life."[3] The author brought his point home by explicitly enjoining readers to "take all just actions necessary (including deadly force) to protect the lives of the unborn."

I tried reading excerpts to my husband, but he lost interest after the first alarming statement and defended his lack of interest by saying that the rest was predictable. At 6 a.m. the next morning that predictability seemed more sinister than boring. We both wondered at the force of that rhetoric after our radio woke us with the news that yet another abortionist had been shot by a pro-lifer--this time a woman, acting in concert, a long time member of the pro-life direct action movement, and not a lone outsider like Griffin.[4] Less than one year later, Paul Hill the author of the article I read that Thursday evening committed the double murder of physician John Britton and James Barrett, his bodyguard, while wounding June Barrett in the process. More recently, there were multiple shootings at two abortion clincs in Brookline, Massacusetts, on December 30, 1994.[5]

In the late 1970s a very few of the first pro-life direct activists concluded that the most logical response to abortion was to kill abortionists, but they had no intention of acting on that conclusion. Their cultural heritage and philosophical commitments precluded murder. During the 1980s the population participating in pro-life direct action altered, changing the range and character of the logic driving their small but persistent movement. While the vast majority of pro-lifers (those involved in either conventional or direct activism) aver they would not consider participating in violent acts, the tenor of rhetoric in their movement has altered and so have the bounds of their activism. These changes may continue to complicate abortion politics. The effects of abortion legislation depend largely on their reception by opponents as well as proponents. In this sense, legal resolutions are contingent on the social and psychological character of the parties who attend to them.

Early on, the abortion debate stalled in a dangerous position; rather than resolving antithetical arguments, each side has persistently attempted to exert power over the other[6] (while women's needs remain underserved). Past arguments need revision but in order to change, we may need to rethink the nature of abortion and pregnancy, the legal basis for abortion, the cumulative effects of abortion on the lives of women who have undergone the procedure, and the role of the abortion debate in our society. The chapters in this volume explore past choices made in support of and in opposition to abortion, current societal and political attitudes toward abortion, and new ways to conceptualize abortion and direct the debate over its legal status. Their authors challenge entrenched arguments and positions, and push thought forward in this contentious area of deliberation and practice.

INDIVIDUALITY AND SOCIAL CONTROL

Debate over the legal status of abortion continues to affect women's lives adversely despite the access to services authorized by *Roe v. Wade* in 1973.[7] This persistent contention circumscribes women's health care and channels their life courses. Having become politicized, women's health care and life choice options depend, in part, on the will of the population and the behavior of politicians.

While *Roe* presumably reduced the incidence of illegal abortion and eliminated the need for women to frame themselves in terms of psychopathologies in order to obtain abortions, *Roe* did not eradicate the negative consequences of the legal status of abortion on women. Rather, *Roe* replaced one set of historically derived (and not inherently necessary) entanglements between legal, political, personal, and health considerations with another. The continuing interaction between societal attitudes and conditions and the experience of women seeking abortion illustrates the imposition that broad social circumstances place on individuals' health, self-identities, and life courses.

Women's access to abortion depends ostensibly on the moral consensus and political will of the voting population expressed through the political behavior of elected officials, yet in the realm of abortion politics, these two factors tend to diverge. In Chapter 3 of this volume, Clyde Wilcox points out that political elites tend to take polar positions on the legal status of abortion. In sharp contrast, most American citizens hold compromised, nuanced positions on abortion's legal (and moral) status; only very small minorities hold polarized views either supporting or opposing access to abortion regardless of the circumstances surrounding a pregnancy.

When state legislation concerning abortion diverges from attitudes toward abortion expressed by the citizenry (in public opinion surveys) women are effectively controlled by a few individuals (usually white males). Such divergence between public opinion and political commitment creates a context that shapes individuals' health care and life choice options but may not represent their will, beliefs, or interests.

RE-EXAMINING THE ICONS

The pressure to recriminalize abortion has encouraged supporters to defend *Roe v. Wade* and to resist criticism of the legal theory upon which it rests. *Roe* established a way of living in our society, and such modifications of practice modify beliefs about what is natural and right.[8] Pre-*Roe* pro-choicers argued that women had the right to abort despite laws and societal norms to the contrary. These early advocates of reproductive freedom *attained Roe*; *Roe* solved problems they either observed or experienced.[9] While *Roe may* have benefitted these supporters, it certainly vindicated them. Since subsequent pro-choicers grew up with *Roe*, they may think of access to abortion as a natural right, a part of their social environment; and this assumption may color their political behavior regarding abortion. While pro-lifers argue that their stance on abortion is a return to the founding principles of our society and pro-choicers fit their stance into a long, historical trend toward liberalization, actual societal attitudes toward abortion may be much more nuanced and fluid than either of the posited histories.

For example, in a study of attitudes toward abortion, Elizabeth Adell Cook, Ted G. Jelen, and Clyde Wilcox found less support for abortion among white people who reached age 18 during the 1970s and 1980s than among cohorts who matured during the 1960s. The authors considered the possibility that (1) the right-to-life movement swayed the Reagan-era cohort with its rhetoric, (2) the Reagan-era cohort was more conservative in general and their attitudes toward abortion were only a part of their general conservatism, (3) young Republicans were persuaded by Reagan and Bush that opposition to abortion was correct policy, and (4) younger whites were influenced by a media message that presented abortion as morally problematic.[10] The authors found some evidence to support the first three explanations but tentatively dismissed them in favor of the fourth. Cook, Jelen, and Wilcox also illustrated more support for abortion among the Great Depression cohort than the World War II cohort, followed by a large increase in support that culminated in the 1960s. They attributed the increased support for abortion across these older cohorts to changes in gender roles.

Along this line, James Mohr has documented widespread use of folk abortifacients in the 1800s, and folklore suggests that such usage continued into the first few decades of the 1900s.[11] Perhaps attitudes toward *legalization* of abortion do not fully reflect attitudes toward abortion *practice* among people with such experiences. I would suggest that (at least at the micro-level of the family) shifts from rural to urban and suburban living during that period altered everyday experiences and reduced communications between generations regarding folk practices, including abortion. Because such changes alter the attitudes that underlie and grow out of earlier practices,[12] postwar cohorts were left to find their own basis for abortion attitudes in the public arena and, consequently, in the discourse of rights. The connection I draw here between demographic trends, individual experiences, and attitudes toward abortion is speculative. It suggests an interplay between experiences and attitudes within a society over time. Further research into the attitudes of individuals in different eras toward abortion gained through micro-historical methods might provide an enlightening comparison of political attitudes and practical approaches to abortion.

As contention over abortion persists, supporters may be wise to continue searching for alternative precedents, policies, and philosophies. Fidelity may undermine victory; a dogmatic defense of *Roe* might leave the faithful clinging to a legal doctrine that could indeed be overturned. In Chapter 5 of this volume, Kent Sezer discusses a legal basis for liberal access to abortion; he supports the pro-choice side, although he begins by examining *Roe*'s weaknesses. Sezer points out that *Roe* fails to clarify why a right to privacy exists, an oversight he attempts to rectify.

Sezer roots his argument for *Roe* in the concept of substantive due process, a controversial concept that asks whether the state has a legitimate interest in imposing a restriction on people. He notes that individual citizens empower the Constitution and, through that document, empower the government. Legislation that restricts citizens' self-definitions would constrain the very source of its own power and create a circularity (in which the government shapes its own source) that should be avoided. Consequently, Sezer argues that individual freedom to define oneself must be protected. He concludes that because parenthood is a fundamental aspect of individuals' self-concepts, it cannot legitimately be regulated by the government.

Could the argument Sezer presents reinforce *Roe* by grounding the concept of a right to privacy? He contends that his argument provides a reliable basis for access to abortion since it rests on a basic (and acknowledged) principle in our nation's legal tradition. Sezer's argument locates the substantive due process concept in history and in *Roe*, which he contends is a piece of progressive jurisprudence. Consequently, his argument comments on the correct application of substantive due process, which was formerly used to strike down progressive legislation.

Eileen McDonagh bases her argument on fundamental concepts in our legal system accepted by both pro-choice and pro-life proponents (see Chapter 2 of this volume). The genius of her analysis is that it examines a medically-based concept of pregnancy in light of concepts integral to our legal tradition and to both pro-choice and pro-life philosophies.

McDonagh examines legal precedents relevant to the relationships pregnancy involves. In the process she provides an alternative conceptual and moral basis supporting free access to abortion. Her rationale could displace current choice rhetoric, de-center the polarized abortion debate, and empower pro-choice advocates seeking broad government funding of abortion.

McDonagh adopts a pro-life concept that is often ignored or poorly contested in pro-choice rhetoric--the personhood of the fetus. Conceding (or acknowledging) the humanity of the fetus, McDonagh brings the pro-life side of the abortion debate into dialogue with the pro-choice concern for individual liberty and autonomy. She provides a basis for reopening discussion that has become polemic and overweighing. McDonagh's model is relational and invites contemplation of the relative scope and authority of personal autonomy and interpersonal obligation.

INADEQUACY

In 1992 pro-choicers began to realize solid political victories, with strong support shown for pro-choice candidates, President Clinton's efforts to reverse restrictions on abortion, shifts in the Supreme Court away from a conservative and toward a liberal stance on abortion, and, in 1994, passage of the Freedom of Access to Clinic Entrances Act (FACE). Indeed, the Republican Congressional majority elected in 1994 has not appeared to place a high priority on reversing these trends. However, legal access to abortion has not been accompanied by sufficient development of the social supports some women need in order to have choices regarding their pregnancies. Unfortunately, values and social institutions change more slowly than leadership and legislation.

Legalization alone is insufficient to provide choice. As journalist Linda Wertheimer observed during a radio broadcast, some women who wanted to carry pregnancies to term were told by their men to "get rid of it or I'll get rid of you" long before *Roe*.[13] Such clandestine coercion continues. For many women, parenting and achieving professional progress conflicted before *Roe*, and the dilemma posed by these dual objectives has not abated. Legalization allows women more control over their professional pathways but does not resolve the conflict between these two potentially desirable objectives. Legalization may, in fact, excuse discriminatory treatment of women who choose to parent; because legalization of abortion has made continuing pregnancies optional, such women may be stigmatized as having chosen against professional advancement. By making childbearing optional without sufficiently altering our society's attitudes, values, and infrastructure, legalization of abortion sometimes appears to validate pressure on women to choose options they might not prefer.

RETRENCHMENT

Polarized politics have resulted in a solid pro-choice political victory, but this victory itself may restrict abortion by excluding its opponents and encouraging drastic responses that effectively reduce the availability of abortion. In the past, political circumstances that favored legal abortion tended to galvanize the pro-life movement's direct action faction and increase its support. For example, in the late 1970s many former conventional pro-lifers came to see direct action as the movement's most logical and effective strategic option. They flooded the nascent direct action movement, displacing its liberal, leftist originators. These activists began to sit-in when they realized that almost a decade of conventional activism had gained them little more than the Hyde Amendment (which forbids federal funding of abortions). Longtime activists joined newcomers to sit-in despite the broad-based, diverse, extensive, and well-developed conventional activism of their time.[14] Pro-life direct action continued but diminished when President Reagan appeared to promise a victory from the top. Participation in direct action expanded in the late 1980s when disillusionment with Reagan and Bush, and with conventional politics in general, set in. As the 1980s wore on, direct activists altered the classic passive sit-in to incorporate more aggressive and destructive tactics.

The extreme violence that arose in 1993-1994 was a logical extension of several trends in the pro-life movement. The roots of this violence were, perhaps, innocuous enough, but demographic and environmental changes converged to produce acts outside the ken of most pro-lifers.

The first pro-life direct activists based their tactics on political and strategic philosophies inspired by Mahatma Gandhi and Dr. Martin Luther King. (Many of the founders of pro-life direct action were originally peace-and-justice Catholics.) These activists formed autonomous local groups that held frequent meetings to cope with the anger and frustration they felt after sitting-in.[15] At such meetings they reaffirmed the ascendant value of nonviolence.

Subsequent direct activists lacked this ideological commitment and the training and organizational practices that had instilled it. Expansion restructured the organization of the movement, and these changes diluted the control early leaders had over the philosophical basis of this activism. In the late 1980s Christian radio programs exposed broad audiences to the idea of pro-life direct action, and this exposure facilitated the advent of Operation Rescue. Newcomers joined a loosely organized, nationwide movement that swept individuals into a sense of belonging and commitment but did not always provide the ongoing interpersonal interactions early activists found so necessary to cope with the emotionality generated by direct action.

From the mid 1980s onward demographic changes in the movement altered its ideological basis and laid the groundwork for an escalation in aggressive tactics and a potential for violence. Pro-life direct activists entering the fray from 1984 onwards either had not sprouted from the movement's Gandhian roots or had rejected them. By the late 1980s, activists said they resented the implication that a philosophy other than Christianity and a leader other than Christ should be recognized.

Operation Rescue dominated this movement during the late 1980s, and aggression and militancy were not altogether foreign to its leadership despite public protests to the contrary. Initially, input from early pro-life direct activists tempered the original exuberance expressed by Operation Rescue's founder, Randall Terry, and directed his activism along nonviolent lines. One of the early pro-life direct action leaders recalled that,

> Randy was a little wild when he first came up with the idea [to organize massive sit-ins]. When we were down in Florida at the end of '86 and everybody kind of got up and [he] started talking about, "Well, we're going to take over the building and we'll hold hostages and we'll throw machines out the window." And everybody's standing there with their mouth open looking at each other and saying, "What's going on here?" Then they all kind of sat down and talked to Randy for a while and got things back on a level keel.[16]

During 1992-1993, Operation Rescue established virtual boot camps to train (paying) volunteers how to stalk and otherwise harass and intimidate abortion providers and patients.

Over time, direct activism came to entail rhetoric and events that may have encouraged the outlier, the fringe supporter, to take violent action. Such politically unaffiliated actors accounted for virtually all abortion-related arsons, bombings, and kidnapping that occurred from the 1970s through the early 1990s.[17] When other avenues of political redress and opportunity close, such behavior can be construed as warranted personal sacrifice or mission. Michael Griffin's decision to shoot Dr. David Gunn, an abortionist in Florida, apparently illustrated this dynamic.[18]

During the spring of 1993 I wrote of the likelihood that previously nonviolent pro-life direct activists would undertake further violence in the near future. In what was for them an adverse political environment, some direct activists' deep personal commitments to stop abortion were likely to continue and their adamancy and militancy were likely to intensify. The "rescue community's" response to Griffin's use of force was ominous. Immediately following Gunn's murder, Hill (and others) wrote and publicly argued that deadly force was justifiable in defense of the *unborn*. A passionate debate took place between activists who condemned lethal violence, those who endorsed it, and others who justified but would not endorse it.

Griffin brought the possibility of deadly force into actuality, and so interjected it into the movement's discourse. Previously, such considerations had remained isolated intellectual arguments, immediately rebuked and dismissed. To the extent that discourse influences thought and action, Griffin's act may have served to increase the level of violence by altering the tenor of rhetoric. Following Gunn's murder, several conventions and publications (promoted by pro-life direct action groups distinct from Operation Rescue) featured messages not only endorsing the use of deadly force to stop abortions but providing Biblical and patriotic justifications for it. This rhetoric overtly enjoined listeners and readers to go beyond their current level of activism and embrace the use of (even deadly) force. Such rhetoric may have inspired or encouraged Shannon's August 19, 1993, assault on Dr. George Tiller, an abortionist in Wichita, Kansas, and surely figured prominently in Hill's deadly assault on Britton and Barrett on July 29, 1994 and the Brookline shootings which took place in late 1994.

Many individuals who joined pro-life direct action during Operation Rescue's groundswell retained the rhetoric of nonviolence without the earlier well-reasoned philosophical basis for it. Their nonviolent rhetoric was in many ways a "survival," a practice initiated by their predecessors but sustained without a coherent, logical basis in their own worldview. By the late 1980s some activists rejected pacifism as a "Hindu philosophy;" but during the debate that followed Gunn's death, activists so completely abandoned the Gandhian ethic that a major pro-life direct activists' magazine carried an article that argued, "The Biblical evidence used to support nonviolent civil disobedience also logically supports violent civil disobedience."[19] Activists noted that the injunction "Thou shalt not kill" was modified by the right and duty to kill in order to defend one's own life or that of an innocent person (especially family and children), to fight in a just war, and to execute criminals (via a legitimate government).

Those who abandoned an absolute ethic of non-violence argued that the central question was whether or not the *unborn* deserve the same standard of defense as the *born*. The right and duty to defend family and innocents found a logical convergence in defending the *unborn*, who were portrayed both as kin and as the ultimate innocents. Direct activists' rhetoric emphasized their kinship with the unborn and their duty to defend helpless "brothers and sisters". Confronted by arguments such as "he [the doctor] was going in there to kill 12 people, and that justified killing him to prevent his crime," they were stymied.[20] Consequently, when confronted with Griffin's murder of Gunn, many direct activists claimed a moral justification for Griffin's actions and could not refute his tactic.[21]

Such arguments severed pro-life direct action from its non-violent heritage in the debate that began in 1993.[22] Throughout the 1980s many direct activists openly criticized pro-lifers for not joining their sit-ins and a few direct activists privately criticized moderates within their movement for not supporting violent acts. When 15 years of sit-ins failed to recriminalize abortion, the voices advocating aggression surfaced. One prominent direct activists' convention included a message blaming the pro-life movement for censorious attitudes that dissuaded those who "might have taken out an abortion clinic."[23] As pro-lifers became increasingly detached from the political philosophy of Gandhi, were sporadically assured that even murder was justifiable, and were repeatedly inundated with Operation Rescue-National's call-to-arms (urging listeners to repent and join a national evangelical, redemptive mission), the likelihood that more individuals would choose to do violence increased throughout 1993-1994.[24] The wave of rhetoric enjoining lethal force grew until Paul Hill acted on his own advice, revisiting the turn to lethal violence that Griffin had initiated somewhat earlier.

The serious consideration of lethal violence during 1993-1994, coupled with the increased penalties FACE imposed for blockading, led direct activists to redefine their movement. In October 1994, *Pearls*, a newsletter published by one of the nation's more adamant pro-life direct action groups, Missionaries to the Preborn, declared, "We have reached a crossroads and there is no map. We need a map and only all of us working together can draw one."[25]

That map appears to be dominated by two lines. One emphasis rallies around the call to *change hearts*, that is, to educate, lobby, and influence judges, to *sidewalk counsel* women going into abortion clinics, to staff *crisis pregnancy centers*, contest media imagery, but most of all to evangelize (with a focus on the country's youth). Some advocates for this strategy openly renounce violence, arguing that "*all* life is sacred, including the life of an abortionist."[26] Others consider violence justifiable, but ineffective, because it does not change *mothers'* hearts. Such activists oppose violence and call for a sacrificial love that follows Christ's example. They argue that by laying down one's life for another (i.e., sitting-in) they both physically defend the *unborn* and witness against abortion (a "radical betrayal of love" and only one aspect of our "culture of death").[27]

A second strategy has emerged from the American Coalition of Life Activists (ACLA) a national organization formed during the summer of 1994 by the leaders of existing direct action groups in an attempt to sustain broad-based activism, reconcile newly formed factions, and eliminate the autocratic organization that Operation Rescue had established. ACLA advocates diminishing the availability of abortion by "targeting particular abortionists and abortion mills for exposure to their communities."[28] This strategy, which centers on frequent or sustained picketing aimed more at specific individuals than at clinics, became increasingly common throughout the 1990s as sit-ins waned. Such tactics have been promoted by those who advocate lethal violence, although ACLA espouses a commitment to nonviolence and "aggressive employment of First Amendment activities."[29]

Either strategy may accommodate individuals who are unwilling to risk stiff jail sentences, but both tactics eliminate the culturally acceptable middle ground between conventionality and outright aggression that sitting-in once provided.[30] As direct activism slides into the relatively conventional activities of pickets, prayer vigils, and "sidewalk counseling," and as the safety valve of sit-ins is all but eliminated, a few individuals may opt again for outright violence. Shortly before Hill killed Britton and Barrett, he and other advocates of violence argued that restrictions on sit-ins impinged "legitimate, nonviolent protest" and were "likely to bring about violence"; they predicted that "they won't be able to put the genie back in the bottle."[31] That near-threat may be far-fetched, but, coupled with the warnings of divine displeasure reiterated in direct activists' discourse, such rhetoric may encourage further violence. The void created by decreasing sit-ins was evident in deParrie's lament that, "With FACE, activism may now wane. If it does, it will reduce that awful and convicting sight of other believers actually doing something for their neighbor."[32] Unlike conventional activism, sitting-in let activists feel they were "actually doing something."[33]

The idea that sit-ins provided an intermediate step between unsatisfactory conventional activism and intolerable violence reappears throughout direct activists' rhetoric. In the 1980s activists spoke of the possibility that conflict over abortion would lead to a gun-toting "civil war." The prospect of reduced options posed by FACE raised a similar specter in which direct action was pitted against violence. For example, one of the first activists to sit-in after FACE was enacted remarked that, "Always the way a social sin comes to an end is either through a massive nonviolent movement or a war. What we have here is a massive nonviolence movement."[34]

INTIMIDATION

The possibility that a small number of violent or very aggressive political actors may be sufficient for a *de facto* victory has not escaped abortion opponents. In an editorial, Andrew Burnett quoted a "noted abortionist" who said, "It doesn't make any difference if abortion is legal if you can't find a place to get one."[35] Even more chilling, *Life Advocate* quoted "the anonymous replacement for the late abortionist David Gunn" as saying, "A bullet will stop me. And psychological violence will stop me....All they need to do is kill a couple more, and then everyone will quit."[36] Indeed, Gunn's death not only killed an abortion provider who had traveled over three states but it also convinced other physicians in Florida and elsewhere to stop providing abortion services.

The number of physicians learning to perform abortions, an elective skill, fell sharply in the years preceding Gunn's murder, and this trend may become more pronounced if violence continues. In 1993, the *Wall Street Journal* reported that "medical schools have been cutting back sharply on abortion training, and medical students appear increasingly unwilling to take such courses." In 1985 as many as 23% of residency programs offered first and second-trimester abortion training; in 1992, 12% offered first-trimester instruction and only 7% trained residents to do second-trimester abortions.[37]

The fear aroused by pro-life violence has been complemented by a campaign to seek out potential plaintiffs in malpractice suits against abortion providers. Such suits drain abortion clinics' resources, even when suits do not succeed. If access to abortion becomes much more restricted, abortion's legal status will be a moot point.

A TOOL FOR HEALING

Currently, victory in the contest over the legal status of abortion appears to be something of a mirage. Restricting opposition to abortion may actually escalate violence and effectively reduce the availability of abortion, leaving the pro-choice side with a rather intangible victory. Similarly, recriminalizing abortion would not stop it; consequently, such a legislative coup would leave the pro-life side without a victory in practice.[38]

In Chapter 4 of this volume, Mary Segers points out that political contexts are not inevitable despite the involvement of a particular cast of actors; she argues, rather, that outcomes are contingent on the accidents and decisions that preceded them. This is a good time to examine the concepts underlying our arguments (both for and against legal access to abortion) and to construct discourse and activism that will promote viable goals embedded in both pro-choice and pro-life projects. The public is open to compromise. Moreover, the interests of women (as well as families and communities in general) would be served by directing more and more energy and resources into healthy, socially-conscious channels and away from a pitched battle with little hope of lasting resolution.

In 1989, shortly after the *Webster* decision, a small group of highly dedicated long-time pro-choice and pro-life activists in St. Louis, Missouri met to discusswhat they had in common; hence, the group's name, *Common Ground*.[39] This group included Loretto Wagner (then board member, legislative chairman, and past president of Missouri Citizens for Life--later Missouri Right to Life), B.J. Isaacson-Jones (then director of Reproductive Health Services), and Andrew Puzder (known for authoring the restrictive Missouri law that led to the *Webster* decision). Shared concern drew them together when they realized that the distress many women and children suffered would not be alleviated by alterations in the legal status of abortion. From the start, they agreed to set aside discussion of their positions on abortion and turn to the task of identifying areas of social concern that could be addressed through the political process. Isaacson-Jones remembered that "After about ten minutes, we identified enough work to keep us busy for the rest of our lives."[40] Those early efforts eventually grew into a nationwide network, with *Common Ground* groups in some 25 cities.

Common Ground is not politics as usual; its founders are attempting to grasp the roots of social problems and find practical ways to alleviate them while maintaining the integrity of their diametrically opposed positions in the area of abortion legislation. In a profound way they are trying to achieve goals common to both pro-life and pro-choice advocates, that is, they are working to provide women with reproductive choices *and* promote family welfare. Although *Common Ground* received accurate, sympathetic, and continuous (although sporadic) national and even international media coverage between 1990 and 1993, its incremental approach to formulating a new politics of reproduction does not make it headline material. *Common Ground* will require patient support from members of the public who are interested in its approach. Wagner warns that, "Cynicism and suspicion are the greatest obstacles to *Common Ground*.[41]

The *Common Ground* steering committee is proceeding with the patience necessary to discover and develop an innovative process; as Isaacson-Jones commented, they began by "embracing the process." They have invested years in developing a solid foundation of trust and understanding in the hope of obtaining long-term success in resolving the social problems they have targeted. This approach has resulted in deep personal relationships that have weathered both time and public exposure.

From the outset, this trust has borne fruit: first in providing client services, then in collaboration on legislation, then in an attempt to redefine adoption policy. After only the first few meetings, Wagner was surprised by a phone call from one of the pro-choice *Common Ground* pioneers. A client had decided to carry to term but needed complete bedrest throughout the remainder of her pregnancy, and therefore, full-time care in her home to do so. Wagner quickly organized the care needed, drawing on an extensive network of pro-life volunteers associated with Our Lady's Inn (a home she helped organize for women in crisis pregnancies). Through such experiences, Isaacson-Jones and Wagner recognized both the trust they were developing and the value of each other's resources. Together, they could provide expanded services to women in need. Shortly after they began meeting, the wider social implication of *Common Ground* became evident when these activists found themselves working together to pass mutually approved legislation that had previously been scuttled by abortion politics. This legislation concerned services for drug-addicted pregnant women and expansion of the Women, Infants, and Children program. Wagner notes that they "support welfare reform that will give women the tools they need to get off welfare and provide a transition so that women can become independent with minimal hardship on their families";[42] they oppose reform that would limit entitlements to women who become pregnant while on welfare--the so-called family caps.

Unfortunately, workers on both sides of the issue must approach these promising efforts with a degree of circumspection because they are often unsupported and even denigrated by their own contingents. Isaacson-Jones remembered the barrage of resentment from her pro-choice colleagues that left her "cuddling up in the fetal position for days" in her office after word of this collaboration leaked to the press. Tiring of harassment from her pro-life colleagues, Wagner eventually resigned her positions with Missouri Right to Life rather than discontinue pursuit of *Common Ground*.

Fortunately, *Common Ground*'s founders were activists of such stature that they were able to remain politically effective despite such contention. How much more might they be able to accomplish with widespread support for their efforts to address long-standing sources of problems for women and children? More than that, Isaacson-Jones explained that *Common Ground* has been "not only a learning tool, an empowering tool, but it's also been a tool of healing for me";[43] it is a "search for common humanity" and common good. Our society needs healing in this area.

CONCLUSION

Clyde Wilcox reports considerable ambiguity and nuance in public opinion on abortion. Perhaps my own responses would appear undefined or equivocal; however, such responses would not derive from vague or tepid feelings on my part. Rather, I find key aspects of both sides of the abortion debate compelling. Consequently, I would rather see energy focused on eliminating factors that result in unwanted or crisis pregnancies.

Such efforts might be facilitated if an alternative (or expanded) legal foundation were to eliminate contention over abortion's legal status and free supporters' time and political will to address other pressing social needs. For example, abortion supporters could eradicate undesirable aspects of current abortion practice (e.g., lack of alternative assistance for women, inadequate counseling or follow-up care, and unsound medical practices where they exist). A political climate in which abortion was less vulnerable to legislative restriction would encourage research on undesirable sequelae; this would improve pre-abortion counseling and help women make fully informed decisions. With the legal issue resolved, people who care about women and families could focus on supporting them. Unfortunately, history suggests that a one-sided legal victory could undermine its own purpose. More likely, activists on both sides will need to refocus their energies away from polemics and toward the resolution of common goals.

Abortion has become the issue; I believe it is a red herring, distracting people from the more profound issues of human suffering and limited life-possibilities. By focusing on the legal status of abortion, we deal with the effect of diverse social problems rather than addressing the problems themselves. More than a decade ago moderates urged that abortion laws be repealed, leaving the moral aspects of abortion to be worked out by individuals within their own social networks and obligating the medical profession to regulate technical aspects of abortion procedures when appropriate.[44] How does current regulation of abortion differ from that of other critical medical procedures? Are any differences justifiable? Currently, both extremes in the abortion debate hold the public's ear but have failed to persuade it. Both pro-choice and pro-life proponents might benefit by reconceptualizing and then reconstructing their arguments in ways that would encourage a convergence of interests and, one hopes, a tolerant attitude toward each other. The current battle drains energy and financial and human resources that might otherwise serve the interests of both sides by solving structural inequities and inadequacies that turn many pregnancies into crises. Solving problems such as the need for child care, fair and adequate remuneration, employment opportunities, reliable long-term birth control, family support, protection from familial violence, changed attitudes and policies regarding adoption, and alternative gender constructs would free more women to focus on the moral rather than the pragmatic aspects of decisions regarding their pregnancies-- and their lives in general.

NOTES

1. Labels for proponents of both sides of the abortion debate are highly political and sometimes ambiguous (e.g, both sides refer to themselves as being pro-women, while accusing their opponents of being anti-women). I will follow the anthropological tradition of calling people by the names they use to refer to themselves.

2. Paul J. Hill, "Who Killed the Innocent--Michael Griffin or Dr. David Gunn?" *Life Advocate* (August, 1993): 41.

3. *Ibid,* p. 42.

4. Rachelle "Shelly" Shannon admitted shooting Dr. George Tiller in Wichita, Kansas, on August 19, 1993. Shannon had a history of activism with both Operation Rescue and Advocates for Life Ministries., one of its predecessors. See Andrew Burnett, ed. "Tiller Shot: Oregon Woman Accused," *Life Advocate* (October 1993): 10-13. As discussed above, militancy has tended to increase among pro-lifers faced with a discouraging political situation; This dynamic may have influenced Shannon's treatment in Oregon, a state that is famed among direct activists for harsh treatment of individuals who sit-in at abortion clinics and punishing sentences for those arrested.

5. Kifner, John, "Gunman Kills Two at Abortion Clinics in Boston Suburb," *New York Times*, (December 31, 1994), A1.

6. Celeste Michelle Condit, *Decoding Abortion Rhetoric* Urbana: University of Illinois Press, 1990; Michele Dillon, "Argumentative Complexity of Abortion Discourse," *Public Opinion Quarterly* 57 (1993): 305-314.

7. Mary W. Armsworth, "Psychological Response to Abortion," *Journal of Counseling and Development* 69 (1991): 377-379.

8. G. Carter Bentley, "Ethnicity and Practice," *Society for Comparative Study of Society and History* 29 (1987):24-55.

9. Elizabeth Adell Cook, Ted G. Jelen, and Clyde Wilcox, "Generational Differences in Attitudes Toward Abortion." *American Politics Quarterly* 21 (1993): 31-53.

10. *Ibid.*, p. 33.

11. James C. Mohr, *Abortion In America: The Origins and Evolution of National Policy, 1800-1900* (New York: Oxford University Press, 1978).

12. Bentley, "Ethnicity and Practice."

13. Linda Wertheimer, "Illegal Abortion: Married Women Who Did," National Public Radio: All Things Considered, April 22, 1992.

14. Carol J.C. Maxwell, "Meaning and Motivation in Pro-Life Direct Action." unpublished Ph.D dissertation, Washington University, St. Louis, Missouri.

15. *Ibid.*

16. Personal communication, March 1991.

17. Dallas A. Blanchard and Terry J. Prewitt, *Religious Violence and Abortion: The Gideon Project* (Gainesville: University Press of Florida, 1993).

18. Personal communication with pro-life direct activists, April 1993.

19. Hill, "Who Killed the Innocent?"

20. Personal communications with pro-life direct activists, April 1991 and April 1993.

21. Many pro-life direct activists were disinclined to accept a moderating, compromising position on abortion because they quite concretely conceptualized abortion as the murder of innocent children.

22. Another disturbing trend in activists' rhetoric indicted women as guilty of murder for having aborted. Even as activists continued to frame women as victims who had been pressured or duped into having an abortion, this message was frequently supplemented by a call to recognize women as guilty--forgivable, but culpable.

23. Golden Ohlhausen and Cathy Ramey, "Rescue and 'Use of Force' Debate Part of Conference," *Life Advocate* (August, 1993): 24-25.

24. Blanchard and Prewitt, *Religious Violence and Abortion.*

25. *Pearls* (October, 1994:) 2.

26. *Pearls* (October 1994).

27. Policy Statement of Citizens for Life, Milwaukee, October, 1993.

28. *Life Advocate* (August, 1994). This strategy was discussed as early as 1990, when it was called "Operation Goliath."

29. Steven Paul Mears, Paul de Parrie, and Andrew Burnett, "ACLA: New National Activists Coalition Begins in Mississippi," *Life Advocate* (October 1994): 15-18.

30. This discussion does not address the distress or burden sit-ins may cause clinic personnel and women attempting to obtain abortions. Such effects merit serious consideration, but are somewhat tangential to the present discussion. Here I focus on abortion opponents' potential responses to a changing legal environment.

31. Paul deParrie, "FACE Bill Passed, Signed by Clinton," *Life Advocate* (July 1994): 8-9.

32. Paul deParrie, "FACE Facts," *Life Advocate* (July 1994): 38.

33. Maxwell, "Meaning and Motivation"

34. deParrie, "FACE Bill Passed."

35. Andrew Burnett "Abortion--Legal, But Not Practiced," *Life Advocate* (August 1994): 2.

36. *Life Advocate* (August 1993): 5.

37. Helen Cooper,"Medical Schools, Students Shun Abortion Study," *Wall Street Journal* (March 12, 1993): B1.

38. Research suggests that pro-life activism is less a matter of status discontent than an attempt to preserve a lifestyle. Consequently, pro-lifers most likely would not be satisfied with public acknowledgment of their moral orientation on laws that were not enforced. See Alan Clarke, "Moral Protest, Status Defence and the Anti-Abortion Campaign," *British Journal of Sociology* 38 (1987): 235-253.

39. Faye Ginsburg reported a short-lived and lower-keyed attempt at rapprochement between pro-life and pro-choice factions in Fargo, North Dakota. See Faye Ginsburg, *Contested Lives: The Abortion Debate in an American Community* (Berkeley: University of California Press, 1989).

40. Personal communication.

41. Personal communication.

42. Personal communication.

43. Personal communication.

44. Margaret Mead, "Rights to Life," in *Abortion: The Moral Issues* Edward Batchelor, Jr, ed. (New York: The Pilgrim Press, 1982), 7-14.

2

Abortion Rights Alchemy and the United States Supreme Court: What's Wrong and How to Fix It

Eileen L. McDonagh

In 1973 in the landmark *Roe v. Wade* case, the Supreme Court ruled that women have a constitutional right to obtain an abortion.[1] At the time, however, two major concepts were missing from the Court's rationale for women's abortion rights: pregnancy and consent. Over 20 years later, these two concepts are still missing. As a consequence, what's wrong is that women's reproductive rights have been undermined--including, most significantly, their right to abortion funding. Let us review the Court record with an eye not only to "what's wrong," but also to why we must add pregnancy and consent to the abortion debate to "fix it."[2]

When the Supreme Court first established a woman's constitutional right to have an abortion in 1973, it adopted the American Bar Association's definition of abortion as "termination of human pregnancy with an intention other than to produce a live birth or to remove a dead fetus."[3] While it has been common to focus on the last part of this definition, "an intention other than to produce a live birth or to remove a dead fetus," we need instead to direct our attention to the first part of the definition, the "termination of human pregnancy."

It would seem obvious that if abortion is the termination of human pregnancy, the Court must have formally considered what constitutes the condition of pregnancy terminated by abortion. Contrary to expectations, however, the Court did not do this in 1973, nor has it yet to do so from legal or medical perspectives in any case dealing with abortion in the intervening decades up to and including the 1992 decision in *Casey*.[4]

Rather, in *Roe* the Court devoted *seventeen pages* to an exploration of the legal status of the "fetus" and the history of attitudes and practices regarding abortion since ancient times in Greece. The result was an impressive journey indeed, encompassing the attitudes of Hippocrates and Aristotle, English common law, and the American Medical Profession, to cite only a few of the many notables referenced. However, a comparable history of what the medical profession, and religious or philosophical authorities thought about "pregnancy," is conspicuously absent.[5]

The Court concluded that the fetus could not be considered a person entitled to constitutional protection under the Fourteenth Amendment, primarily because the fetus was not yet "born" and the Fourteenth Amendment specifically refers to "born" people. As the Court put it in *Roe*,

> The Constitution does not define "person"' in so many words. Section 1 of the Fourteenth Amendment . . . in defining "citizens," speaks of "persons born or naturalized in the United States." The word also appears both in the Due Process Clause and in the Equal Protection Clause. "Person" [also] is used in other places in the Constitution . . . But in nearly all these instances, the use of the word is such that it has application only postnatally. None indicates, with any assurance, that it has any possible prenatal application. . . All this, together with our observation . . . that throughout the major portion of the 19th century prevailing legal abortion practices were far freer than they are today, persuades us that the word "person," as used in the Fourteenth Amendment, does not include the unborn.[6]

The Court ruled, therefore, that the fetus was not a person covered by the Fourteenth Amendment. It refused, however, to rule on the more general question of when life begins.

> We [the Court] need not resolve the difficult question of when life begins. When those trained in the respective disciplines of medicine, philosophy, and theology are unable to arrive at any consensus, the judiciary, at this point in the development of man's knowledge, is not in a position to speculate as to the answer.[7]

In contrast to the extensive review of abortion and the personhood status of the fetus, the Court utterly failed to conduct a systematic analysis of what constitutes the condition of pregnancy. Rather, it referenced this condition using only the most loosely constructed cultural representations of the meaning of pregnancy--so loose and so culturally derived, in fact, that they replicate what undergraduate students will say, if asked to define what pregnancy means to them. I have asked my students over the years to do this, and they have come up with five different definitions of pregnancy.

CULTURAL CONSTRUCTIONS OF PREGNANCY

1. *Women as vessels.* Students will most often define pregnancy in terms of women as vessels. As one student put it, "Pregnancy is having a living person inside of you." The basic idea underlying this definition is that women "carry" fetuses around, and that is what pregnancy "is."

2. *Fetal development.* Another definition of pregnancy that students offer relates to fetal development. One student defined it as "that joyous nine-month incubation period that a woman must go through in order for a child to be born." Here, the idea is that pregnancy is a time period during which something--the fetus--develops. This time period is marked and calibrated in terms of the developmental stages of fetal growth, culminating in birth.

3. *Result of sex.* A third definition is that pregnancy is something that is caused by having sex. In the words of one such student, "Pregnancy is what happens to a woman when she has sex with a man and his sperm fertilizes her egg."

4. *Burdensome condition.* A fourth definition of pregnancy given by students is that pregnancy is a burdensome condition. The depiction of pregnancy as a burden ranges from a mere "inconvenience" to something that constitutes a major "sacrifice." Representing of the latter end of the continuum, one student stated that, "pregnancy is a strain for a female who must go through the pain and agony of the 9-month process."

5. *Value to society.* Finally, students define pregnancy in terms of its value, particularly in relation to the survival of society. One student expressed this idea by stating that "pregnancy is a gift from God."

Another said pregnancy is "the way society reproduces; it's a role given to women as a link to the growth of society."

TRANSFORMING CULTURE INTO LEGAL DOCTRINE

I recommend to everyone that you ask yourself, other people, and your own students to define pregnancy. Chances are, the collection of depictions will fall into one or more of the five cultural metaphors for pregnancy catalogued here. What is striking, however, is that these categories are the same ones used by the Supreme Court to define pregnancy when assessing the rights of women to have abortions and receive state funding for abortions.

The difference between the general public and the Supreme Court, however, is the Court's authority to transform these cultural assumptions about pregnancy into law. It is this very transformation that has become the legal foundation for women's reproductive rights as constructed by the Supreme Court over the last 20 years in the context of the abortion issue.

As we shall see, the Court's process of transforming each of the five cultural assumptions about pregnancy into law has led to a set of five specific legal doctrines. In the resulting alchemy constituting abortion rights, what is "wrong" is that these doctrines, established without reference to formal legal or medical definitions of pregnancy, have been the foundation for policies that have devastating consequences for the implementation of women's reproductive rights. To correct this situation, we must examine how the Court transformed culture into law in the first place.

"Women as Vessels" and "Privacy Is Not Sole" Doctrine

In 1973 the Court sought to expand abortion rights for women in *Roe* on the basis of the right to privacy defined by decisional autonomy. The right of decisional autonomy guarantees that a person has the right to make choices about fundamental areas of private life without interference from the state. Prior to *Roe*, the Court had established not only that there was a fundamental right to privacy protected by the

Constitution but that this right to privacy included family life, decisions about marriage, the education of one's children, and the use of contraceptives.[8]

The *Roe* decision was famous for expanding the right of privacy to include the right of a woman to choose to terminate her pregnancy by having an abortion. As the Court put it in *Roe*, the "right of privacy . . . is broad enough to encompass a woman's decision whether or not to terminate her pregnancy."[9] This was no small feat, as later Court decisions were to show. In 1986, for example, the Court failed to declare that this same right of privacy was broad enough to cover the right to engage in consensual homosexual sodomy.[10] We can well appreciate, therefore, why those who care about women's rights correctly rank *Roe* as the landmark victory it surely was.

As the Court expanded the right of privacy to include a woman's decision to terminate her pregnancy with an abortion, however, it adopted the "women as vessels" cultural depiction of pregnancy. As the Court put it, when a woman is pregnant "[s]he *carries an embryo* and, later, a *fetus*."[11]

The stunning legal consequence of depicting pregnancy in terms of the cultural metaphor of "women as vessels" is the codification of this cultural metaphor into legal doctrine "restricting" the very right of privacy *Roe* established for women in the first place. Specifically, the Court's adoption of the "women as vessels" metaphor led to its conclusion that because a pregnant woman "*carries life within her*,"[12] she "*cannot be isolated in her privacy*" and, hence, her "*privacy is no longer sole*."[13]

Based on a "women as vessels" metaphor, therefore, the Court ruled that a pregnant woman's right of privacy "is inherently different" from other examples of privacy, such as "marital intimacy, or bedroom possession of obscene material, or marriage, or procreation, or education."[14] Consequently, as the Court put it, because she "carries" a fetus, "any right of privacy she possesses must be measured accordingly."[15]

What the Court meant by this is that a woman's right of privacy would have to be limited by, or balanced against, the rights of the fetus that she "carries." The question was, of course, how? The answer turned out to be based on yet another cultural metaphor about pregnancy: that of fetal development.

"Fetal Development" and "Viability" Doctrine

In figuring out how to effect a balance between the privacy rights of a pregnant woman and the fetus she "carries," the Court invoked the cultural definition of pregnancy based on fetal development. Pregnancy defined in terms of fetal development was bedrock to the *Roe* decision, and has provided the foundation for the Court's assessment of women's abortion rights ever since.

The Court referred to the "*developing young* a woman carries when pregnant" in *Roe*, and, as Justice Blackmun stated in the majority opinion, "it is reasonable and appropriate for a State to decide that at some point in time in *fetal development* another interest, that of the health of the mother or that of the potential life becomes significantly involved."[16]

The consequence of the Supreme Court's embracing the cultural assumption that pregnancy is a condition defined by what happens to the fetus's body over a period of time, rather than what happens to the woman's body, is the doctrine of the trimester system established in *Roe*, later modified as the doctrine of viability.[17]

Viability is the stage of fetal development at which there is a good chance that the fetus could live outside the woman's body, though it may require artificial support.[18] It is at this stage of fetal development, viability, that the Court decided that the balance between the State's interest in protecting potential life and the State's interest in protecting a woman's right of privacy to choose an abortion tips from the woman to the fetus.[19] In other words, it is at a particular point in fetal development--viability-- that the State's interest in the fetus becomes "compelling," regardless of the difficulties involved in determining if a fetus actually is viable or not. As reiterated in *Casey*, the *viability standard* takes account of the undeniable fact that as the *fetus evolves into its postnatal form*, and as it loses its dependence on the uterine environment, the *State's interest in the fetus' potential human life, becomes compelling.*[20]

"Sex Causes Pregnancy" and "Rape/Incest Exception" Doctrine

We also see in Supreme Court reasoning on abortion the idea that sex causes pregnancy. This assertion is established as early as *Roe*, when

Justice Blackmun cited the American Bar Association's 1972 Uniform Abortion Act, without questioning it, as follows:

> an abortion may be performed after 20 weeks if the physician has reasonable cause to believe that the that "the *pregnancy resulted from rape or incest*, or illicit intercourse with a girl under the age of 16 years."[21]

Also, in *Doe v. Bolton*, which was a companion case to *Roe* in 1973, Chief Justice Burger referred to "*nonconsensual pregnancies*" as "those *resulting from rape and incest*."[22]

The Court transformed the cultural presumption that pregnancy is caused by sex into a "rape and incest exceptions" doctrine. According to this rule, a woman's right to terminate a pregnancy is based on the context of sexual intercourse that preceded the pregnancy. If a woman did not consent to sexual intercourse, as in the contexts of rape or incest, the Court is willing to acknowledge that she should not be forced to continue her pregnancy and even takes seriously arguments that she should be entitled to State funding for an abortion.

"Burdensome Condition" and "Therapeutic Abortion"

In its review of the abortion issue in *Roe* in 1973, the Court acknowledged a definition of pregnancy as a burdensome condition. Initially these burdens were recognized as "the specific and direct medical harm, medically diagnosable even in early pregnancy, which "may be involved in pregnancy."[23]

In *Casey* the Court elevated these "normal" conditions of pregnancy to almost pedestal level. As the Court put it, pregnancy entails "anxieties," "physical constraints," "intimate and personal" "suffering," and "pain" which "only she [the pregnant woman]" bears. The Court stated that, "these sacrifices have from the beginning of the human race been endured by woman with a pride that ennobles her in the eyes of others."[24]

Yet the Court views the burdens of pregnancy, even when depicted in dramatic terms, as "normal" as long as they do not threaten a woman's very life. From the Court's vantage point, therefore, burdens of pregnancy that are "expected" and non-life threatening may "ennoble" women, but legally they do not constitute "harm" to women. As the Court stated in *Harris*, "Surely the government may properly presume that *no harm will ensue from normal childbirth*."[25]

The Court uses this "pregnancy as burden" definition to develop its notion of "therapeutic" and "nontherapeutic" abortions. If a woman is experiencing only the "normal" burdens of pregnancy--that is, anything and everything that stops short of a threat to her life or permanent injury to her health--her abortion is considered medically "unnecessary" and, therefore, "nontherapeutic." Only when the burdens of pregnancy become life threatening does the Court view an abortion as medically "necessary" and concomitantly as "therapeutic."

As the Court stated in *Beal*, "treatment for *therapeutic abortions*" constitutes "necessary medical services," but that for "elective abortions" does not.[26] The policy consequence has been the Court's finding that it is constitutional for a State to withhold funding for "elective" nontherapeutic abortions because they entail only burdens that are not life-threatening and, therefore, an abortion that is not medically "necessary."

"Value to Society" and "Childbirth Preference" Doctrine

Finally, we find in Supreme Court cases the adoption of the cultural definition of pregnancy as a value to society. In 1973 this was stated outright in *Roe* when Justice Blackmun, writing the majority opinion, referred to the fact that pregnancy is something the Court must address because not only does it "come often" to women, but it must come "if man [sic] is to survive."[27]

The Court's use of the cultural definition of pregnancy as a "value to society" is the foundation for the construction of its "childbirth preference" doctrine. It is reasonable, as the Court put it, for a State "to further . . . [its] unquestionably strong and legitimate interest in encouraging normal childbirth,"[28] which is "an interest honored over the centuries."[29] Pregnancy as a value to society, therefore, results in the legal doctrine of a preference for childbirth, which means that the State may withhold funds for abortions even while providing funds for childbirth.

As the Court stated in *Maher*, *Roe* "implies no limitation on the authority of a State to make a *value judgment favoring childbirth* over abortion, and to implement that judgment by the allocation of public funds."[30] A regulation that fails to fund abortions for indigent women even while funding childbirth, therefore, is constitutional because it is "rationally related to and furthers its [the State's] strong and legitimate interest in encouraging normal childbirth.'"[31]

POLICY CONSEQUENCES OF ABORTION RIGHTS ALCHEMY

In my experience, everyone, all groups, and the general public--ranging from students, pro-life and pro-choice advocates, to the Supreme Court--premise their stance on abortion in terms of one or more of the five cultural metaphors for pregnancy. However, the Court has used these cultural representations of pregnancy to construct a powerful edifice for defining women's abortions rights. And it is this authority of the Court to codify culture that has transformed these cultural views of pregnancy into an alchemist's nightmare. Rather than "gold," the result has been pernicious legal doctrines creating devastating policy consequences for millions of women.

The cultural assumption that "women are vessels" who carry fetuses has been transformed by the Court into the doctrine that a pregnant woman's "privacy is not sole." The policy consequence of this doctrine is limitations upon a woman's right to terminate her pregnancy. The cultural view of pregnancy in terms of "fetal development" has been transformed by the Court into the doctrine of "viability" that sets the cut-off point at which women lose their constitutional right to an abortion. The cultural assumption that pregnancy is "caused by sex" has been transformed by the Court into the "rape and incest exception" to prohibitions on abortion, a doctrine that consequently serves to rationalize policies refusing abortions to pregnant women who have not suffered from rape or incest.

The cultural assumption that pregnancy can be defined as a "burdensome condition" has been transformed by the Court into notions of "normal" and "abnormal" pregnancy and the concomitant doctrine of "therapeutic" and "nontherapeutic" abortions. The policy result has been the Court's finding that it is constitutional to deny abortion funding for "nontherapeutic" abortions for "normal" pregnancies whose burdens do not constitute medically necessary termination.

Finally, the cultural view that pregnancy is a "value to society" has been transformed by the Court into the legal doctrine of a State "preference for childbirth." The policy consequence of this doctrine has been the Court's finding that it is constitutional for a State to deny to

Table 2.1
The Alchemy of Abortion Rights: The Supreme Court's Transformation of Culture into Law and Policy

Cultural Assumptions about Pregnancy	Legal Doctrines	Policy Consequences
Women as Vessels	Pregnant woman's "privacy is not sole"	"Balance" privacy rights of pregnant woman against value of potential life
Fetal Development	"Viability" as the stage of fetal development having legal significance	Viability of fetus is the point where legal protection switches from a woman's right of privacy to State protection of potential life
Sex Causes Pregnancy	Rape and incest "exceptions" to abortion restriction	Abortions allowed and/or funded when preceded by rape or incest
Burdensome Condition	Normal/abnormal pregnancy categorization; concomitant nontherapeutic/ therapeutic abortions categorization	State funding provided only for therapeutic abortions terminating abnormal pregnancies
Value to Society	Preference for childbirth	It is constitutional for State medical benefits to cover pregnancy and childbirth but not abortions

indigent women Medicaid funding for "nontherapeutic abortions" even while providing funds for pregnancy and childbirth.

Each cultural assumption, its doctrinal transformation, and its policy consequence is summarized in Table 2.1.

ABORTION RIGHTS: WHAT MUST BE (UN)DONE

Roe has been criticized on many grounds. However, the most serious grounds have been all but ignored: the Court's failure to use formal legal or medical definitions of pregnancy in its assessment of women's right to terminate their pregnant condition. What's wrong, therefore, is what is missing from Supreme Court reasoning on abortion rights: a formal definition of pregnancy.

Legal Definition of Pregnancy

According to a law dictionary, pregnancy is defined as the "condition [in a woman's body] *resulting from the fetilized ovum* . . . beginning at the moment of conception and terminating with the delivery of the child."[32] The key aspect of this definition is that it posits pregnancy as a condition in a woman's body that results from something else--in this case, the fertilized ovum throughout its developmental stages.

Introducing this definition of pregnancy into the abortion debate immediately recasts the issue of women's rights. Rather than a right solely to *decisional autonomy* (i.e., a right to choose what to do with her own body) pregnancy invokes a woman's right to *bodily integrity* (i.e., her right to consent to what is done to her body by another entity, namely, the fertilized ovum). This is because it is not merely that she "carries" the entity, the fertilized ovum, or that it "grows" and "develops" while she carries it, or that society "values" her "carrying" of the fetus. Rather, it is because the fertilized ovum throughout its developmental stages "does" something to her body while it is being carried. It makes her pregnant.

Arguments for women's right to terminate their pregnant condition, therefore, must shift to whether women "consent" to what is done to their bodies by fetuses to make them pregnant in the first place. Shifting to the right to "consent to pregnancy" rather than solely the right to "choose an abortion," underscores the obvious "relational reality" of the condition of pregnancy. Pregnancy is a condition in a woman's body that only occurs if and when a fertilized ovum implants itself in a woman's uterus. It is not merely that a woman's privacy is not sole when she is pregnant; rather, it is that her privacy, represented by her own body, has been *intruded upon* by another entity, the fertilized ovum, which has made her body pregnant.[33]

Pregnancy: Woman-Centered or Fetus-Centered?

It is true, of course, that a woman's pregnant condition benefits and serves the fetus. It is by virtue of her pregnant condition that the fertilized ovum is able to grow and develop. Yet pregnancy itself is a condition referencing the *woman's body*, not that of the fetus itself. It is the woman who is pregnant, not the fetus.

Currently, however, cultural assumptions and Court reasoning about abortion invoke fetus-centered definitions of pregnancy. They focus on what happens to the *fetus* as a *consequence of pregnancy*, rather than what happens to the *woman* as a *consequence of the fetus*. Therefore, we lack woman-centered definitions of pregnancy that focus on what happens to a woman as a consequence of what the fertilized ovum must do to her to make her pregnant.

Medical Definition of Pregnancy

Medically, a woman is pregnant at the point of implantation of a fertilized ovum in her uterus, according to the American College of Obstetricians and Gynecologists.[34] Consent to pregnancy means that a woman has a right to consent (or not) to this implantation, or intrusion, by a fertilized ovum upon her body.

Consent

Legally, the definition of "consent" is an "act of reason," that must be a "voluntary agreement by a person in the possession and exercise of sufficient mental capacity to make an intelligent choice to do something proposed by another." More simply, consent is the willingness that "an act or an invasion of interest shall take place" based on "a choice between resistance and assent."[35]

Consent, therefore, denotes a relationship. For consent to be meaningful and legally valid, a person must be able to choose whether to consent (or not) to an invasion of her/his interest by someone (or something) else. If there is no choice about whether to consent (or not), there can be no consent.[36]

Choice, however, does not necessarily entail consent. Individuals can make choices that reference only themselves and therefore, do not involve the idea of consenting to an agreement with another person, potential person, or "thing." If I say I "choose" to use contraceptives, for example, I am making a choice that primarily references only myself. If I say, on the other hand, that I "consent" to use contraceptives, this means that I have agreed with another person or entity, such as the State, to use contraceptives.

While consent, therefore, necessarily involves choice, choice does not necessarily involve consent. In the context of pregnancy, to say that a woman has a right to "choose an abortion" references her right to make an individual choice about how to live her own life. On the other hand, to say that a woman has a right to "consent to pregnancy" means that she has a right to consent to how her interest is invaded by another person or entity. Specifically, a woman's right to consent to pregnancy references a woman's explicit willingness, based on her choice between resistance and assent, that the fertilized ovum invade her interest by implanting itself in her body.

DISAGGREGATION OF SEX AND PREGNANCY

One of the first consequences of introducing the "consent to be pregnant" into the abortion debate is the disaggregation of sexual intercourse and pregnancy. Consent to sexual intercourse references a relationship between a man and woman. It is consent to engage in what is medically referred to as "gamete transport."

Gamete transport. Gamete transport refers to the bringing together of male and female gametes--that is, sperm and ova--into a *proximate location* to each other. This is necessary if the sperm and ova are to unite to produce a fertilized ovum, or conception. The most common form of gamete transport is sexual intercourse in which sperm and ova are brought to a proximate location within the body of a woman. However, gamete transport also can be accomplished by means of artificial insemination and *in vitro fertilization* (IVF).

Conception. Conception, however, is *not* pregnancy. Consent to engage in gamete transport--whether through sexual intercourse, artificial insemination, or IVF--is consent to engage in simply that: the moving around of sperm and ova. Reproductively, the most that can be accomplished by any and all forms of "moving male and female gametes around" is the union of two of them--a sperm and ovum--in other words, conception.

Medically, however, the mere existence of a fertilized ovum, (i.e., conception) does not constitute pregnancy. Medically, pregnancy is defined by what the fertilized ovum *does* to a woman's body, not by whether it exists or not. Specifically, a woman's body is not in a pregnant condition until, or unless, the fertilized ovum implants itself in her uterus. Therefore, there are *two* reproductive relationships requiring a woman's consent: (1) a *sexual relationship with a man* and, (2) a *pregnancy relationship with a fertilized ovum*.

Sexual penetration. Consent to engage in a sexual relationship with a man references a woman's right to consent to a man's sexual penetration of her body during sexual intercourse. Legally, a woman's consent to sex with a man entitles him to deposit his sperm inside her body. The most that can reproductively result from such a deposit, however, is that a sperm and an ovum--due to a new, proximate location to each other--can unite. The most that a woman can accomplish reproductively, therefore, in relation to a man, is conception, or the joining of a sperm and ovum.

Pregnancy penetration. Consent to engage in a pregnancy relationship references a woman's right to consent to a fertilized ovum's "pregnancy penetration" of her body by means of its implantation in her uterus.[37] It is only if, or when, the fertilized ovum implants itself in a woman's body that she is medically considered to be pregnant. Therefore, only in relation to an implanting fertilized ovum can a woman reproductively accomplish her pregnant condition.

Fetus as the legal cause of pregnancy. Therefore, legally and medically, sex and pregnancy are disaggregated. Whereas the law defines sexual intercourse as a *sexual relationship* between a *man and a woman*,[38] a *pregnancy relationship* necessarily must be one between a *fetus and a woman*, where the fetus causes a woman's pregnancy.

By law, therefore, the fertilized ovum is the legal or "proximate" cause of a woman's pregnancy.[39] Whereas there are many other causal links that must occur in order to make it possible for a fertilized ovum to implant itself, no woman is actually pregnant until it does implant itself. Although it is obvious that a fertilized ovum must exist or be conceived before it can implant itself, it is not the conception itself that defines the condition of pregnancy or, in that sense, causes pregnancy. Rather, a woman's body is in a pregnant condition only when a fertilized ovum implants itself in her body, thereby initiating and maintaining her pregnant condition throughout its developmental stages.[40]

The key question, therefore, is not merely a woman's decisional autonomy to decide how to use her own body. Rather, the key question is a woman's right of bodily integrity to consent (or not) to the penetrating implantation of her body by a fertilized ovum.

WHO DOES WHAT TO WHOM IN THE WOMB?

Although it is common to depict what happens to the fetus while a woman is pregnant, medical texts point instead to the massive changes initiated and maintained by a fetus in the *woman's body*.[41] When we conisder representations of pregnancy typical of the medical profession, we find a picture of fetal activity that hardly can be labeled anything other than aggression. The metaphorical language used by some medical texts is graphic in its choice of words to describe what the fetus must do to a woman to produce the condition of pregnancy in her body.

At various stages of fetal development, medical texts describe the intruding fertilized ovum as "eating a hole" in the lining of a woman's uterus; as "maintaining" its "implantation" by secreting cells from itself; as "penetrating" tissues in the woman's uterus with its own cells; thereby making it possible to "colonize" parts of her body; as using tactics of "invasion" and "attack" to "destroy" and "replace" her own cells with those of its own, thereby "converting" the woman's vessels to suit its own needs.[42]

Entire chapters in medical texts are devoted to the major transformations that occur in a woman's body when pregnant. For example, the implantation of the fetus causes a massive new organ to be constructed in a woman's body: the placenta. In addition, some parts of a woman's body are actually reconstructed during pregnancy: her circulatory system is rerouted to allow all of her blood to flow through and be made available to the fetus in support of its own growth and development.

Women's hormonal levels also undergo massive alterations during the course of pregnancy, in some cases jumping to 400 times their baseline levels. This monumental change provides the most common, and reliable, diagnosis that a fertilized ovum has implanted itself and caused a pregnant condition in a woman's body. When she is pregnant, a woman's uterus expands 500 to 1000 times its normal size. Typically, she gains 25 pounds or more. In addition, pregnant women usually experience other symptoms related to the way in which their body has been altered by the fetus; these symptoms include frequent urination, water retention, nausea and vomiting, labored breathing, back pain, and fatigue.[43]

What we must keep in mind is that all of the changes medically defining the condition of pregnancy are a result of the implantation and maintenance of a fertilized ovum throughout its developmental stages. No women will, or can, experience a pregnant condition unless or until such an implantation takes place. This is why it is misleading to say that a woman "chooses" to be pregnant. No woman can make such a choice. Women can choose whether to minimize or maximize the probabilities that a fertilized ovum will implant itself. However, no person, including the pregnant woman herself, can actually control whether or not a fertilized ovum *does* implant itself, as those who deal with infertility problems can testify.

Why do metaphors matter? Feminist scholars, such as Mary Jo Frug, have long warned us about the liabilities of metaphors, which often do no more than reproduce men's power and authority over women in our patri-saturated society.[44] We must be careful, therefore, that we do not construct the world using stories that express typically masculine and male rather than feminine and female experiences, not to mention human perspectives. As Emily Martin has brilliantly demonstrated, too often the social world of male aggression is superimposed upon certain biological issues, thereby recapitulating stereotypical views of how men generally relate to women.[45]

Three penetrations. One way of analyzing the representations of pregnancy cited above, therefore, is to say that the language of aggression attributed to the fetus in medical texts is simply the product of a male profession (medicine) imposing its own social stereotypes upon women, who are typically conceptualized as the "objects" of male aggression. As a result, perhaps what we are really talking about is not pregnancy, but the social construction of pregnancy by a medical profession which extends the view that (1) a man penetrates a woman in sexual intercourse, (2) a sperm penetrates an ovum in conception, and (3) a fertilized ovum penetrates a woman in pregnancy by implanting itself in her body to make her pregnant.

Consent to altruism. While we must be mindful that all that we know to be real comes to us in the form of some sort of social construction, we also must think through what might, or must, be common denominators in the variety of ways we could metaphorically represent pregnancy. For example, we could construct pregnancy in *altrustic* terms, by saying that the fertilized ovum "bestows" itself to the woman and "gives" itself to her by "activating" her capacity to be pregnant. Even so, the issue would still be whether a woman consents or not to "pregnancy activation" or to her receipt of pregnancy as a "gift." That is, a woman would have the right to *consent to altruism*.

The common denominator to pregnancy metaphors, therefore, is that it is a condition *resulting from* the fertilized ovum, however one wishes to characterize the process. Consequently, whatever might be the metaphorical range used to depict pregnancy, the key legal issue that remains is whether women *consent (or not) to pregnancy*.

IMMACULATE PREGNANCY

Of all the many ways to depict pregnancy, however, recognition that it is the fertilized ovum that *causes* a woman's pregnant condition is the one that is glaringly missing, not only from culture in general but specifically from the Supreme Court. The Court completely missed the reality of "pregnancy penetration" by the fertilized ovum in its initial ruling on abortion rights in *Roe* in 1973. What is more, recognition that it is the fertilized ovum that intrudes upon a woman to initiate and maintain a pregnant condition in her body has remained missing throughout the intervening years, including the 1992 *Casey* decision. In *Casey*, for example, the Court depicted pregnancy in this way:

The mother who carries a child to full term *is subject* to anxieties, to physical constraints, to pain that only she must bear.[46]

What we see in this passage is the Court's *passive construction* designating what is *causing* the burden of pregnancy, even in 1992 in *Casey*. Of course a pregnant woman is subject to burdens. The relevant question, however, is who or what subjects a woman to the burdens of anxieties, physical constraints, and pain when she is pregnant? In other words, who or what is the causal agent responsible for her pregnant condition?

Despite the many cases the Court has heard on abortion rights over the last twenty years, the causal agency of the fertilized ovum is missing in Supreme Court reasoning on abortion. The Court has failed to identify the fertilized ovum as the causal agent that must do something to a woman to initiate and maintain a pregnant condition in her body. Even while acknowledging at times the extreme degree of burden pregnancy can pose, including a woman's death, the Court nonetheless treats pregnancy as if it were an "immaculate condition" occurring in the absence of an identifiable physical causal agent.[47]

As a result, the Court has failed to develop the idea of the right of a woman to consent to pregnancy penetration by a fertilized ovum, her right to consent to a pregnancy relationship with a fetus, or, more generally, a woman's right to consent to pregnancy rather than solely her right to choose an abortion.

ABORTION FUNDING: STATE INTERFERENCE OR STATE ASSISTANCE?

We can fix what's wrong with Supreme Court reasoning on abortion rights by adding in a woman's right to consent to pregnancy, rather than solely her choice to have an abortion. By doing so, we move the abortion debate to new grounds.

Rather than focusing solely on the right of a woman to be free from *State interference* when exercising her right to choose an abortion, we can ask a new question: To what degree is she entitled to *State assistance* to defend herself from nonconsensual bodily intrusion by a fertilized ovum?

There are no precedents that allow people, once they are born, to intrude upon the bodies of other people.[48] This includes private relationships within kinship groups. A born child, for example, does not have a right to take a pint of blood from a parent without consent. What is more, if a child tried to do so, it would be the parent, not the child, that the State would be obligated to protect.[49]

On what grounds, therefore, would we privilege pre-born life, which may or may not be a person, to take someone's body without that person's consent? I will argue that there are no grounds that allow any born person to intrude nonconsensually upon the body of another private person. According to this standard, even if (or when) pre-born life is considered to be a person, it still would have no right to intrude upon the bodily integrity of another person without consent.

Rather than "freedom from" State interference when making private choices about one's own life, such as whether to have an abortion, what women are entitled to instead is "State assistance" in defense against a fetus intruding upon their bodies without consent. To the extent that the State offers its police protection to defend some people against nonconsensual bodily intrusion by other people, the equal protection clause of the Fourteenth Amendment requires that the State extend that assistance to women when their bodies are nonconsensually intruded upon by a fetus.

GOOD, BAD, AND CAPTIVE SAMARITANS

Many have pointed out that a woman has a right to be a "bad Samaritan" and refuse "to give" her body to a fetus. In a classic article, Judith Jarvis Thomson argued that the burdens required of a woman in pregnancy exceed the morally minimal standard required of Samaritan behavior. For this reason, she concluded, a pregnant woman has a moral right to be a "bad" Samaritan by refusing to give her body to a fetus.[50] Legal scholars support Thomson's view. Donald Regan showed how the law bolsters Thomson's position.[51] There is no legal precedent requiring that one private person donate her/his body, or a part therein, to another person, whatever might be the life-threatening need of the recipient.

Frances Kamm has since developed Thomson's argument from philosophical perspectives, and major legal scholars--such as Laurence Tribe, Cass Sunstein, and Deborah Rhode-- have asserted that there are no legal precedents that would support the view that women should be legally bound to donate their bodies to a fetus during pregnancy.[52]

Yet, as we have seen, it is not so much that women are forced to "give" their bodies as it is that fetuses "take" women's bodies. In this sense, a woman who does not consent to a pregnant condition caused by the fetus is in the position of being a "captive" Samaritan rather than a "bad" or "good" Samaritan.[53] What is at stake, therefore, is not merely women's right to refuse to donate their bodies, but their right to State protection against the nonconsensual *taking* of their bodies by pre-born life.

Reconstructing innocence. Although it is common to depict the fertilized ovum as "innocent," introducing a woman's right to consent to its pregnancy penetration of her body recasts our understanding of this term. The fertilized ovum is *dependent* on a pregnant woman's body; before viability it will die without her pregnant body, and even after viability her pregnant body serves its continued growth and develop prior to birth. The extreme dependency of the fetus, its utter helplessness to provide for its own needs without the assistance of the woman's body, is one way that it comes to be seen as "innocent."

The fetus is also viewed as innocent because it is *not in control* of its behavior. Its implantation in a woman's uterus is not the result of a conscious decision or intended behavior. It cannot "intend" to intrude upon her, and it can not control its behavior whether to intrude or not. In this sense, in the eyes of the law, it is innocent of criminal behavior and also innocent of negligent behavior.

But is the fetus really "innocent"? The fact that the fetus is dependent, helpless, unable to consciously make decisions, and "not in control" of itself does not alter the fact of what it *does*. It is the physical agent that causes pregnancy in a woman's body, regardless of whether it intends to do this, can control itself from doing this, or needs to do this to survive. In the sense of being the causal agent of a woman's pregnancy, therefore, the fetus is anything but innocent. It is causally responsible for a woman's pregnancy.

Risks versus rights. Many will argue that it is a woman who is responsible for her pregnancy if she consents to the risk of pregnancy by consenting to sexual intercourse with a man. Yet the law recognizes that even when a person exposes her/himself to risks, she/he does not loose the right to State protection against those risks. A person who consents to walk down a dark street at night, for example, does not have to consent to a mugging that may occur subsequent to taking such a risk. What is more, if a person exposing her/himself to such a risk is mugged, the police power of the State comes to the assistance of the person who is mugged--even if that person consented to the risk of being mugged in the first place.

FROM DUE PROCESS TO EQUAL PROTECTION

Introducing the idea that a fertilized ovum is the cause of a woman's pregnancy, reframes the abortion issue. Whereas the fetus is dependent upon a woman's body to sustain its own growth and development, it is not innocent of causing pregnancy. Rather, it is the woman who is the innocent victim of the pregnancy caused by a fertilized ovum, should this occur without her consent. Though a woman is responsible for incurring the risks that a fertilized ovum will implant itself, she is not responsible for that implantation any more than a person is responsible for a mugging who walks down a dark street at night and exposes herself to that mugging.

Abortion as Self-Defense

Rather than ceasing the "giving" of a woman's body to the fetus, abortion ceases the "taking" of a woman's body by a fetus. Cast in this framework, abortion is a form of self-defense against the massive bodily intrusion of a fetus.[54] The law recognizes the justifiable use of deadly force in situations where a person's life is in danger, where there is massive bodily invasion, or where there is a *qualitative* invasion which violates a fundamental liberty which may or may not be accompanied by physical harm as well. Examples of such categorical injuries are rape, kidnapping, and slavery.[55]

What makes rape an injury, for example, is not the physical experience of sexual intercourse per se; rather, it is the imposition of *nonconsensual* sexual intercourse upon women that turns a "normal" physical experience into an "injury." Similarly, what makes kidnapping an injury is not the act of traveling somewhere with another person; rather, it is *the forcing* of someone to travel with you without consent. Finally, even in the case of slavery, it is not the use of one's body to do work that makes it an injury; rather, it is the *coercive* use of someone's body without consent that makes this an unconstitutional act.

The purpose of the police power of the State is to provide protection to people against nonconsensual bodily intrusion by other people, not to mention potential people. Because the fetus uses a woman's body for its own purposes, some argue that when a state coerces a woman to be pregnant it in effect enslaves her.[56] A more accurate way to depict coercive pregnancy, however, is to first examine what the fetus itself does to make a woman pregnant. This examination reveals that women are entitled to the protection of the police power of the state in relation to the intrusion of the fetus upon their bodies, if and when this occurs without consent.

Rather than merely the Due Process Clause of the Fourteenth Amendment guaranteeing decisional autonomy to make choices free of state interference, therefore, a pro-consent approach to abortion rights activates the Equal Protection Clause of the Fourteenth Amendment guaranteeing people the equal protection of the State. Accroding to the Fourteenth Amendment, "No State shall . . . deny to any person within its jurisdiction the equal protection of the laws."

All states have laws protecting people from nonconsensual bodily intrusion. It is time these laws were applied to pregnant women in the form of abortion funding in compliance with the equal protection mandate of the Constitution.[57]

FUNDAMENTAL VALUES: LIFE AND LOVE

Pregnancy and abortion are emotional and political concerns as well as legal ones. Central to how we think and feel about these issues is not merely the value of the physical life of a fetus but also the value we place on love as an underpinning of our human community. Physical life sustained without human nurturing or connection becomes a paltry, if not fearful, prospect.

I wish to conclude, therefore, by emphasizing that my pro-consent approach to pregnancy and abortion rights is meant to expand the continuum about how we socially and legally construct pregnancy, not to substitute for other valuable ways by which we imbue meaning to these terms. My goal has been to identify hitherto hidden coercive dimensions of pregnancy in order to activate principles of law to which women are entitled, including State assistance in the form of abortion funding. If or when a fertilized ovum intrudes upon a woman's body without her consent, she not only has a right of decisional autonomy to make choices free of State interference, she also has the right to State assistance to help in defense of her bodily integrity.

However, we can continue to celebrate women's reproductive powers, as did the Court in *Roe*, noting that society would not survive without them.[58] Further, it is a deep desire, goal, and wish of many women to have a capacity to be pregnant and to exercise that capacity. Moreover, it is critical to recognize the value of the commitment of individuals to meet the needs of others as well as for greater public support to care for people in general, and pregnant women, fetuses, newborns, and children in particular.[59]

Ironically, however, the valorization of women's reproductive power is often used to enslave them, as when the physical power to be pregnant is equated with the legal mandate to remain pregnant.[60] What is more, the morality of care, the public funding of care, and the priceless value that care will always have for both those who give and those who benefit still stand in distinction to legal requirements designating who is to provide care. Recognition of the vital care disproportionately contributed by women is not equivalent to establishing legal coercion for such care from women.

The view of pregnancy presented here focuses on the necessity of a fertilized ovum to intrude upon the body of a woman in order to make her pregnant. We might well ask, of course, whatever the validity, what is the value or utility of conceptualizing pregnancy in these terms? Specifically, why would any woman ever consent to pregnancy defined as intrusive aggression upon herself? Further, does not attributing such aggression to a fertilized ovum substitute an ugly, conflict-constructed relationship for the beauty of a symbiotic one expressive of the mother-child bond, thereby robbing pregnancy of its positive, relational meanings?[61]

Such questions are particularly potent in the context of reproductive relationships. Surely, no species would survive if mothers were to view offspring solely as aggressors upon their bodies. The key word, however, is "solely." The goal here is not to argue that this view of pregnancy should replace all others. Rather, the goal is to expand the way we legally and socially construct pregnancy so that we newly appreciate why it, too, has a latitude comparable to that defining other intimate relationships, such as sexual intercourse.

It is time to frame pregnancy, therefore, much as sexual intercourse has become framed: as an experience requiring a woman's explicit consent in order to be, at a minimum, legal, leaving wide open consideration of what else makes its value maximum. Sexual intercourse, of course, runs the gamut between positive and negative extremes. Highly romanticized under some conditions, intercourse is a criminal offense in other contexts. What makes the difference between a Valentine (or, at least neutrality) on the one hand, and a law suit on the other, is consent. The fact that sexual intercourse is recognized not only as a crime without consent on the part of the woman but also as a disgusting, degrading, physically intrusive, and massively objectionable violent injury does not, and should not, in any way detract from the positive dimensions of the physicality of this act under conditions rendering it not only a consensual experience but one esteemed for the value of its intimacy.

So it is with pregnancy. The depiction here has emphasized the physical nature of pregnancy as a massive intrusion upon a woman's body resulting from a fertilized ovum. Surely, any human being has a fundamental right to say "no" to such physical invasion. Yet the right to say "no" to a fertilized ovum, for which women should have the full support of the State, does not negate the fundamental value pregnancy can also have. When a woman not only consents to be pregnant but actively wishes, desires, and seeks to be pregnant, such a union of rights and values surely produces the best of all possible worlds. That this unfortunately is not always the case, however, also requires legal recognition.

There is more than enough room for full recognition of the joy and value that endow our attitudes toward such fundamental and intimate relationships as sexual intercourse and pregnancy, even while adding legal guarantees to ensure that no woman must experience either without her consent.

NOTES

Social Politics (1994) 1:2, 130, 156. **Reprinted with permission.** Awarded "Best Paper" on "Women and Politics" delivered at the 1993 annual meeting of the American Political Science Association by the Women and Politics section of APSA at the 1994 annual meeting.

This is a revision of papers presented at the Symposium on the Politics of Abortion, Illinois Benedictine College, April 1993, and at the 1993 annual meetings of the American Political Science Association and Social Science History Association.

For their advice and interest, the author thanks Kathryn Abrams, Marcia Angell, Judith Baer, Nonnie Burnes, Barbara Craig, Robert Cord, Cynthia Daniels, Robert Davoli, Laura Frader, David Garrow, Richard Harris, Hilda Hein, Ted Jelen, Wendy Kaminer, Mary Katzenstein, W.D. Kay, Sally Kenney, Andrew Koppelman, Sanford Levinson, Kirstie McClure, Sidney Milkis, Martha Minow, Stephen Nathanson, Jennifer Nedelsky, Lynn Paltrow, H.W. Perry, Edward Price, Robert Price, David Rochefort, Mary Lyndon Shanley, Michael Tolley, Laurence Tribe, and Adam Wolff; and Kim Christensen, Rachel Harris, Susan Lee, Virginia McVarish, and Adam Wolff for research assistance.

The author thanks the Murray Research Center, Radcliffe College, for research support.

1. *Roe v. Wade* 410 U.S. 113 (1973).

2. This is part of a larger project by Eileen McDonagh, *The Captive Samaritan: Abortion and the Politics of Consent* (Oxford University Press, forthcoming). This research draws upon related themes published by McDonagh; see "Good, Bad, and Captive Samaritans," *Women and Politics* 13 (1993): 31-49 and "From Pro-choice to Pro-Consent in the Abortion Debate," *Studies in Law, Policy, and Society* 14 (1994), pp. 245-287.

3. *Roe*, note 1 at 146.

4. *Planned Parenthood of Southeastern Pennsylvania v. Casey* 112 S.Ct. 2791 (1992).

5. See *Roe*, 129-152, 160-163.

6. *Roe*, pg. 157 (1973).

7. *Roe*, pg. 158 (1973).

8. *Griswold v. Connecticut* 381 U.S. 479, pp. 494-495 (1965). *Griswold* affirmed the right of married couples to use contraceptives on the basis of a right to privacy defined by decisional autonomy. *Eisenstadt v. Baird* 405 U.S. 438 (1972) expanded the right of privacy to include the right to use contraceptives by adults whether married or not.

9. *Roe*, pg. 152.

10. *Bowers v. Hardwick* 478 U.S. 186 (1986).

11. *Roe*, pg. 158, emphasis added.

12. *Roe*, pg. 150, emphasis added.

13. *Roe*, pg. 158, emphasis added.

14. *Roe*, pg. 158.

15. *Roe*, pg. 158.

16. *Roe*, pg. 159.

17. The doctrine of viability was mapped onto a trimester framework of fetal development in *Roe*. In subsequent cases, particularly *Webster*, the notion of the trimester development of the fetus as a standard for determining women's abortion rights was discarded in favor of a standard of viability itself. See *Webster v. Reproductive Health Services* 492 U.S. 490, (1989).

18. The Court defines viability as "the point at which the fetus 'has the capability of meaningful life outside the mother's womb,'" *Webster v. Reproductive Health Services*, pg. 515.

19. As the Court stated in *Webster*, "For both logical and biological reasons, we indicated in [in *Roe*] that the State's interest in the potential life of the fetus reaches the compelling point at the stage of viability. Hence, prior to viability, the State may not seek to further this interest by directly restricting a woman's decision whether or not to terminate her pregnancy . . . [but after viability the] State's interest in protecting potential human life 'becomes compelling'" and the State may restrict a woman's decision to terminate her pregnancy. *Webster*, pg. 515.

20. *Casey*, pg. 58, emphasis added.

21. *Roe*, pg. 145, emphasis added.

22. *Doe v. Bolton*, 410 U.S. 179, (1973), pg. 207, emphasis added.

23. *Roe*, pg. 152.

24. *Casey*, pg. 13.

25. *Harris v. McRae*, 448 U.S. 297, (1980), pg. 354, emphasis added.

26. *Beal v. Doe*, 432 U.S. 438,(1977), pg. 448-49, emphasis added.

27. *Roe*, pg. 125.

28. *Beal*, pg. 446; *Maher v. Roe*, 432 U.S. 464, (1977), pg 478.

29. *Maher*, pg. 478.

30. *Maher*, pp. 473-474, emphasis added.

31. *Maher*, pg. 464.

32. H.C. Black, *Black's Law Dictionary* (St. Paul, Minnesota: West Publishing Company, 1990) pg. 1179, emphasis added.

33. As Laurence Tribe notes, what if women automatically miscarried unless they took an "anti-miscarriage" drug? He argues that it would be unconstitutional to pass a law forcing women to take such a drug, "in order to save the lives of whatever unborn children they might be carrying," because it would be "gender-specific on its face." He argues that this type of law would be "more difficult to sustain than would an antiabortion law or a refusal to fund abortions" even though the effect of the law is the same as current rulings by the Court that fail to offer state support to women seeking abortions, since failure to fund abortions for indigent women is equivalent to forcing these women to remain pregnant. Laurence Tribe, *Constitutional Choices*, (Cambridge, Massachusetts: Harvard University Press, 1985) pp 243-345.

34. "Morning-After Use for Abortion Pill," *New York Times*, Oct. 11, 1992, sect. 4 at 2.

35. Black, pg 305.

36. It is exactly this point, for example, that has led some feminist theorists to discount the idea of consent as a guarantee of women's rights. Carole Pateman, for example, views the patriarchal structure of society as undermining women's choice so severely as to render women's consent all but meaningless, Carole Pateman, *The Sexual Contract*, (Stanford, California: Stanford University Press, 1988). Similarly, Catherine MacKinnon argues that women's subordination to men on the basis of patriarchal social structures buttressed by law renders distinctions between rape and consensual sexual intercourse so ephemeral as to be nonexistent, leading to her provocative position that, in this sense, all sexual intercourse can be considered rape. See Catherin McKinnon, "Feminism, Marxism, Method, and the State: Toward a Feminist Jurisprudence," in *Feminist Legal Theory*, K. Bartlett and R. Kennedy, eds. (Boulder, Colorado: Westview Press, 1991) pp. 187-195. While I agree that women's ability to choose often is so constrained as to render their "consent" to be virtually meaningless, nevertheless, I believe that "consent" remains a powerful legal concept in courtroom contexts that needs to be utilized to strengthen women's right to an abortion as well as abortion funding.

37. Implantation of the fertilized ovum can occur in many other parts of a woman's body other than her uterus, such as in a woman's fallopian tubes. Implantation by the fertilized ovum in sites other than the uterus often poses grave and immediate dangers to a woman's health, usually requiring surgery to remove the fertilized ovum.

38. Black, pg. 811.

39. Legal scholars define two types of causes: "factual" causes and legal, or "proximate," causes. An act is a factual cause of an event if the event would not have occurred "but for" the act. We can trace what caused an event back through time, and for this reason all events have a multitude of factual causes. Consequently, the law seeks to identify among the many factual causes one dominant or primary cause of the event. This is what is meant by the "legal" cause of an event, often termed the "proximate" cause. See William L. Prosser and W. Page Keeton, *The Law of Torts* (St. Paul, MN: West Publishing, 1984) pg. 265.

In the context of pregnancy, sexual intercourse usually is a factual cause of pregnancy--meaning it is one of many events that contribute to the condition of pregnancy occurring in a woman's body. Sexual intercourse, however, is not the proximate cause of pregnancy, since it need not occur in order for a woman to be pregnant. Sexual intercourse, as one form of gamete transport, relocates sperm into a proximate location to ova. Sexual intercourse therefore cannot be considered the "proximate" cause of a woman's pregnant condition. Rather, it is only if and when a fertilized ovum implants itself that a woman becomes pregnant. In other words, without the implantation of the fertilized ovum, a woman is never pregnant. The fertilized ovum is, and must be considered, therefore, the legal or "proximate" cause of a woman's pregnant condition, whereas sexual intercourse, gamete transport in general, or men in particular are part of a large category of "factual" causes that contribute to the conditions producing pregnancy but are not the primary causes of pregnancy.

40. The right to an abortion references the right of a woman to terminate a pregnancy. From a medical standpoint, a woman is not in a pregnant condition until a fertilized ovum implants itself in her body. Prior to this implantation, the woman's right to expel a fertilized ovum references her right to use contraceptives, that is, devices and techniques designed to prevent pregnancy.

41. For a more complete analysis, see McDonagh, "From Pro-Choice to Pro-Consent in the Abortion Debate," *Studies in Law, Policy, and Society* (1994); McDonagh, "Good, Bad, and Captive Samaritans," *Women and Politics* (1993); and McDonagh, *The Captive Samaritan: Abortion Rights and the Politics of Consent* (Oxford University Press, forthcoming).

42. J. Knight and J. Callahan, *Preventing Birth: Contemporary Methods and Related Moral Controversies* (1989), pg. 100; and H. Fox, "Placental Structure in Health and Disease," in *Modern Antenatal Care of the Fetus* G. Chamberlain, ed. (Oxford: Blackwell Scientific Publications, 1990), pp. 35-36.

43. Fox, "Placental Structure," pp 38-41; P. McParland and J.M. Pearce, "Uteroplacental and Fetal Blood Flow," in *Modern Antenatal Care of the Fetus* G. Chamberlain, ed. (Oxford: Blackwell Scientific Publications, 1990) pp. 89-126.

44. M.J. Frug, *Postmodern Legal Feminism* (1992). (I an indebted to an anonymous reviewer of *Studies in Law, Policy and Society* for the term, "patri-saturated.") For a brilliant analysis of how "judicial rhetoric perpetuates disempowering images of women and therefore, indirectly, gender discrimination itself," see Sherry F. Colb, "Words That Deny, Devalue, and Punish: Judicial Responses To Fetus-Envy?" *B.U. L. Rev.* 72 (1992): 101.

45. E. Martin, "The Egg and the Sperm: How Science Has Constructed a Romance Based on Stereotypical Male-Female Roles," *Signs* 16 (1991): 485-501; E. Martin, *The Woman in the Body: A Cultural Analysis of Reproduction* (Boston: Beacon Press, 1992), pp. xii, 61.

46. *Casey*, pg. 13, emphasis added.

47. "Immaculate conception" in religious theology refers to the conception of Mary without original sin rather than the virgin birth of Jesus who was conceived without the physical agency of a man in relation to a virgin woman, Mary. However, some theologians, such as Episcopal Bishop John Shelby Spong, point out that the notion of Mary's immaculate conception developed in response to the Augustinian premise that the sin in life, evil, was "located in the flesh" and "transmitted through sex"; see John Shelby Spong, *Born of a Woman: A Bishop Rethinks the Birth of Jesus*, New York: Harper, pg. 216. As Spong characterizes Augustine"s views, "The sins of the fathers and mothers were quite literally passed to the new life through sexual intercourse that resulted in conception." (pg. 216).

The only way to equip Jesus with sinlessness, therefore, was to base his birth on the "virgin status" of his mother, Mary. This premise led inevitably backwards to the "doctrine of the immaculate Conception, which guaranteed that Mary's human flesh was not corrupted by Eve's sin." This meant that Mary herself had been conceived without the agency of a human man and, therefore, that Mary was "pure" of original sin as a precondition for her preparation "to be the womb of the new creation [Jesus]" (Spong, pp. 216-217). As Spong notes, "When the dogma of the Immaculate Conception was promulgated in 1854 by Pius IX, Mary was said to have been 'preserved immaculate from all stain of original sin by the singular grace and privilege granted her by Almighty God'" (Spong, pp. 217-218).

The use of the term "immaculate pregnancy" in this context is meant to connote allusions to representations of biological conception taking place without the necessary involvement of physical agents.

48. The sole exception may be the few states that refuse to recognize marital rape as a crime. Part of the reasoning here, however, is that a married couple has agreed to a contract, a component of which is sexual relations. Without a contract between a fertilized ovum and a woman, marital rape exemptions have no analogy to pregnancy.

49. In an infamous case, *DeShaney v. Winnebago County Department of Social Services*, 489 U.S. 189 (1989), a mother brought suit against her community's social workers and other officials alleging a violation of her son's liberty interest under the Fourteenth Amendment's due process clause; her contention was that the social workers had good reason to believe that the child's father was beating him and had an affirmative duty to prevent that beating, which they did not perform. The father did beat the child and inflict severe damage upon him. Although the majority of the Court agreed with the terrible facts of the situation, they concluded that the State had no obligation to *prevent* harm in this situation because it was too early to be sure of the danger to the child and because affirmative steps by the social service agency could

have infringed on the father's constitutional liberty to control the parent-child relationship (*DeShaney* at 203); see reference to *DeShaney* in *Horton v. Flenory*, 889 F.2d 454, 457 (3rd Cir. [Pa.] 1989) regarding the "prevention" of harm.

DeShaney, therefore, dealt with the issue of the obligation of the State to *prevent* one person from harming another. Presumably, if someone had called upon the State for assistance *while the beating was in progress* in the *DeShaney* case, the police power of the State would have been mobilized to assist the victim.

A pregnant woman *is in the process* of having her body taken and used by a fertilized ovum. If she does not consent, she is clearly the victim of bodily intrusion. The issue is no longer how to *prevent* harm, but how to *assist* her while harm is in progress.

50. J. Thomson, "In Defense of Abortion," reprinted in *Rights, Restitution, and Risk*, W. Parent (ed). (Cambridge, Massachusetts: Harvard University Press, 1986).

51. D. Regan, "Rewriting *Roe v. Wade*," *Mich. L. Rev*. 77 (1979): 1569-1646.

52. Frances Kamm, *Creation and Abortion* (Oxford: Oxford University Press, 1992); Laurence Tribe, *American Constitutional Law*, (New York: Foundation Press, 1988, 2nd edition), pp. 1340, 1349; see also by Laurence Tribe, *Abortion: The Clash of Absolutes* (New York: W. W. Norton, 1990); Cass Sunstein, *The Partial Constitution*, (Cambridge: Harvard University Press, 1993), note 21, pg. 395; Deborah Rhode, *Justice and Gender: Sex Discrimination and the Law* (Cambridge: Harvard University Press, 1989), pg. 212.

53. For a more complete analysis of this point, see McDonagh, "Good, Bad, and Captive Samaritans," *Women and Politics* (1993).

54. See Regan, "Rewriting *Roe*." Also see Jane English, "Abortion and the Concept of a Person," in *The Problem of Abortion*, 2nd ed., Joel Feinberg ed. (Belmont, CA: Wadsworth Publishing Co., 1984) English presents a moral argument for abortion based on the degree of injury suffered by a pregnant woman rather than the personhood status. However, she does not frame abortion rights in terms of a woman's right to "consent to pregnancy," nor does she develop the idea of what constitutes injury in pregnancy or the fetus as the causal agent of that injury.

55. *Model Penal Code*, Part I, General Provisions, vol. 1, Section 3.04, (Philadelphia: The American Law Institute. 1985).

56. A. Koppelman, "Force Labor: A Thirteenth Amendment Defense of Abortion," *Northwestern Law Review* 84 (1990), pp. 480-535.

57. This argument as constructed applies to those abortions already deemed constitutional by the Supreme Court: abortions prior to fetal viability. The main goal of my approach is to uncover new grounds justifying funding for women seeking abortions during the stage of pregnancy where abortion is a constitutional right.

This general approach, however, raises the issue of late, third trimester abortions. Does a woman retain a right of consent to continue, or terminate, pregnancy throughout its duration? This is a vexing theoretical question, even though it has little practical significance. Only the minutest fraction of women seeking abortions do so in the last trimester. It is a distortion, therefore, to skew the articulation of abortion rights and funding to cover what is an almost irrelevant, empty context.

Women's own interests are best served when they seek and obtain needed abortions at the earliest stages of pregnancy. As Laurence Tribe notes, after viability it is often safer for a woman to carry a fetus to term than to abort it (Tribe, *Abortion: The Clash of Absolutes*, p. 103). For this and other reasons, the overwhelmingly vast numbers of women do just that; if they choose an abortion, they seek and obtain one as early as possible into their pregnancy.

On the basis of strict logic, however, some might attempt to apply a "pro-consent" argument to third trimester abortions. If a woman has a continuing right to consent to the intrusion and use of her body by a fetus, then on what grounds would, or could, she ever be deprived of exercising such a right? The strict answer is probably "never," but why ask the question? Nowhere in the abortion debate are pro-choice advocates arguing that the "real" policy problem is that women are denied third trimester abortions. After all, third trimester abortions are not the goal of reproductive rights advocates and will not be a policy consequence of expanding the grounds for women's rights to abortions and funding by means of a pro-consent approach, since "late abortions" are not a policy that serves anyone's interests, including women.

Pro-choice advocates do seek a way to secure women's access to and funding for abortions during that period of pregnancy when women have a constitutional right to an abortion. It is with this policy goal that my pro-consent approach can be effective. It develops self-defense grounds for women's right to an abortion that are consistent with the way in which abortion rights originally were legislated. By so doing, it taps into privacy defined as the right to bodily integrity, which includes the right to State assistance in defending one's body.

The result is a stronger justification for both women's right to an abortion and to funding.

58. *Roe,* pg .125.

59. J. Baer, "Beyond Rights: Fetal Protection and Sexual Equity," presented at Midwest Political Science Association Annual Meeting, (1991), p. 19.; R. Goldstein, *Mother-Love and Abortion: A Legal Interpretation* (1988).

60. "Enslave" may seem too strong a term, and D. Regan, (*supra* note 51), pg. 1619, questions the applicability of the Thirteenth Amendment to the abortion issue. Other scholars, however, do invoke the Thirteenth Amendment in defense of women's abortion rights. See A. Koppelman, "Forced Labor: A Thirteenth Amendment Defense of Abortion," (1990); J. Baer, "What We Know as Women: A New Look at *Roe v. Wade*," *National Women's Studies Association Journal*, 2 (1990):558-582; Laurence H. Tribe, "Foreword: Toward a Model of Roles in the Due Process of life and Law," *Harvard Law Review*, 87 (1973), pp. 18-29.

61. Some might argue that the definition of pregnancy proffered here also resurrects old-fashioned legal reasoning premised upon rigid principles of boundaries, ownership, and individual power, a tactic of dubious merit just at the time when legal reasoning that appealsto relational, contextual references is making some inroads. J. Singer, "Sovereignty and Property," *Northwestern University Law Review*, 86 (1991), pp. 1-56; J. Beermann and J. Singer, "Baseline Questions in Legal Reasoning: The Example of Property in Jobs," *Georgia Law Review*, 23 (1989), pp. 911-995 (1989); J. Singer, "Property and Coercion in Federal Indian Law: The Conflict between Critical and Complacent Pragmatism," *Southern California Law Review*, 63 (1990), pp. 1821-1841; and M. Minow, *Making All the Difference: Inclusion, Exclusion, and American Law* (Ithaca, New York: Cornell University Press, 1990).

On the other hand, while noting the gains to be made by relational feminism eschewing "autonomy-talk," Daniel Ortiz makes the point that relational feminism "cannot well achieve much of what the feminist legal agenda demands" on the abortion issue. As a result, feminists must smuggle in autonomy-talk to resolve inherent tensions between relational feminism and abortion rights as the only response that can work. D. Ortiz, "In a Diffident Voice: Relational Feminism, Abortion Rights, and the Feminist Legal Agenda," paper presented at Cornell Law School, April 1992.

3

The Sources and Consequences of Public Attitudes Toward Abortion

Clyde Wilcox

In 1993, several events illustrated the changing politics of abortion. The Republican Party was deeply involved in a divisive fight over the abortion issue, with pro-choice candidates more frequently winning their party's nomination. Rev. Marion (Pat) Robertson indicated that his efforts would henceforth be focused on persuading women to choose not to have abortions rather than in marshaling the power of the state to forbid them from having abortions. This seeming abandonment of the pro-life movement left activists feeling increasingly politically isolated, and two doctors were shot by marginal members of pro-life organizations. Newly elected Bill Clinton reversed the pro-life policies of previous Republican presidents in several areas, including allowing doctors in family planning clinics that receive federal funds to counsel women on abortion, and mandating that state governments pay for abortions under certain circumstances under Medicaid.

The recent history of the politics of abortion in the United States can be divided into four periods, each demarcated by a major decision by the U.S. Supreme Court. The 1960s were a decade of abortion reform. During this period states began to liberalize their abortion laws, primarily in response to pressure by a variety of interest groups including associations of medical professionals. California governor Ronald Reagan signed into law the nation's most liberal abortion law, which essentially provided for abortion on demand. Yet by 1972 many states still banned most abortions, and most states imposed restrictions on abortion access.

In 1973, the U.S. Supreme Court radically transformed the politics of abortion. The Court struck down all state laws that restricted access to abortion during the first trimester of pregnancy, allowed state regulations only to protect the health of the woman during the second trimester, and permitted states to regulate abortion access to preserve fetal life only in the final trimester of pregnancy. In most states, the *Roe v. Wade* and *Doe v. Bolton* decisions overturned the state laws that dealt with the abortion issue.

The *Roe* decision caught opponents of legal abortion by surprise, and they responded by rapidly forming a plethora of political organizations aimed at restricting abortion.[1] These pro-life groups differed in their tactics but shared the goal of banning abortions. Some sought to pass a right-to-life amendment to the U.S. Constitution, others worked in the political arena to support pro-life members of Congress and presidential candidates, and still others worked primarily at the state level.

From 1973 until 1989, the pro-life forces had organizational and financial advantages over their pro-choice counterparts.[2] One measure of this advantage is total contributions to political action committees (PACs) that focus on the abortion issue. Figure 3.1 shows the total amount raised by pro-life and pro-choice PACs from 1978 through 1988. The pro-life side had a clear and growing advantage in the number of PACs and in total PAC receipts.

There is some evidence that the pro-life forces had an advantage in intensity as well. When Kristin Luker identified pro-life and pro-choice activists for her insightful in-depth interviews, she used somewhat more lax criteria for activism among pro-choice forces: her pro-life activists volunteered 20 hours each week, but her pro-choice activists volunteered only 10 hours a week.[3] This discrepancy was due to the fact that few pro-choice activists volunteered as many hours as did the pro-life organizers. Conventional wisdom in the 1970s and early 1980s held that in the general public, pro-life forces were also far more likely than their pro-choice counterparts to cast a single-issue vote.

This imbalance in intensity on the abortion issue during the 1970s and early 1980s is understandable in light of the string of pro-choice decisions by the U.S. Supreme Court. From 1973 to 1989, the Court consistently overturned efforts by state legislatures to impose restrictions on abortion access. For pro-choice activists, the status quo was acceptable, while for pro-life activists, it was intolerable.[4] Moreover, pro-choice voters could assume that despite the strong pro-life rhetoric of Republican presidents Reagan and Bush, abortion access was guaranteed by the Court and there was very little that a president or the

Figure 3.1
Pro-Choice and Pro-Life PAC Receipts, 1978-1988

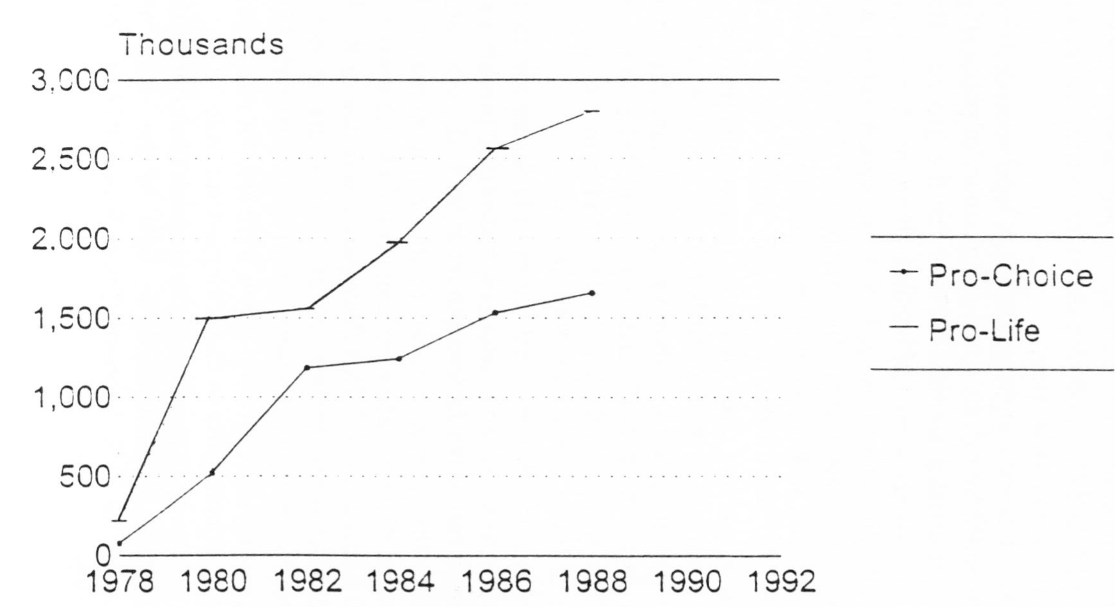

Source: Federal Election Commission

Congress could do to alter that fact. Similarly, there was little that pro-life governors or state legislatures could do to limit abortion access.

Yet presidents do replace justices on the Supreme Court, contingent only on the consent of the Senate. Reagan and Bush both promised pro-life groups to appoint anti-abortion justices, and by 1989 most of the justices from the original *Roe* majority had been replaced by men and women who were more conservative. In 1989, the Court dramatically changed its direction on abortion by upholding restrictions on abortion recently adopted in the state of Missouri. In *Webster v. Reproductive Health Services*, the Court allowed Missouri to ban state hospitals from performing most abortions, to require doctors to perform tests of fetal viability before performing abortions, and to maintain a preamble to the law that declared that life begins at conception.

The primary importance of the *Webster* decision was not in the content of the Missouri law, however. Four justices signaled a willingness to overturn *Roe*, and a fifth appeared to consider the possibility of doing so in later decisions. It appeared that the Court was at best one justice away from overturning *Roe*, with three years left in Bush's first term. If *Roe* was overturned, pro-choice forces would need to pass a national abortion rights law, probably over a Republican veto, or face an unending series of battles to preserve abortion rights in state legislatures and city councils.

Moreover, because *Webster* did not articulate a clear definition of the sorts of restrictions that the Court would find acceptable, it was interpreted as inviting states to experiment with abortion regulations to test the limits of the new conservative majority. Many states did just that: In Louisiana, Utah, and Guam, the legislatures passed laws that would ban most abortions. Although some states moved to codify *Roe* protections and some state courts held that the state constitution protected abortion rights, it appeared to pro-choice voters that they could no longer be sanguine about abortion rights.

The *Webster* decision stimulated organizational and financial efforts by pro-choice groups. Fundraising by the National Abortion Rights Action League increased sharply,[5] and new groups formed to protect and promote abortion rights.[6] Figure 3.2 again shows the fundraising of pro-choice and pro-life PACs, this time through the 1992 election. The data show that pro-choice PACs passed pro-life PACs in fundraising in 1989, the year of the Webster decision, and by 1992 had a substantial advantage. Much of this advantage came from the activity

Figure 3.2
Pro-Choice and Pro-Life PAC Receipts, 1978-1992

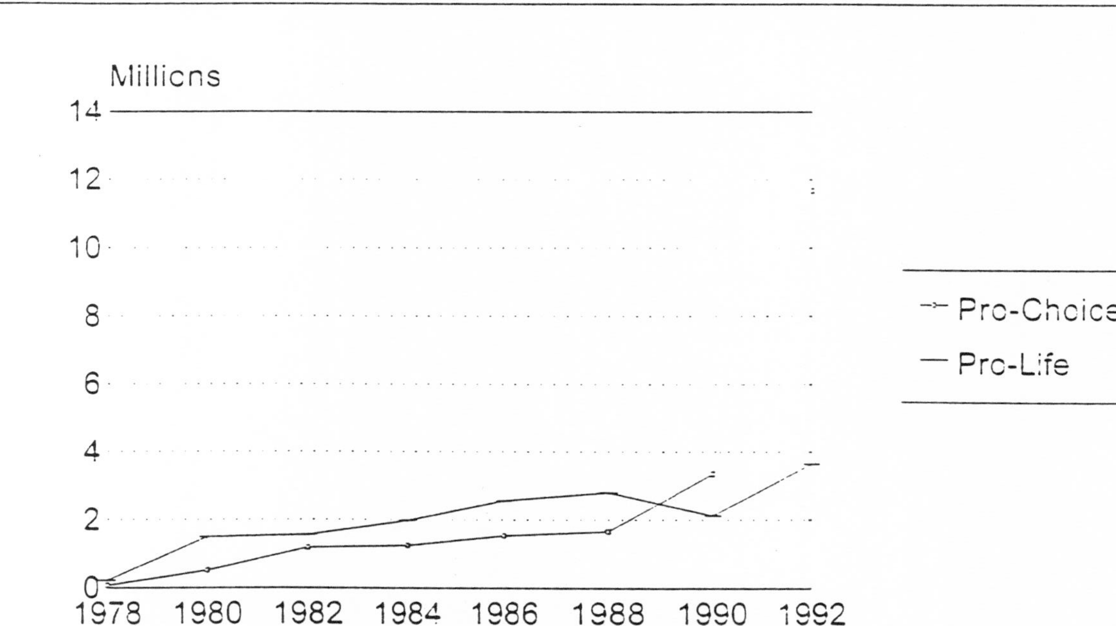

Source: Federal Election Commission.

of pro-choice groups that sought primarily to elect women to Congress,[7] but a variety of other pro-choice groups also formed or grew.

The financial mobilization was mirrored at the polls as well. In 1989, gubernatorial elections in Virginia and New Jersey resulted in the election of pro-choice Democrats who defeated pro-life Republicans. In both states pro-choice voters appear to have been mobilized by the *Webster* decision.[8] Prior to *Webster*, pro-choice Republicans in these states might have voted for the pro-life candidates of their party, safe in the assurance that the Supreme Court guaranteed their abortion rights. In 1989, it appeared that state governments would soon have substantial authority to regulate abortion policy and that the abortion position of a gubernatorial candidate did matter. Indeed, the abortion issue appears to have been influential in other state elections as well, including that for lieutenant governor in Virginia.[9]

It is likely that the 1992 Court decision in *Casey v. Planned Parenthood* and the presidential-election victory of Bill Clinton may have ushered in a fourth period in abortion politics. In response to the *Webster* decision, the Pennsylvania legislature had passed a law that imposed a variety of restrictions on abortion access, including waiting periods, parental consent, and viability tests. In *Casey*, the Court has upheld many of these provisions, while leaving the core constitutional claim of the *Roe* decision intact.

Although the Court upheld most of the restrictions in the Pennsylvania law, it struck down the requirement that women notify their husbands before obtaining an abortion. Moreover, Justice Sandra Day O'Connor articulated a new doctrine for reviewing state abortion restrictions, holding that state laws cannot pose an "undue burden" on women seeking abortions. Although pro-choice activists were outraged that the Court upheld the Pennsylvania restrictions, it was obvious that *Roe* was in no danger of immanent demise. The election of pro-choice Democrat Bill Clinton to the presidency provided further safeguards for *Roe*. In his first year, Clinton replaced Justice White, who had dissented in *Roe* and consistently voted to overturn the decision, with pro-choice justice Ginsburg. The subsequent appointment of Justice Breyer by President Clinton would appear to guarantee that *Roe* will remain the law of the land for many years.

The *Casey* decision and the election of Clinton quieted the worst fears of pro-choice citizens. States will remain free to pass some types of restrictive legislation, but there are clear limits on those regulations. The basic abortion right articulated in *Roe* appears safe for several years. These events may lead to greater complacency among pro-choice forces and a return to pre-*Webster* politics remains to be seen.

PUBLIC OPINION ON ABORTION

The politics of abortion have been shaped by the Court and driven by interest-group activity, but public opinion has played a vital role in the post-*Webster* politics. Although activists on the abortion issue take uncompromising positions and have worldviews that differ radically,[10] the public is more ambivalent on abortion. A *CBS News/New York Times* poll in 1989 showed that one fourth of Americans simultaneously believe that abortion is murder, and that it is sometimes the best choice.[11]

Since 1972, the General Social Survey (GSS), which is conducted by the National Opinion Research Center at the University of Chicago, has asked Americans whether abortion should be allowed under several different circumstances: when the woman's health is in seriously in danger because of the pregnancy, when there is a strong chance of a serious defect in the baby, when the woman becomes pregnant as a result of rape, when the family has a very low income and cannot afford any more children, when the woman is single and does not want to marry the man, and when the woman is married and wants no more children. These six items allow us to see (1) the types of rationales the public finds most persuasive, and (2) trends in abortion attitudes over time.

Since 1972, approximately three in four Americans have supported legal abortions in all three circumstances that involve physical trauma--threats to the health of the woman, danger of fetal defect, and rape. The public has been more divided on the social rationales for abortion--poverty, single women, and families who want no more children--with nearly half opposing abortions under all three circumstances and four in ten favoring allowing abortions under all three occasions.[12]

If we count the number of circumstances of which each survey respondent approves, we get a measure of the strength of support for legal abortion. Figure 3.3 shows the trends in abortion attitudes since 1972. Between 1972 and 1991, the average number of these

Figure 3.3
Support for Legal Abortion, 1972-1991

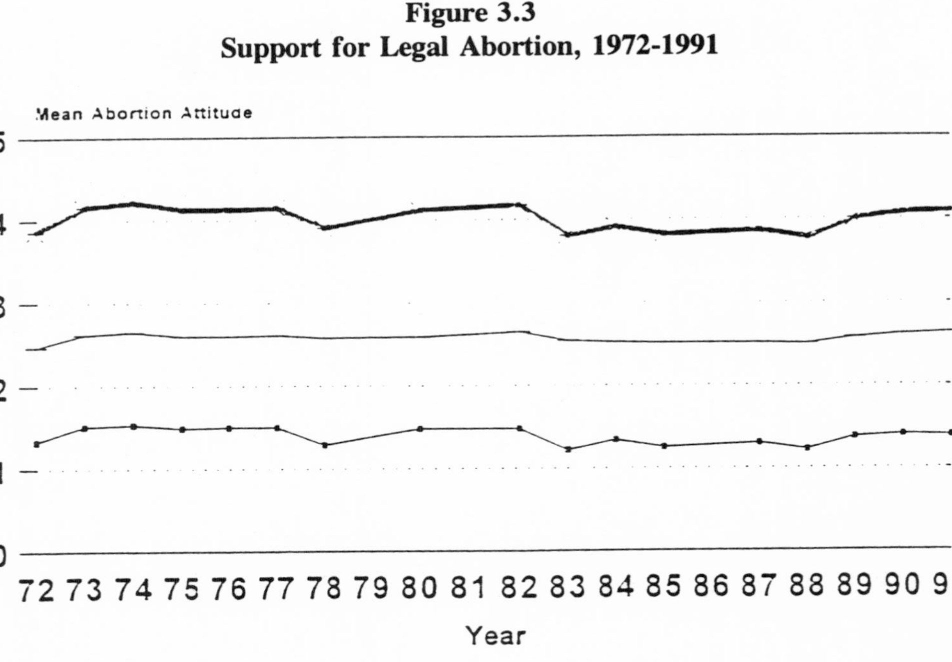

Source: General Social Survey.

circumstances supported by the public is between 4 and 5--that is, the public appears to favor allowing abortion in most but not in all circumstances. Since 1988, the GSS data show that approximately 8% oppose abortion in all circumstances and 39% favor allowing abortions under all six conditions.

Since 1972, public opinion on abortion has been remarkably stable. There have been small shifts in abortion opinion: the public became somewhat more pro-choice in the mid 1970s after *Roe*,[13] and became more conservative in the mid-1980s in the middle of the Reagan presidency. In 1989, shortly before the *Webster* decision, public opinion polls began to show increasing support for legal abortion, and the 1992 National Election Study shows that the trend continued through the 1992 election. Although the 1988 survey found approximately 38% of the public wanting abortion to remain legal under all circumstances, the 1992 survey found 47% of the public in the pro-choice camp.

The public response to these items differs sharply from the positions taken by activists, but surveys that ask additional questions show an even more moderate public. A 1989 *CBS News/New York Times* survey asked respondents a series of questions very similar to those in the GSS, and in addition asked many other questions about abortion restrictions. Approximately 3% of respondents consistently opposed abortion under all circumstances, and a similar percentage favored legal abortion with no restrictions. The modal (most common) position was to support keeping abortion legal in all circumstances but imposing a series of restrictions such as waiting periods, parental notification and consent, and tests for fetal viability. In short, the public seems to support a position very similar to that articulated by the Court in *Casey*. Table 3.1 shows the responses to various items in the *CBS News/New York Times* survey administered to a random sample of Americans, and to samples in several states. The first set of items mirror those in the GSS, with a couple of exceptions. The GSS item on married couples who want no more children was not asked in this survey; instead two additional items were included: whether abortions should be legal if childbirth would require a teenaged girl to drop out of school, and if the birth would interrupt the mother's career. The public is especially unwilling to allow abortions that would interrupt a woman's career, suggesting that most Americans believe that abortion is a morally troubling choice that should not be made merely for convenience.[14] At the bottom of the table, support for various restrictions on abortion access is assessed. Note that

Table 3.1
Support for Abortion Laws, 1989

	US	CA	FL	IL	OH	PA	TX
Should abortion be legal:							
Woman's health in danger	91	94	94	94	92	92	92
Woman is raped	87	86	88	86	86	85	84
Fetus has serious defect	76	79	79	75	73	75	72
Family cannot afford child	51	60	60	57	49	52	47
Woman is unmarried	51	61	59	58	50	54	49
Birth would force school dropout	50	56	56	52	46	50	46
Birth would interrupt career	35	46	47	42	37	37	35
None of above	6	6	4	4	7	7	8
All of above	31	40	41	36	31	32	31
Favor restrictions:							
Parental notification	86	82	86	86	89	87	86
Parent consent	74	67	70	74	75	75	75
Fetal viability tests	73	69	75	68	61	73	69
More regulations on private clinics	75	68	77	70	74	47	78
Ban abortions in public hospitals	38	31	35	35	39	34	38
None of the above	5	7	5	6	3	8	4
Four or more of above	50	40	49	45	50	37	49
Among those who favor legal abortion in all seven circumstances:							
Approve four or more restrictions	31	22	27	27	30	15	29

Source: CBS News/New York Times Surveys, 1989.

among those who supported legal abortion in all seven circumstances at the top of the table, a substantial number favored at least four of the restrictions. Only a small minority of these otherwise pro-choice citizens opposed all the restrictions.

The distribution of public opinion has political consequences. Because a large majority of Americans favor allowing abortions for circumstances involving physical trauma, candidates who favor banning abortions under these circumstances are poorly positioned on the issue. In the 1989 gubernatorial election in Virginia, Republican candidate Marshall Coleman took a strong pro-life position that would ban abortions except to save the life of the mother. Earlier he had supported allowing abortion for rape, incest, and fetal defect, but he moved to the right to win the Republican nomination. After *Webster*, he was poorly positioned for the general election. Similarly, the pro-life platform in the Republican presidential platforms since 1980 has become far more conservative than the general public.

Because the public also favors a number of restrictions including parental notification, waiting periods, and fetal viability tests, however, candidates who oppose these policies are also poorly positioned to win election. When the public is forced to choose between two poorly positioned candidates, the winner will often be the candidate who best frames the issue. For pro-choice candidates, the best "frame" for the abortion issue is around government intrusion into the private lives of citizens. "Who chooses?" is perhaps the most potent pro-choice theme. For pro-life candidates, issues of parental notification and waiting periods are the best foci for the campaigns, for most Americans support these policies.

POLITICAL IMPLICATIONS OF THE SOURCES OF ABORTION ATTITUDES

The distribution of abortion attitudes is an important factor in determining the politics of abortion, but it also matters who takes pro-choice and pro-life positions. The kinds of people who favor legal abortion are very different from those who oppose abortion, and they have different resources to bring to the abortion battle.

The main demographic source of pro-choice attitudes is education. Those with higher levels of education are far more likely than other Americans to take a pro-choice position. Among those citizens who did not graduate from high school, pro-choice forces hold a small numeric advantage. Among those with post-graduate education, the pro-choice advantage is vast. Fully 63% of those with postgraduate education are consistently pro-choice, and only 3% are pro-life.[15]

Pro-choice citizens are also more affluent, for a variety of reasons. In part this is because of the educational advantage described above, in part because pro-choice women are more likely to work outside the home and therefore to live in a family with two wage earners, and in part because pro-choice women have smaller families. The pro-choice advantage in education and income is mirrored in occupational prestige. Pro-choice men and women are more likely to be professionals or managers than their pro-life counterparts.

These demographic differences between the pro-choice and pro-life camps mean that when the pro-choice community is fully mobilized, it commands a wide array of resources that are less available to the pro-life side. If pro-choice women and pro-life women were both to give an equal share of their income to political action committees, the larger numbers of the pro-choice side combined with their greater affluence would produce a huge financial advantage. The quick mobilization of pro-choice money evident in Figure 3.2 shows the impact of these numerical and demographic advantages.

The principal source of opposition to legal abortion is religion. Pro-life activists are almost all deeply religious and actively involved in religious networks, and this characteristic is shared to a lesser extent by pro-life citizens who are not active in abortion politics. Several religious characteristics independently influence abortion attitudes: religious involvement, religious doctrine, and religious denomination. In addition, attitudes toward sexual permissiveness and the sanctity of life are important predictors of abortion attitudes, and these are directly related to religious characteristics.[16] Most pro-life men and women believe that their position is anchored in Biblical or papal authority, and that God is on their side. This gives the pro-life side an intensity that exceeds that of the pro-choice forces.

Even in the pre-*Webster* politics, pro-life voters were more likely than pro-choice voters to support a candidate with an abortion position similar to their own.[17] After *Webster*, the magnitude of this intensity advantage was reduced, which allowed the greater numbers of pro-choice voters to prevail in most elections. Yet the pro-life side maintained an advantage in intensity, presumably rooted in the religious sources of their beliefs.

The religious involvement of pro-life Americans is a source of strength in yet another way. Churches are political as well as religious communities,[18] and in many communities local congregations of the Assemblies of God, of various Baptist churches, and local Catholic parishes provide organizational and financial resources for the pro-life forces. Pastors in evangelical and Catholic churches have various resources that help them mold the attitudes of their congregants.[19] There is evidence that pro-life groups recruit new members in churches, even in mainstream Protestant churches that are nominally pro-choice.[20]

Of course, the characterization of pro-choice and pro-life activists and supporters above does not imply that *all* people who take these positions fit these categories. There are many highly educated pro-life activists and many deeply religious pro-choice activists. There are almost as many pro-life citizens with college degrees as there are pro-life citizens who failed to enter high school, and there are more pro-choice than pro-life Catholics and evangelical Protestants, even among those who attend church regularly.[21] Yet the resources that each side brings to the abortion battle differ in part because people who are pro-life and pro-choice differ in their characteristics. On one side of the issue is a relatively large, well-educated and affluent set of Americans, and on the other side is a much smaller, less-educated and less-affluent group who organize through religious networks and hold intense beliefs that inspire their activism.

Finally, it is important to note that a narrow majority of Americans are *situationalists*--that is, they support legal abortion in some circumstances, not in others. These citizens ultimately hold the balance of power in the abortion debate. In general, they do not want sharp restrictions on legal abortion, yet they are uneasy about the frequency of abortions in America and are ambivalent about the moral rights of the fetus. Most believe that the fetus has some rights, and that abortion is a difficult decision that is best avoided if at all possible. Ultimately, a majority of situationalists believe that the government should not dictate the moral decisions of citizens, but that too many women today choose abortions.

ABORTION AND THE PARTY SYSTEM

In an important deductive analysis of the dynamics of party systems, Anthony Downs has argued that in a two-party system with a politically

Table 3.2
Abortion Positions of Primary Voter and Other Partisans--1988

	Pro-life	Situationalist	Pro-choice
Democrats:			
Voted in primary	12%	50%	38%
Did not vote	15%	49%	36%
Republicans:			
Voted in primary	11%	58%	31%
Did not vote	13%	53%	35%

Source: 1988 National Election Study

moderate public, both parties tend toward the middle position on the distribution. If a party nominates a candidate who takes a position that is far from the middle of the distribution, she or he will lose.[22] Downs' analysis suggests that presidential candidates usually echo each other and not provide clearly divergent choices on policy issues.

On most issues, Downs' analysis seems to fit the American system quite well. In 1988 Dukakis and Bush debated the details of health care, family leave, military reductions, and aid to the homeless, but took similar positions on the basic direction of policy. In 1992 Clinton and Bush differed in their positions on fiscal stimulus and national health care, but the differences on these issues were far smaller than on abortion. Clinton favored legal abortion with no restrictions, and the Republican platform contained a plank that would have banned all abortions with the possible exception of those that would save the woman's life.[23]

Indeed, since 1980 the Republican platform has contained a plank that has the support of perhaps 10% of the American public, and the Democratic nominee has taken a position that also represents a minority position. Some presidential candidates whose initial positions on abortion did not fit the party orthodoxy in the 1980s changed their positions: They include George Bush, Jesse Jackson, and Richard Gephardt. Why have the positions of the two parties diverged so widely at the national level, despite a generally ambivalent public opinion that supports legal abortion with restrictions? Several possible explanations exist. It may be that the parties take more extreme positions because those who vote in primary elections are more ideologically extreme.[24] If pro-life and pro-choice activists are more likely than situationalists to vote in presidential primaries, the candidates might adopt more extreme positions in order to win the nomination. Yet the data in Table 3.2 from 1988 National Election Studies (NES) show that primary election voters are no more extreme on the abortion issue than other partisans. There were more pro-choice Republican primary election voters in both elections than pro-life voters, yet every Republican candidate in both elections took strong pro-life positions. Indeed, what is striking is the similarity between Democratic and Republican primary voters.

It is also possible that party elites hold more extreme positions, and candidates take positions to appeal to party activists. Perhaps those who contribute to presidential candidates are more likely to be consistently pro-life or pro-choice, or those who serve as delegates to the party conventions are more extreme on the abortion issue. However, the data in Table 3.3 show that this explanation also fails. The data from polls of convention delegates shows that more Republican delegates took a pro-choice than a pro-life position, although a clear majority were situationalists. The party was sharply divided, with delegates for Bush and Dole being far more supportive of abortion rights than delegates who supported Robertson or Kemp. Among the Democratic delegates there was a strong pro-choice consensus, although substantial minorities of delegates for Simon, Gephardt, and Gore took a pro-life or situationalist position.

The data in Table 3.3 for campaign contributors comes from a national mail survey of those who gave $200 or more to a presidential candidate in 1988. The data show more pro-choice than pro-life Republicans, although the Robertson contributors were strongly pro-life. Again the Democratic elites were generally pro-choice, although minorities of contributors to Gephardt, Gore, and Jackson took situationalist or pro-life positions.

The data in Table 3.3 show that party elites are more polarized on abortion than are the primary election voters characterized in Table 3.2. Yet the difference is not between a strongly pro-choice Democratic Party and a pro-life Republican Party; instead Republican elites are more likely to adopt situationalist positions. Democratic elites are strongly pro-choice but not significantly more so than other highly educated, affluent Americans.

Taken together, the data in Tables 3.2 and 3.3 show that primary election voters, party delegates, and contributors are not as extreme on

Table 3.3
Party Elites and Abortion Attitudes, 1988

	Pro-life	Situationalist	Pro-choice
Convention Delegates			
All Democrats	5%	18%	78%
Dukakis	6%	14%	81%
Gephardt	5%	28%	67%
Gore	3%	31%	66%
Jackson	2%	13%	85%
Simon	7%	31%	62%
All Republicans	12%	55%	33%
Bush	8%	55%	37%
Dole	9%	57%	33%
Kemp	46%	42%	13%
Robertson	44%	54%	2%
Campaign Contributors	**Government Should Prohibit Abortion**		
	Strongly Agree	**Intermediate**	**Strongly Disagree**
Babbitt	7%	13%	85%
Dukakis	9%	15%	76%
Gephardt	8%	35%	57%
Gore	3%	23%	74%
Jackson	4%	20%	76%
Bush	10%	41%	49%
Dole	15%	42%	43%
DuPont	10%	24%	66%
Kemp	32%	36%	32%
Robertson	85%	12%	3%

Source: CBS News/New York Times Delegate Polls; Data from a survey of presidential contributors compiled by Clifford Brown, Jr., Lynda Powell, and Clyde Wilcox.

the abortion issue as are the positions taken by presidential candidates. Yet it is likely that candidates take these positions to attract votes, money, and delegates. Prior to *Webster*, candidates could appeal to abortion activists with little fear that their positions would repel more moderate voters or elites, for only activists were likely to assign the abortion issue a position of high salience in their political calculations. Thus, a Republican presidential candidate could win primary election votes and campaign contributions by taking a strong pro-life position, even though there were more pro-choice Republicans than pro-life Republicans. Democrats could likewise win support from pro-choice activists by taking very strong pro-choice positions, even though a majority of Democratic voters and activists support parental notification and waiting periods.

ABORTION, PARTISANSHIP, AND PRESIDENTIAL VOTING

The salience of the abortion issue for presidential elections is evident in the expenditures of pro-life PACs,[25] which focused their efforts in 1992 on keeping a pro-life Republican in the White House. Presidents can influence abortion policy in several ways: in their Supreme Court nominees, in signing or vetoing legislation that regulates or funds abortions, and in executive orders that interpret various federal statutes. In a few hours during his first week in office, Bill Clinton changed national abortion policy more dramatically than could have several additional pro-choice senators had George Bush won the election.

Although in 1972 and 1976 the major-party presidential candidates took similar positions on abortion, beginning in 1980 the party platforms became widely divergent. Yet most political science research suggests that voters rely on candidate evaluations and partisanship in making their vote decisions far more often than on political issues. Indeed, one important line of research has argued that issues are relatively unimportant in vote decisions.[26] This is true for at least two reasons. First, most citizens are relatively uninvolved in politics and inattentive to the issue positions taken by candidates. Second, in a two-party system with a generally moderate public, candidates tend to take centrist positions and obscure, rather than highlight, their differences on issues.

When issues do matter in vote decisions, they are frequently "easy" issues--issues that (1) have been long on the political agenda, where the

Table 3.4
Democratic Presidential Voting and the Abortion Issue

	1972	1976	1980	1984	1988	1992
Pro-life	37	58	45	36	46	46
Many restrictions	31	49	44	37	39	45
Few restrictions	38	47	33	38	46	48
Pro-choice	41	53	49	50	55	72

Note: Table shows the percentage of respondents with each position on abortion for the Democratic candidate in each year.
Source: National Election Studies.

focus is on ends and not means, and (2) contain a heavy symbolic component. In addition, issues matter most when candidates take clear and distinct positions and emphasize the issues in their campaigns. The abortion issue is a clear example of an easy issue. The issue has been on the agenda since the 1960s, it is about whether to allow abortions, not how to prevent unwanted pregnancies or to decrease childbirth among teenagers. Finally, the abortion debate symbolizes a much wider discussion about the proper role of women in society and the proper role of sexuality.[27]

Table 3.4 shows that over time, citizens appear to have learned the positions of the presidential candidates, and to have cast votes for candidates who took positions similar to their own. From 1972 through 1980 there were only small differences in the percentage of pro-life and pro-choice voters who cast Democratic ballots, but beginning in 1984 there has been a widening gap. This learning appears to have occurred primarily among pro-choice voters, who have cast Democratic ballots in increasing numbers. The 1992 National Election Study data show that Bush beat Clinton among each set of voters who did not take a pro-choice position, but that Clinton won handily among those who took a consistent pro-choice position.

Of course, the data in Table 3.4 do not prove that abortion attitudes are the source of these vote decisions. Pro-choice voters are more likely than pro-life voters to be liberals on other issues, and it may be these other issues, not abortion, that have influenced vote decision. To determine the effects of the abortion issue on vote choice, it is necessary to *control* for other factors such as partisanship, ideology, and other issue attitudes. In one study of the 1992 presidential election, Alan Abramowitz reported that abortion was the single strongest issue in determining vote choice--stronger even than evaluations of the economy.[28] Other research suggests that the importance of the abortion issue in presidential elections has increased over time. According to the NES, in the 1984 election, abortion was not a significant predictor of vote choice after controlling for other attitudes, but in 1988 abortion was an important source of vote decisions.[29]

The data presented here show that American voters gradually have become aware of the wide difference in the positions of the presidential parties on the abortion issue. Of course, the positions by the presidential candidates are not always shared by congressional, state, or local candidates. There are prominent dissenters in both parties in state offices and in Congress. Yet there is evidence that the public has gradually aligned its partisanship with the positions of the presidential parties on abortion. The correlation between abortion attitudes and partisanship in the 1970s was essentially 0. By 1984, the correlation had grown to .05, and this modest correlation was large enough to inspire confidence that it is not attributable to sampling error. In the 1992 NES data, the correlation between party identification and abortion attitudes was .12, more than twice as high as in 1984.[30]

How might this growing alignment take place? One explanation for the growing congruence between partisanship and abortion attitudes is that pro-life Democrats and pro-choice Republicans have begun to change their partisanship because of the abortion issue. There is substantial evidence of changing aggregate partisanship among pro-life evangelicals in the South,[31] and Celinda Lake, who was one of Clinton's key pollsters in 1992, reported that she found evidence that pro-choice Republican women began to change their partisanship after *Webster*.[32]

There is also some evidence that some citizens have changed their attitudes on abortion as a result of the policy leadership of their party's candidates.[33] It seems likely that this type of persuasion is not especially widespread, for abortion attitudes are among the most stable attitudes at the individual level.[34]

In 1992, the abortion issue appears to have hurt George Bush. Although the Voter Research Surveys exit polls showed that a majority of voters who mentioned abortion voted for Bush (a statistic widely reported in the media), a more subtle reading of the data suggests that

Bush lost as much as 2% of the general election vote on the abortion issue. Many of those who mentioned the abortion issue were strong partisans who would have supported the candidate of their party regardless of their abortion positions. Rich Bond, former chairman of the Republican party under Bush, noted that the abortion issue was for many suburban voters "the straw that broke the camel's back." Abramowitz showed that abortion was a source of vote defection among well-educated Republicans, wheras pro-life Democrats were less likely to be aware of Clinton's pro-choice stand and were therefore less likely to defect to Bush.

ABORTION AND VOTE DECISIONS IN GUBERNATORIAL ELECTIONS

Although the president can influence abortion policy at the national level, governors play an increasingly important role in abortion politics. In the aftermath of *Webster*, governors in a number of states vetoed or signed additional abortion restrictions, and others called for their state legislatures to pass restrictions or abortion-rights guarantees. One governor called a special session of the legislature to seek additional abortion restrictions, although the legislature did not comply.

The data presented above shows that there is a substantial pro-choice plurality at the national level, states differ in their political cultures, their religious cultures, and their attitudes on abortion. Figure 3.4 shows abortion attitudes by state, taken from data from the 1988-1992 NES Senate study.[35] In some states there is a substantial pro-choice advantage, in others opinion is more closely divided, and in a few states, there is a small pro-life plurality. The most conservative states are in the border south (Kentucky, West Virginia) or deep south (Mississippi, Louisiana), in the central West (North Dakota, Kansas, Utah). The most liberal states are in the Northeast (Vermont, New Hampshire, New Jersey, New York), the West (California, Oregon, Colorado, Arizona). Surprisingly, the states with the most liberal attitudes are those with the largest number of Catholics.[36]

Of course, interest groups are very important in mobilizing abortion attitudes in state elections. Although there have been several attempts to measure interest group activity on the abortion issue across the states,[37] all available measures have problems. Nevertheless, all measures show that there are large differences across states in the organizational muscle

Figure 3.4
Pro-Choice/Pro-Life Advantage by State

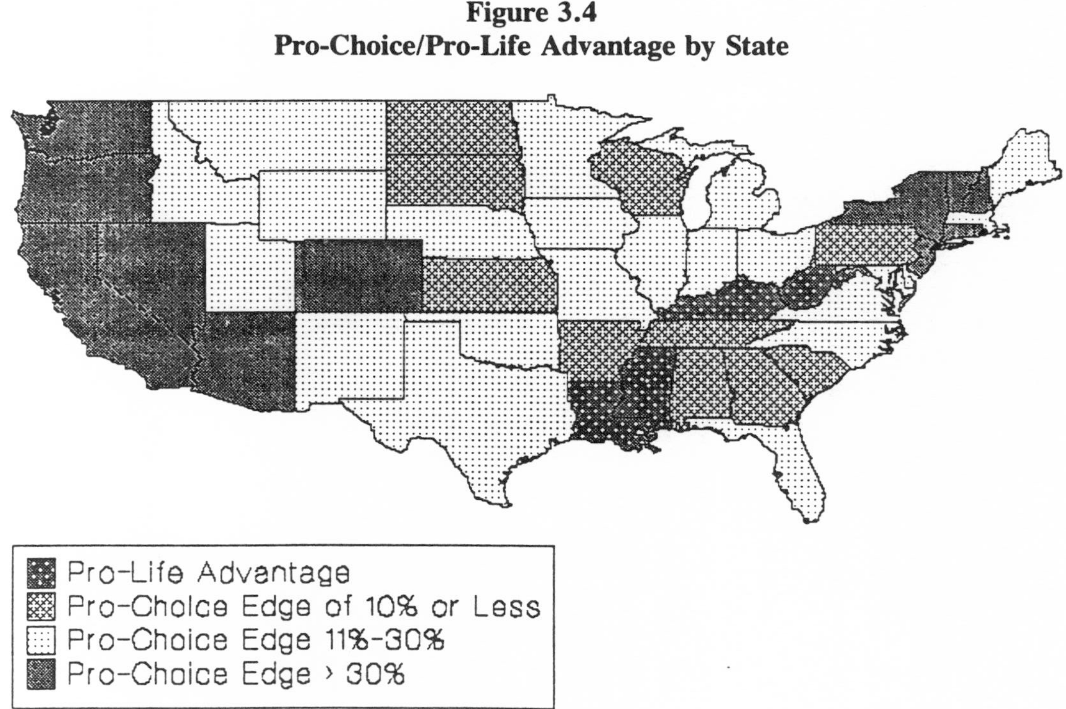

of the pro-life and pro-choice movements, and that interest group activity does not perfectly correlate with state public opinion.

The substantial differences in abortion attitudes and interest group activity across the states suggest that the abortion issue might play differently in elections in California than in Louisiana. The abortion issue might also have a different impact on the elections in 1990 than in 1992. The 1990 elections were conducted after *Webster* and prior to *Casey*, a period of maximum uncertainty about the ability of states to regulate abortion. The *Casey* decision in 1992 showed the limits of state authority to regulate abortion, although states do retain considerable leeway to pass procedural barriers to abortion access. The data in Table 3.5 show the impact of the abortion issue on vote decisions in a number of governor's elections in 1989-1992, controlling for partisanship. The data show that abortion was an important issue in most states. In two states, Massachusetts and Pennsylvania, the Democratic candidate took a more conservative position on the abortion issue than the Republican candidate, and in both states voters appear to have been sufficiently aware of these positions to alter their voting behavior.

In Virginia, the abortion issue was especially important. Fully 70% of pro-choice voters in Virginia voted for Douglas Wilder, compared to only 18% of pro-life voters. The Virginia race was held soon after the *Webster* decision, and the Democratic ticket emphasized the abortion issue. The National Abortion Rights Action League (NARAL) spent substantial sums in independent expenditures in Virginia to advocate the election of the Democrats. It is worth noting, however, that a strong pro-choice position on abortion does not guarantee an automatic victory in Virginia. In 1993, Democratic pro-choice candidate Mary Sue Terry lost to Republican George Allen, whose vague position on abortion appeared to include an endorsement of at least some procedural restrictions.

Of course, some of the reason for the pattern in Table 3.5 may be that Democrats, liberals, and other groups are more likely to be both pro-choice and Democrats. Yet multivariate analysis controlling for a variety of factors found that in 1990, abortion was a very important issue in most state gubernatorial elections.[38] Indeed, in Pennsylvania abortion attitudes were a stronger predictor of vote choice than even partisanship, and in several states abortion was more important than attitudes toward the economy.

Table 3.5
Abortion in Gubernatorial Elections, 1989-1992

	1989		1990								1992	
	VA	NJ	FL	TX	CA	MA	IL	MI	OH	PA	MO	WA
Democrats:												
Legal	92	90	95	91	87	60	78	80	84	62	92	90
Limited	81	87	79	82	78	71	71	79	70	85	89	83
Not legal	51	84	79	73	74	78	85	76	74	92	64	72
Independents:												
Legal	68	76	67	68	62	39	51	42	53	41	81	70
Limited	38	63	52	40	40	48	41	45	33	75	47	43
Not legal	21	48	40	23	29	48	45	37	17	97	16	19
Republicans:												
Legal	35	35	40	31	17	21	29	17	20	27	38	28
Limited	13	22	18	15	11	21	14	27	15	51	30	15
Not legal	2	13	16	12	4	42	16	23	5	77	21	14

Source: Voter Research and Surveys Exit Polls.

In 1992, only a few exit polls contained a question on abortion. Two states had gubernatorial elections and abortion questions in their exit polls, and in both states abortion was a factor in vote choice. In both states abortion played a much larger role in the vote choice of independents than of partisans. In both states the abortion issue was especially salient, for there were also Senate elections in which abortion differences were aired.

Taken together, these data suggest that the abortion issue has become an important one in gubernatorial elections in the post-*Webster* era. Whether this will continue in future elections is not clear. In 1993, two gubernatorial elections resulted in Republicans replacing Democratic governors. In New Jersey, the Republican candidate took a pro-choice position and won over an unpopular incumbent governor. In Virginia, the Republican gubernatorial candidate hedged on abortion but appeared to endorse procedural restrictions on abortion, and he won an easy victory over a weak candidate who opposed these restrictions. The Republican candidate for lieutenant governor took a strong pro-life position, and he lost badly in an otherwise Republican sweep. This suggests that when candidates take widely divergent positions, and when the issue is salient in the election, abortion may continue to influence gubernatorial voting. However, if Republicans begin to either nominate pro-choice candidates or else hedge their abortion positions, then issue voting on abortion will become less likely.

ABORTION AS AN ISSUE IN U.S. SENATE ELECTIONS

Governors obviously have a role in state abortion policy, so issue voting on the abortion issue was relatively common after *Webster*. Several U.S. Senate elections in 1990 and to a lesser extent 1992 also addressed the issue. The Senate has voted on a variety of bills relating to abortion: legislation that would have overturned the *Rust v. Sullivan* decision banning health professionals in family planning clinics that accept federal funds from discussing abortion with their patients, and other abortion issues as well.[39] As some states adopted stringent abortion regulations, pro-choice forces lobbied Congress for passage of the Freedom of Choice Act, which would guarantee access to abortion to all women until the point of fetal viability and would allow abortions

Table 3.6
Abortion in Senate Elections, 1990-1992

	1990									1992			
	CO	HI	ID	IL	IA	NH	NC	OR	RI	IL	MO	NY	WA
Democrats:													
Legal	84	77	81	92	93	86	88	63	81	90	88	79	87
Limited	63	75	66	89	87	66	64	50	81	85	72	67	88
Not legal	68	81	55	90	71	45	69	59	75	89	53	61	89
Independents:													
Legal	51	37	49	72	68	48	65	66	54	67	72	66	74
Limited	35	43	38	59	52	27	39	44	50	60	43	40	54
Not legal	47	53	25	59	27	16	20	34	57	32	11	25	27
Republicans:													
Legal	19	14	29	35	34	13	35	41	25	28	26	34	30
Limited	12	25	9	35	16	6	13	21	36	17	12	14	13
Not legal	10	15	9	34	11	7	8	4	43	14	3	13	6

Source: Voter Research and Surveys Exit Polls.

after viability to save the life or health of the mother. Thus retrospective and/or prospective voting on the abortion issue was possible in 1990 and 1992. Some Senate campaigns focused heavily on the abortion issue,[40] providing voters with sufficient information on candidate positions to allow an issue vote.

The data in Table 3.6 shows the impact of abortion issues on Senate voting, controlling for partisanship. In states in which the candidates took diverse positions on abortion, in which both candidates had sufficient money to get their messages across, and in which one or both candidates emphasized the abortion issue, abortion influenced vote choice. The impact was especially large in 1990 in Iowa, Idaho, New Hampshire, and North Carolina, where abortion was a featured issue. In Hawaii and Rhode Island the pro-choice Republican women candidates were more liberal than the generally pro-choice Democrats, and in both states the voters appear to have perceived this reversal of the national party positions. In states where the candidates took similar positions, such as Illinois, abortion played only a minor role.

In 1992 abortion played a significant role in the Senate election in Missouri, but far less of a role in other states. Abortion was most important in determining the votes of Independents, although there were substantial defections of pro-life Democrats in Missouri and New York and of pro-choice Republicans in Missouri, New York, Illinois, and Washington.

THE PAST AND FUTURE POLITICS OF ABORTION

As the Senate prepared to hold hearings to confirm pro-choice justice Ruth Bader Ginsburg to the U.S. Supreme Court, pro-choice groups worried about her public statements that the *Roe* decision had interrupted a process of ongoing legislative compromise and stimulated the pro-life movement. Ginsburg is almost certainly correct. The abortion reform movement in the 1960s was gradually liberalizing abortion laws, and would probably have succeeded in many and perhaps most states.

The *Roe* decision transformed the debate. Many pro-choice citizens were content with the fundamental abortion right guaranteed by the decision, and only the activists were motivated to fight on issues such as abortion access and funding. Pro-life citizens, in contrast, were strongly motivated to attempt to overturn the decision, and with the active support of church networks they formed a number of organizations and voted the abortion issue in many elections. Although the number of those who oppose abortion in all circumstances was relatively small, they were politically powerful in part because of the very Court decision that inspired their anger. Because pro-choice and situationalist voters believed the abortion right was safe, they were less motivated to organize and vote the abortion issue. The Republican Party embraced the pro-life activists in an effort to woo formerly Democratic evangelicals and Catholics on the issue.

The *Webster* decision again transformed the politics of abortion. For almost three years the exact limits of state authority to regulate abortion were undefined, and state legislatures and governors in many states deliberated or acted to restrict or guarantee abortion rights. Between 1989 and 1992, it appeared that the Supreme Court was only one justice short of overturning *Roe*. Pro-choice Americans perceived a threat to their reproductive rights, and they mobilized. With larger numbers and deeper pockets, they were able to affect the outcomes of a number of gubernatorial elections, Senate elections, and even the presidential election.

In response to the pro-choice mobilization, the Republican party began and internal debate on its position on abortion,[41] and many candidates began to moderate their position. The *Webster* decision altered the abortion issue to fit more closely the pattern described by Downs, in which the two parties nominate candidates close to the middle of the public opinion. Republican candidates scrambled to reposition themselves on the abortion issue, and prominent party elites began a major effort to redefine the party position. Even national leaders of the Christian Right began to deemphasize the abortion issue in favor of other, more promising topics.

This movement by the Republican mainstream left the pro-life movement isolated. Recently, there have been troubling signs of violence from marginal members of the pro-life ranks, and many pro-life activists have been hesitant to condemn the violence. With prominent conservatives declaring the abortion issue "won" by the opposition and abandoning the cause, the movement is increasingly dominated by the most extreme elements. Indeed, a number of abortion providers in Florida and Massachusetts have been murdered in recent years.

Meanwhile, President Clinton has replaced one of the four pro-life justices on the Supreme Court, and has added another pro-choice justice as well. President Clinton may well replace at least one more justice before his term is over. This would appear to guarantee a Court that will continue to uphold the basic outline of *Roe*, even as it allows states to impose a variety of procedural restrictions to make abortions more difficult to obtain. The basic right to abortion seems secure, if no longer fundamental. Whatever the limitations of an "undue burden" to women's right to choose, the "undue burden" test is far from the Republican party pro-life platform and close to the position of the average American.

Several possible scenarios for the future of abortion politics seem possible. First, it is possible that the pro-choice forces will continue to win elections in which the Republicans nominate strongly pro-life candidates. The Republicans would then almost totally abandon the pro-life plank in their platform, leaving the pro-life movement to the most extreme element. If violence becomes more common, then the government will crack down on the pro-life movement much as it did to the vestiges of the New Left when it went underground and resorted to violence.

Second, it is possible that the abortion issue will become less salient, now that the *Casey* decision has at least partially demarcated the limitations of state authority to regulate abortion. Pro-life candidates will learn to hedge their position or to "spin" the issue on their own terms, and both parties will more frequently nominate moderates on abortion. Under this scenario, the pro-choice mobilization will gradually erode, and pro-life forces will be able to pass procedural restrictions in many states.

Finally, it is possible that the abortion issue will be settled by the national legislature. If Congress passes a Freedom of Choice Act, then only a few state restrictions will be possible. This latter scenario seems unlikely as of late 1994. Some pro-choice members of Congress have promised to vote against the Freedom of Choice Act if it allows states to impose waiting periods or parental notification, and because these policies have the support of more than 80% of Americans in most states, it is difficult to imagine the bill passing without the states being allowed these options.

Whatever the future of abortion politics, it is unlikely that either side will be fully happy with national or state policy. For 17 years abortion activists have focused their rhetoric on the "rights" of life or choice, and debates about rights are usually not prone to compromise. Although the general public and politicians may be able and willing to work out a compromise that encompasses elements of the *Casey* decision, pro-choice activists will correctly note that many of the restrictions passed by states pose hardships on women seeking abortions, especially in rural states with few providers, and pro-life activists will correctly note that these restrictions will do little to decrease the numbers of abortions in America. It seems likely that abortion activists will be fighting this issue for many years to come.

NOTES

1. Kristin Luker, *Abortion and the Politics of Motherhood* (Berkeley: University of California Press, 1984).

2. Clyde Wilcox, "Political Action Committees and Abortion: A Longitudinal Analysis," *Women and Politics* 9 (1988): 1-20.

3. Luker, *Abortion and the Politics of Motherhood.*

4. Pro-choice activists did not find the status quo ideal, however. The Court did allow Congress to forbid the use of national government Medicaid funds to pay for abortions for poor women, and in some states abortion providers were few and far between.

5. Sue Thomas, "NARAL," in Robert Biersack, Paul Herrnson, and Clyde Wilcox, eds. *Risky Business: Political Action Committees in the 1992 Elections* (Armonk, N.Y.: M. E. Sharpe, 1994), 103-116.

6. Craig Rimmerman, "New Kids on the Block: The WISH List and the Gay and Lesbian Victory Fund in the 1992 Elections," in Biersack, Herrnson, and Wilcox, eds, *Risky Business: Political Action Committees in the 1992 Elections*, 214-224.

7. Candice J. Nelson, "Women's PACs in the Year of the Woman," in Elizabeth Adell Cook, Sue Thomas, and Clyde Wilcox, eds., *The Year of the Woman: Myths and Realities* (Boulder, CO: Westview, 1994), 181-196.

8. Debra Dodson and Lauren Burnbauer, with Katherine Kleeman, *Election 1989: The Abortion Issue in New Jersey and Virginia* (New Brunswick, NJ: Eagleton Institute, 1991) and Elizabeth Adell Cook, Ted G. Jelen, and Clyde

Wilcox, *Between Two Absolutes: Public Opinion and the Politics of Abortion* (Boulder, CO: Westview, 1992).

9. Elizabeth Adell Cook, Frederick Hartwig, and Clyde Wilcox. "The Abortion Issue Down Ticket: The Virginia Lieutenant Governor's Race in 1989," *Women & Politics* 12 (1992): 5-19.

10. Luker, *Abortion and the Politics of Motherhood*; Donald Granberg, "A Comparison of Members of Pro and AntiAbortion Organizations in Missouri," *Social Biology* 28 (1982): 239-252; and Donald Granberg, "Family Size Preference and Sexual Permissiveness as Factors Differentiating Abortion Activists," *Social Psychology Quarterly* 45 (1982): 15-23.

11. Elizabeth Adell Cook, Ted G. Jelen, and Clyde Wilcox, "Measuring Public Attitudes on Abortion: Methodological and Substantive Considerations," *Family Planning Perspectives* 25 (1993): 118-121, 145.

12. Cook, Jelen, and Wilcox, *Between Two Absolutes*.

13. Charles Franklin and Liane Kosaki, "Republican Schoolmaster: The U.S. Supreme Court, Public Opinion, and Abortion," *American Political Science Review* 83 (1989): 751-771.

14. Of course, these data also show how many Americans perceive career women negatively, and suggest an anti-feminist backlash.

15. Cook, Jelen, and Wilcox, *Between Two Absolutes*.

16. Ibid.

17. Elizabeth Adell Cook, Ted G. Jelen, and Clyde Wilcox, "Issue Voting in Gubernatorial Elections: Abortion and Post-*Webster* Politics," *Journal of Politics* 56 (1994): 187-199.

18. Ted G. Jelen, *The Political Mobilization of Religious Beliefs* (New York: Praeger, 1991).

19. Ted G. Jelen, *The Political World of the Clergy* (Westport, CT: Praeger, 1993).

20. Jerome Himmelstein, "The Social Basis of Anti-Feminism," *Journal for the Scientific Study of Religion* 25 (1986): 1-15.

21. Cook, Jelen, and Wilcox, *Between Two Absolutes*.

22. Anthony Downs, *An Economic Theory of Democracy* New York: Harper, 1957.

23. Bush himself took a somewhat more moderate position, favoring abortions to protect the health of the mother and in cases of rape and fetal defect. Bush's wife told a national media audience that she would support the decision of any of her grandchildren to have an abortion.

24. James Lengle, *Representativeness and Presidential Primaries: The Democratic Party in the Post-Reform Era* (Westport, CT: Greenwood, 1981). For a contrary view, see Barbara Norrander, "Ideological Representativeness of Presidential Primary Voters," *American Journal of Political Science* 33 (1989): 570-587.

25. Roland Gunn, "The National Right to Life Committee," in Biersack, Herrnson, and Wilcox, eds., *Risky Business: Political Action Committees in the 1992 Elections*, 130-140.

26. Angus Campbell, Phillip Converse, Warren Miller, and Donald Stokes, *The American Voter* (New York: John Wiley and Sons, 1960).

27. Amy Fried, "Abortion Politics as Symbolic Politics: An Investigation into Belief Systems," *Social Science Quarterly* 69 (1988): 137-154.

28. Alan Abramowitz, "It's Abortion, Stupid: Policy Voting in the 1992 Presidential Election," *Journal of Politics* 57 (1995): 176-186.

29. Elizabeth Adell Cook, Ted G. Jelen, and Clyde Wilcox, "The Electoral Politics of Abortion," presented at the annual meeting of the American Political Science Association, Washington, D.C., September 1991.

30. These fiures were computed from the National Election Studies.

31. Lyman Kellstedt, "Evangelicals and Political Realignment," presented at the annual meeting of the American Political Science Association, Washington, DC, September 1986; and Lyman A. Kellstedt and John C. Green, "Religion, Partisanship, and Political Behavior: Regional Variation," presented at the Citadel Symposium on Southern Politics, Charleston, SC, March 1990.

32. Personal communication, August, 1993.

33. John E. Jackson, and Maris A. Vinovkis, "Public Opinion,Elections, and the 'Single-Issue' Issue," in Gilbert Steiner, ed, *The Abortion Dispute and the American System* (Washington, DC: Brookings, 1983).

34. Phillip E. Converse and Gregory Markus, "'Plus ca Change' The New CPS Election Panel Study," *American Political Science Review* 73 (1979): 32-49.

35. Barbara Norrander and Clyde Wilcox, "State Differences in Abortion Attitudes," presented at the annual meeting of the American Political Science Association, Washington, DC, September 1993.

36. Elizabeth Adell Cook, Ted G. Jelen, and Clyde Wilcox, "Catholicism and Abortion Attitudes in the American States: A Contextual Analysis," *Journal for the Scientific Study of Religion* 32 (1993): 223-230.

37. See Norrander and Wilcox, "State Differences;" Jeffrey E. Cohen and Charles Barrilleaux, "Public Opinion, Interest Groups, and Public Policymaking: Abortion Policy in the American States," in Malcolm Goggin, ed., *Understanding the New Politics of Abortion*(Newbury Park, CA: Sage, 1993), 203-221; Kenneth Meier and Deborah McFarlane, "Abortion Politics and Abortion Funding Policy," in Malcolm Goggin, ed., *Understanding the New Politics of Abortion*, 249-267; and Christopher Wlezien and Malcolm Goggin, "The Courts, Interest Groups, and Public Opinion about Abortion," *Political Behavior* 15 (1993): 381-405.

38. Cook, Jelen, and Wilcox, "Issue Voting in Gubernatorial Elections."

39. Julie Rovner, "Hill Faces Trench Warfare over Abortion Rights," *Congressional Quarterly Weekly Report* (August 25, 1991): 2713-2720.

40. Beth Donovan, "Open 2nd District Contest Tests Partisan Trends," *Congressional Quarterly Weekly Report* (April 7, 1990): 1090-1091.

41. See Fred Barnes, "Pregnant Silence," *New Republic* (August 19 & 26, 1991): 11-12; Eleanor Clift, "The GOP's Civil War Over Abortion," *Newsweek* (August 5, 1991): 31; and Cal Thomas, "Is the Pro-Life Position Proving Harmful to Republicans?" *Washington Times* July 29, 1991, D3.

4

The Catholic Church as a Political Actor

Mary C. Segers

An incident at the founding of our country illustrates the enduring tension American Catholics feel over the participation of their church in the American political process. In 1784, Benjamin Franklin, then ambassador to France, was consulted by the papal nuncio to Versailles for advice as to who should lead the fledgling American Catholic Church. After consulting Congress, Franklin replied that the government of the United States would *not* recommend in the matter of Catholic Church leadership. In contrast to the customary European pattern of monarchs nominating bishops who were then consecrated by Rome, Franklin advised the nuncio that the new American republic viewed the matter as "purely spiritual" and beyond "the jurisdiction and powers of Congress." In the tradition of church-state separation, the Vatican was free to name whomever it judged appropriate to head the new American church. For his part, Rev. John Carroll (who had accompanied Franklin on a mission to Canada in 1776) thought the American church should be "free of the least taint of foreign jurisdiction," and he took democratic principles so seriously that he requested that American priests be permitted to choose their own bishop at least initially. A natural leader, Carroll was appointed superior of the North American mission in 1784 and indeed was elected the first American bishop (of Baltimore) in 1789.[1]

To me, this vignette from our early history illustrates the complexity of American Catholic experience. On one hand, our national government, true to the tradition of church-state separation, seeks to avoid religious establishment and institutional entanglement while promoting toleration and religious freedom. On the other hand, American Catholics, like Bishop Carroll, being steeped in traditions of self-government and religious liberty, have sought to harmonize the demands of a hierarchically structured church with the spirit of democratic governance in a pluralistic society. Secular authority takes great pains to acknowledge church autonomy, while generations of Catholics have struggled to reconcile the claims of religious dogma with civic duties of tolerance and respect for the rights of non-Catholic Americans.

The Carroll-Franklin episode highlights the fact that being an American Catholic has never been easy. The challenge has been to integrate fidelity to church authority with allegiance to a democratic polity, to demonstrate love of country while looking to Rome for spiritual leadership, to integrate the truth-claims of a hierarchical church with one's obligations to respect the rights of non-Catholic citizens to disagree. Inevitably, the challenge involves resisting the expressions of anti-Catholicism that predictably greet the entrance of the Catholic Church into the political arena.

In this chapter, I want to examine the challenge of being Catholic and American in the context of the church's unprecedented political efforts to shape public policy on abortion. Over the last 30 years, the Catholic Church in the United States has been a major player in the movement to restrict abortion. As a political scientist, I am fascinated by the degree of church involvement in the politics of abortion. From the perspective of political science, of course, the Catholic Church may be seen as yet another interest group or religious lobby using the political process to advance its views and protect its interests. Viewed as a "special interest," the church has distinct advantages in American politics--chiefly its quasi-federal organizational structure, which enables it to lobby effectively at national, state, and local levels. However, the church's role as a political lobby raises normative questions concerning representation and accountability--questions political scientists ask about all pressure groups. For whom do the Catholic bishops speak? To whom are they accountable? And how effective are they in delivering votes?

This chapter examines the American Catholic effort to restrict abortion from two perspectives: the external viewpoint of a political scientist who analyzes the church as a religious lobby, and the internal viewpoint of a believer who sees the church as a Christian community. The chapter itself is divided into three parts. The first, more analytical part of the chapter examines the church's anti-abortion campaign through the prism of political science. After a brief explanation of interest group theory as it applies to the church, this section reviews typical interest group strategies the bishops have employed in their anti-abortion efforts. The second, more critical or evaluative part of the chapter addresses questions raised by the church's unprecedented lobbying effort on abortion. These questions include issues of representation and accountability, as well as the church's uneven treatment of political issues such as abortion, economic justice, and nuclear war. I also discuss the implications of the church's anti-abortion campaign for Catholic lawmakers and citizens.

Finally, in the third part of the chapter, I shift vantage points from that of professional political scientist to that of an American Catholic in order to evaluate the church's anti-abortion efforts from the internal viewpoint of a believer. From this perspective, churches are more than mere interest groups. They have a special duty to attend to the common good and to universal values of peace and justice. In the United States, we expect religious communities to avoid sectarian strife and to rise above partisan politics. In this section I apply normative considerations such as these to an evaluation of the church's anti-abortion activity.

A few caveats are in order. First, in speaking of the Catholic Church as a political actor, I am referring to the American church, not to the 800 million adherents of worldwide Roman Catholicism. Second, I am referring to the official institutional church in the United States, the National Conference of Catholic Bishops (NCCB) and the United States Catholic Conference (USCC) in Washington as well as state Catholic conferences, individual bishops, and diocesan officials at the local level.[2] Third, the term "church" here is used to refer to the hierarchy of bishops, archbishops, cardinals, and their staffs. The bishops' conference is not the only Catholic lobby working Capitol Hill. It is important to realize that many groups constitute the Catholic lobbying effort in Washington (for example, Catholic Relief Services, Network, Catholic Charities, the Catholic Health Association, the Leadership Conference of Women Religious, the National Catholic Conference for Interracial Justice). Moreover, these groups lobby on many different issues, sometimes in opposition to the institutional church lobby (the NCCB/USCC).[3] Like many American institutions, the Catholic lobby in Washington is not monolithic but is characterized by pluralism and diversity. So it is important to clarify my meaning here: in referring to the Catholic Church as an interest group or religious lobby, I am pointing to the episcopal hierarchy, the institutional church leadership. Fourth, although the bishops' conference has a multi-issue political agenda, this chapter focuses on the church's efforts to influence abortion policy. I do this not only because this volume is devoted to the subject of abortion but also because the abortion issue has consumed the Catholic hierarchy in recent years. No other issue has commanded the priority the bishops have accorded abortion in the last 30 years. A fifth caveat is that this chapter addresses primarily questions of abortion *politics and policy* rather than the morality of abortion. As a political scientist, I am less concerned with the church's position on the morality of abortion and more interested in the church's stance in the political arena, its willingness to work hard to translate its moral position into public policy. Where necessary, I will advert to the church's position on the morality of abortion, but my primary focus is on the bishops' political activism on this issue.

One final cautionary note: I assume that the argument for the Catholic Church's participation in the American political process is well known and requires no lengthy justification. As citizens, Catholic clergy and laity have the *right* to participate in the democratic process and to press for public policies they judge appropriate in a well-ordered society. Moreover, the church and individual Catholics have, as do all citizens, a moral *duty* to voice their views and to contribute their moral perspective to public debate. The NCCB/USCC, like other churches and temples, has social and economic interests to be protected. And historically, the American church has had to lobby to protect the rights of its members against periodic waves of anti-Catholicism in American society. I mention all this because whenever the Catholic bishops publicly advocate their pro-life position, there is the predictable, simplistic, knee-jerk reaction on the part of some in the media that "those Catholics are at it again"--trying to impose their moral views on others in violation of the constitutional separation of church and state.

THE POLITICS OF ABORTION: THE CATHOLIC CHURCH AS AN INTEREST GROUP

I approach this topic from the perspective of a political scientist interested in religious lobbies or interest groups. Many churches with government relations offices in Washington hire lobbyists--usually from their own ranks--to represent them in the policymaking process. Indeed, within the field of political science it is difficult to characterize religious lobbies. The political science literature on pressure groups tends to classify interest groups into *membership interest groups* (such as the American Association of Retired Persons), *institutional interest groups* (a hierarchical institution such as a corporation, university, or church which may have its own Washington office or hire a Washington law firm to represent it), and *public interest groups* (such as Common Cause), that seek a collective good and do not stand to benefit selectively or materially from the achievement of that common good. Churches could certainly be considered membership organizations, although a political scientist would want to know whether church leaders consult their members and are accountable to them in some concrete way.[4]

The American Catholic church may be categorized as an institutional interest group, that is, a hierarchical organization with tremendous resources that is able to maintain a consistent lobbying presence in Washington. At the same time, the American Catholic Church may be categorized as a membership association. With almost 60 million members, this church is the largest religious denomination in the United States (it is twice the size of the American Association of Retired Persons, the largest nondenominational membership interest group in American society). However, issues of representation and accountability are clearly not central for the American Catholic hierarchy. Catholic bishops do not regularly consult rank and file church members prior to lobbying on Capitol Hill. As one United States Catholic Conference lobbyist explained his role, "I'm the hired gun of the Bishops."[5] With a group such as this, a political scientist will want to know "whether the generals have any troops," that is, whether church leaders in this particular denomination can deliver a block of votes in elections, for example, or generate grassroots pressure on legislators.

To be sure, religious organizations are not mere lobby groups like the AFL-CIO, the National Rifle Association, or the U.S. Chambers of Commerce. Churches are clearly more than interest groups; they have a special duty to attend to the common good and to universal values of peace and justice. They often fall, then, into the category of a public interest group which pursues a collective good or policy in which the group itself has no material or economic interest. However, even this characterization is inadequate. Churches differ from public interest groups in that they engage in a much broader range of activities (pastoral care, social services) than does a public interest lobby such as Common Cause. Churches have purposes that transcend politics. Thus a political scientist analyzing the attempts of churches to contribute a moral dimension to public debate must be careful not to trivialize religion or ignore the unique character of churches.

Nevertheless, from the vantage point of political science, churches can at times operate as institutional interest groups seeking to protect their own narrow interests, and as membership organizations mobilizing congregants to influence public policy. At other times they may be acting as public interest groups, seeking the enactment of public policies that will benefit all in society. Lobbying by church representatives for passage of the 1964 Civil Rights Act is a good example of the latter. On the issue of national health care reform, the American Catholic Church combined all three roles, operating as an institutional interest group on behalf of its own health care institutions, mobilizing parishioners to lobby Congress to exclude abortion coverage from the health plan, and seeking passage of a universal health care policy that will benefit everyone, especially the poor and the vulnerable.

The American Catholic Church brings several distinct organizational and structural advantages to its participation in the political process. Of fundamental importance is the fact that the church is a hierarchical institution with impressive resources at both the national and state levels. The National Conference of Catholic Bishops/United States Catholic Conference represents the church's interest in Washington, D.C., while 28 state conferences and hundreds of diocesan offices do so in the states and localities. Robert Salisbury has argued that "hierarchical structures which exercise authority over people within their jurisdiction" are different "in crucial ways from our conventional notion of interest groups." Hierarchical institutions, like corporations, think-tanks, universities, and of course the Catholic Church, have longevity, resources, and a fundamental freedom of action that member-based or issue-based groups generally lack. These institutions, Salisbury claims, have come to "dominate the processes of interest representation in American national politics" because of these structural advantages.[6]

Salisbury's insight helps to illuminate the Catholic Church's leading role in the politics of abortion in the United States. The church is a major player in public debates over abortion not because it represents the views of its members (indeed, poll data indicate that it does not) but because it is uniquely positioned, as an institution, to contend with what David Truman called the "multiplicity of co-ordinate or nearly co-ordinate points of access to governmental decision in the United States."[7] Truman argued that the federal division of jurisdiction between national and state governments and the constitutional separation of powers between three branches of government together create many points of access to political decisionmaking. An interest group denied access at one level or branch of government can seek redress at other branches or other levels. Moreover, any group that is able credibly to seek access at *all* levels and at *all* branches will have an advantage over those that cannot.

The Catholic Church has such an advantage with respect to its efforts to restrict legal abortion. In particular, the church's own quasi-federal structure has allowed it to respond immediately to the movement of abortion first from the state to the national level and then back again to the states. Whether the arena of abortion politics has been the state legislatures, congressional politics, the Supreme Court, or presidential politics, the leaders of the church have been able to enter each arena bearing the legitimacy, resources, and freedom of action that belong to leaders of permanent, hierarchical institutions.

Moreover, the American Catholic Church is organizationally equipped to engage in the full range of interest group activity. In its 30 year anti-abortion campaign, the church has used many strategies typically employed by pressure groups in American politics. The church is institutionally capable of grassroots mobilization activities, of a judicial strategy of court litigation, of an elite "insider" approach, of public information campaigns, of legislative lobbying, and of direct intervention in electoral campaigns. This first part of my essay reviews how the church has employed these strategies nationally and in the states to shape abortion policy.

An Overview of Anti-Abortion Activities of the American Catholic Bishops

The Catholic Church was the institutional home for the pro-life movement in the years before and immediately following *Roe v. Wade*. From 1966 to 1973, the Family Life Bureau of the USCC, acting under instructions from the NCCB and led by staff director Rev. (later Bishop)

James McHugh, monitored legal developments concerning abortion in the states, provided information to a rudimentary network of pro-life activists across the country, and coordinated a series of episcopal statements expressing church opposition to legalized abortion. Both organizationally and ideologically, the Roman Catholic Church provided resources for a fledgling right-to-life movement. The USCC became a communications center for many state right-to-life groups, and the Catholic teaching that all direct abortions were immoral was a major ideological resource in the mobilization of pro-life activists.[8]

The church's national opposition to legal abortion also included organizational initiatives. In 1966, Father McHugh invited a small number of already active abortion opponents to serve as advisors to a "National Right to Life Committee" (legally incorporated and separated from the USCC after *Roe* and now the nation's paramount anti-abortion organization). In 1974, Robert Lynch (now Monsignor Lynch, general secretary of the NCCB/USCC) organized the National Committee for a Human Life Amendment (NCHLA) to mobilize grassroots opposition to *Roe* and to provide information on national policymaking to state Catholic conferences and diocesan pro-life committees. NCHLA is funded through a one-cent per Catholic assessment each year.[9] The NCHLA plays an important role as a communications link between national, state, and local Catholic groups working to restrict abortion.

In the pre-*Roe* period of abortion reform in individual states, the Catholic Church spearheaded opposition to liberalization of restrictive laws. From 1966 to 1973, strict nineteenth century abortion statutes were reformed by 14 states and repealed by 4 others. Individual bishops and diocesan officials relied upon grassroots mobilization techniques, elite lobbying, and public information campaigns to stem the tide of abortion reform. Although these strategies were successful in many states (New Hampshire, Arizona, Minnesota, Michigan, Pennsylvania, and North Dakota), Catholic opposition was ineffective in other states such as California, New York, Hawaii, Washington, Florida, and Alaska.[10]

The case of Hawaii provides a good illustration of the Catholic Church's strategy and tactics in opposing liberalization of abortion laws. In March 1970, Hawaii became the first state in the nation to repeal all criminal sanctions against abortions done by licensed physicians.[11] From the beginning, the Catholic Church led the opposition to abortion reform and repeal (in 1970, Hawaii's population was 28% Catholic). While a broad range of groups supported abortion liberalization, the opposition relied heavily upon Catholic-affiliated groups: Catholic Physicians' Guild, Catholic Social Services, Knights of Columbus, Catholic Women's Guild, and the Roman Catholic Diocese of Honolulu.

A key figure was Honolulu Bishop John Scanlan, who took a strong stand against any change in the existing abortion law. Bishop Scanlan relied upon Catholic media and an elite lobbying strategy to articulate the official Catholic position. He used the diocesan newspaper and Catholic ceremonial functions to communicate to Catholics the church's teaching against abortion. He also focused considerable attention on the state legislature, sending representatives to testify at committee hearings and using the diocesan newspaper to address statements to lawmakers. He argued that people do not always know what is good for them, that laws provide part of the support people need in order to be good, and that legislators should therefore keep in mind the teaching function of the law. Later in the campaign, he requested and received a special meeting with members of the legislature.

Despite the church's efforts, Hawaii's abortion law was repealed. Moreover, the key legislator supporting the bill, State Senator Vincent Yano, was Catholic, and the Catholic Governor, John Burns, refused to veto the bill, allowing it to be enacted without his signature. Why did these Catholic lawmakers support legal change rather than the existing restrictive law?

Patricia Diamond and Milton Steinhoff suggest that although these political leaders were practicing Catholics, they "felt duty-bound to reach a personal decision on the abortion issue and not to accept the bishop's pronouncements solely because of his position as an officer of the Church."[12] Each of these lawmakers gave study and careful thought to the issue. They were also influenced by the legal arguments of Father Robert Drinan, S.J., then dean of Boston College Law School and later a congressman from Massachusetts. In 1967, in order to forestall the coming of elective abortion, Father Drinan tried to make the notion of therapeutic abortion more acceptable to the Catholic community.[13] Recognizing public support for liberalization in the "hard" cases of rape-incest-fetal deformity, he supported abortion reform as the lesser of two evils. However, by 1970, Father Drinan had concluded that abortion *repeal* was preferable to abortion *reform*, that complete decriminalization was preferable to having moderately permissive abortion laws.[14] In his no-law position, he reasoned that the law should remain mute on the abortion issue rather than sanction it in some cases.

Father Drinan's argument convinced State Senator Yano and Governor Burns that repeal was the least evil of the various unsatisfactory solutions to the abortion problem. Senator Yano had read recent studies arguing that the 1967 Colorado and California reform laws had not solved the abortion problem in those states. And Governor Burns, in tacitly consenting to Hawaii's repeal bill, argued that the law should be silent on abortion to respect church-state separation and to prevent the maiming and death caused by dangerous illegal abortions.

Hawaii thus offered an example of two leading Catholic lawmakers who shared their hurch's strong moral opposition to abortion, yet disagreed with the policy implications drawn by their bishop. Senator Yano and Governor Burns personally embodied the argument that abortion law repeal would leave the moral decision to the individual's conscience. Their presence in the Hawaii abortion debate "undercut the Church's opposition more effectively than any amount of anti-Catholic invective could have."[15]

As we shall see, once the Supreme Court ruled in *Roe v. Wade* that abortion was legal, the NCCB/USCC went into high gear, forcefully opposing all laws, policies, and candidates who favored legal abortion. Father Drinan's position appeared less practical and less realistic. Throughout the 1980s and 1990s, the bishops grew less tolerant and accepting of Catholic lawmakers who refused to translate the church's moral proscription of abortion into public law--until, by the early 1990s, they were imposing sanctions against such Catholic politicians. These politicians were censured in sermons, barred from ministerial activities, refused sacraments, removed from parish councils, denied invitations to speak at church functions, expelled from the Knights of Columbus, and threatened with excommunication. Individual Catholic citizens were told that it was immoral to vote for pro-choice candidates.[16]

In the 20-plus years since *Roe v. Wade*, the church has committed its vast institutional resources to an all-out campaign to roll back permissive abortion laws. Space here does not permit a full description of the church's many anti-abortion initiatives. However, I have selected a few examples of the bishops' tactics to illustrate the church's behavior as an interest group.

Elite Lobbying. Elite lobbying is the process through which the leadership of an interest group attempts to influence public policy by communicating directly with, or putting pressure directly on, policy makers. An elite interaction strategy is a standard tactic of the American

Catholic Church. At the national level, the NCCB/USCC has its office of governmental liaison, with at least 6 staff representatives who regularly lobby members of Congress and officials in the executive branch. At the state level, each of the 28 state Catholic conferences has at least one staff member whose job is to communicate that conference's views to state legislators.

There are many examples of elite lobbying on the abortion issue by the National Conference of Catholic Bishops. The NCCB reacted immediately to what it perceived to be the Supreme Court's sweeping opinion in *Roe v. Wade*. Cardinal John Krol, president of the bishops' conference, condemned the Court's ruling as an "unspeakable tragedy" and was instantly supported by formal statements of the NCCB's Administrative Committee and its Ad Hoc Committee on Pro-Life Activities. The church then quickly affirmed its commitment to a constitutional amendment in defense of unborn human life. On March 7, 1974, four cardinals (John Krol of Philadelphia, Humberto Medeiros of Boston, John Cody of Chicago, and Timothy Manning of Los Angeles) testified in support of this constitutional amendment before the subcommittee on constitutional amendments of the Senate Judiciary Committee.[17] The appearance of such high-level church officials testifying before Congress was unprecedented and indicates, I think, the bishops' commitment to reversing *Roe* and restricting abortion. The NCCB repeated this performance in 1976 when the NCCB president, Archbishop Joseph Bernardin, and Cardinal Terence Cooke of New York offered their testimony before a U.S. House of Representatives subcommittee.[18]

In addition to the testimony of these cardinal-archbishops, lobbyists and other staff members of the United States Catholic Conference were busy on Capitol Hill asserting the church's institutional and policy interest in the subject of abortion. In April 1973, the bishops declared that the over 600 Catholic hospitals in the United States could not comply with laws requiring them to provide abortion services, nor could Catholic physicians and nurses participate in abortion procedures in good conscience. As a result of the efforts of USCC lobbyists, Congress passed legislation in June 1973 designed to protect the integrity of Catholic hospitals and Catholic personnel.[19]

In this case, the official church acted to protect its hospitals and health personnel from potential legal harm--being forced to perform abortions. In terms of legislation concerning abortion, however, the church has gone well beyond protecting its institutional autonomy and integrity. It has also played a central role in efforts to restrict access to abortion more generally. The two most noteworthy instances of church lobbying in this sense are passage of the Hyde Amendment (voted annually by Congress since 1977) and the Civil Rights Restoration Act of 1988.

The Hyde Amendment, named after Rep. Henry Hyde (R.-IL), restricts Medicaid funding of abortion for poor women. This amendment has usually been attached as a rider to appropriations bills for the Departments of Labor and Health and Human Services. When first passed in the late 1970s, it was the occasion for protracted, acrimonious political battles over which, if any, exceptions to the funding ban would be allowed. During these struggles, lobbyists for the church-founded and church-funded National Committee for a Human Life Amendment (NCHLA) were prominent actors in the negotiations and legislative maneuverings surrounding the Hyde Amendment.[20]

During the 1980s, the bishops' conference continued its congressional lobbying against abortion, most notably in the case of the 1988 Civil Rights Restoration Act (CRRA).[21] This civil rights bill was an effort to circumvent a narrow Supreme Court interpretation of Title IX of the Education Amendments of 1972, which forbade discrimination against women by educational institutions receiving federal support. Under Title IX, educational institutions receiving federal funds had to treat medical services related to pregnancy and termination of pregnancy in the same way. At first, the church joined with a broad civil rights coalition to support passage of the CRRA. On second thought, however, the USCC distanced itself from the coalition while lobbyists for the bishops' conference offered an "abortion neutral" amendment to remove abortion-related services from those covered under the anti-discrimination language of Title IX. This proposed amendment precipitated protracted argument and deep divisions within the civil rights coalition and delayed passage of the CRRA for three years.

The USCC's success at having its "abortion-neutral" amendment included in the bill that was finally passed three years later is testimony to the church's tenacity and effectiveness as a participant in the national legislative process. The effect of the church's lobbying was to allow federally assisted educational institutions to offer health and leave plans that do not cover abortion. More recently, lobbyists for the bishops' conference used the same tactic to delay the Religious Freedom Restoration Act for two years (1991-1993) until they were satisfied that it was abortion-neutral and would not alter the tax-exempt status of religious organizations.[22]

The bishops' conference continues to lobby and testify in Congress, an example being the testimony of Helen Alvare against the Freedom of Choice Act in March 1992. (Alvare is Director of Planning and Public Information for the NCCB/USCC Secretariat for Pro-Life Activities.) Also in March 1992, Cardinal John O'Connor, then chair of the NCCB's Pro-Life Committee, sent a letter to every member of Congress stating forcefully the church's opposition to the Freedom of Choice Act. The bishops and their representatives are actively lobbying on health care reform. In April 1993, a delegation of church leaders, led by Cardinal James Hickey of Washington, met with Hillary Rodham Clinton for more than an hour and stressed that the country needs universal health coverage--without abortion.[23]

Interest group lobbying is not limited, of course, to the kind of elite interaction I have been discussing. Interest groups use a variety of strategies to influence public policy. An increasingly important arena in which these tactics and strategies are used is the federal judiciary.

Judicial Strategy. Courts are a major point of access to governmental decisionmaking for interest groups who are unsuccessful in the legislative or executive arenas. It is no surprise that the American Catholic Church, like other pro-life interest groups, has actively pursued its anti-abortion agenda in the courts. It has participated in the judicial process through the filing of *amicus curiae* briefs in abortion-related cases. And it has gone to court when necessary to defend its institutional interests, in particular its tax-exemption, when those interests were challenged by outside forces.

Federal cases related to abortion invariably trigger submission of a "friend of court" brief by the legal staff of the United States Catholic Conference. The USCC's Office of General Counsel has filed briefs, for example, in *Planned Parenthood v. Danforth* (1976), *Harris v. McRae* (1980), *Webster v. Reproductive Health Services* (1989), *Rust v. Sullivan* (1991), and *Planned Parenthood v. Casey* (1992). These briefs do not simply recapitulate the church's moral opposition to abortion; instead, they are rather sophisticated legal arguments appealing to reigning Supreme Court judicial doctrines and trends in constitutional interpretation.

While the church files *amicus* briefs to shape general abortion policy, it also uses the courts to defend its own institutional interests. The most noteworthy recent example of such a defense came in response to the Abortion Rights Mobilization's (ARM) effort to strip the Catholic Church of its religious tax exemption because of its participation in partisan political campaigns. Throughout the decade from 1980 to 1990, this lawsuit bounced back and forth between federal district and appeals courts as lawyers raised a variety of procedural questions. Ultimately, the Supreme Court let stand a lower court ruling that ARM lacked standing to sue; ARM had not established that it had been injured in any tangible way by the Catholic Church's tax exemption.[24]

What is remarkable about the ARM lawsuit is that the church had the resources necessary to engage in a 10-year legal struggle over one of its most fundamental institutional interests. Like corporations and universities and other agencies, the Catholic Church operates in some contexts as an institutional interest group. At other times, however, in other contexts, the church operates as a membership organization mobilizing its members to shape public policy. It engages, in other words, in grassroots political lobbying.

Grassroots Mobilization. The Catholic Church has played a major role in mobilizing public opposition to abortion over the last 30 years. As already noted, the bishops' conference created and funded two national anti-abortion groups, the National Right to Life Committee (NLRC) and the National Committee for a Human Life Amendment. The NRLC severed all official ties to the church in 1973, but originally it was in all respects a Catholic organization. The NCHLA remains church-funded and church-affiliated, the bishops' own lobbying arm on the issue of abortion.

In addition to creating these two lobbying organizations, the bishops have drawn up the most ambitious grassroots lobbying plan ever to have emerged from the offices of the NCCB/USCC. This effort, first announced in 1975 in the Pastoral Plan for Pro-Life Activities and reissued in 1985, aims to educate American Catholics and non-Catholics to the evils of permissive abortion, and to mobilize the American Catholic population, 55 million strong, into an organized and effective anti-abortion force in the United States. The plan consists of three parts: (1) an educational/public information effort; (2) a pastoral effort to assist women with problem pregnancies; and (3) "a public policy effort directed toward the legislative, judicial, and administrative arenas so as to ensure effective legal protection for the right to life." In terms of grassroots lobbying, the key to the plan is this third element, the public policy effort. The bishops called for a "systematic organization of the church's resources" involving a pro-life coordinating committee in each state under the auspices of the state Catholic Conference; a pro-life committee in each diocese; and the "development in each congressional district of an identifiable, tightly knit, and well-organized pro-life unit."[25]

My colleague, fellow political scientist Tim Byrnes, has argued that nothing so clearly illustrates the institutional breadth and political potential of the Catholic Church in the United States as this last provision. As he noted,

> It is hard to come up with very many other organizations of any kind, that could speak realistically of establishing politically viable cells, if you will, in all 435 congressional districts. The bishops were not completely successful in implementing this very ambitious plan, but the blueprint itself is testimony to the church's reach and viability as an organization. The *Pastoral Plan* was a statement of this organization's leadership that its members should think of themselves as members not only of a church with all its attendant spiritual implications, but also of a social movement of sorts, working towards influencing public policy in an area of central political concern.[26]

Needless to say, the church has not hesitated to use its more than 19,000 parish units as mobilization centers for grassroots lobbying. In January 1993, to mark the anniversary of *Roe*, Catholic parishes distributed to churchgoers 5 million postcards to mail to legislators urging Congress to oppose the Freedom of Choice Act. The same tactics were used again in January 1994. The bishops' Pro-Life Secretariat and the National Committee for a Human Life Amendment printed and distributed in parishes 18.9 million postcards urging Congress to exclude abortion coverage from the national health plan.[27] These mobilization campaigns, conducted by the NCHLA, illustrate how the church uses a powerful political resource--its own parochial and diocesan network--to influence public policy.

Perhaps such grassroots lobbying has been surpassed only by the church's decision to hire professional consultants to launch a media campaign to change public opinion on abortion. In 1990, the NCCB/USCC contracted with Hill & Knowlton, one of the largest public relations firms in the world, and with a polling firm, the Wirthlin Group, to launch a 5-year, $5 million media campaign against abortion. The Knights of Columbus agreed to contribute $3 million toward funding the campaign. In an age of media manipulation, the bishops, like other interest and advocacy groups, are able and willing to use public relations techniques, focus groups, and all the other trappings of contemporary high-tech politics to shape public opinion and mobilize opposition to abortion.

Electoral Politics. Another way in which American interest groups participate in the political process is through direct intervention in electoral campaigns. This can occur either through direct endorsement of candidates or through indirect means such as photo opportunities or invitations to candidates to speak at group functions. Here too, the Catholic Church has aggressively pursued its anti-abortion agenda, although as a tax-exempt, nonprofit organization the church has had to be extremely careful about partisan endorsement of candidates. However, such precautions have not prevented the bishops from intervening in electoral politics at the national, state, and local levels. Individual bishops have advised parishioners to use the vote to "defend the innocent life of that little baby in its mother's womb," or to "look at each and every candidate in light of his or her position on protecting the life of the unborn."[28] Other bishops have called abortion the most critical issue in national elections or have asserted in no uncertain terms that it is "immoral for church members to vote for candidates who favor abortion rights."[29] Perhaps the most famous of these exhortations came from New York's Cardinal John O'Connor who once declared, "I don't understand how a Catholic in good conscience can vote for a candidate who explicitly supports abortion."[30] This is the same Cardinal O'Connor who initiated a celebrated intellectual debate with New York governor Mario Cuomo about the duties of Catholic politicians on the abortion issue; who accused Geraldine Ferraro in 1984, in the middle of her historic race for the vice presidency, of "misrepresenting Catholic teaching on abortion;" and who warned pro-choice Catholic politicians in 1990 that "they are at risk of excommunication" if they persist in pro-choice advocacy.[31]

A review of recent presidential campaigns shows the extent of the bishops' interventions in electoral politics. The 1976 election campaign provided the first opportunity after *Roe* for the Catholic bishops to evaluate presidential candidates views on abortion policy. In this instance, the bishops acted *collectively* to impress upon the candidates how seriously the church took the issue of abortion. The NCCB arranged formal meetings between each of the two major candidates,

Jimmy Carter and Gerald Ford, and the Executive Committee of the bishops' conference. In subsequent press conferences, the bishops came embarrassingly close to partisan endorsement of Ford's candidacy.[32] The bishops themselves never denied that their efforts in 1976 were designed to further their anti-abortion cause *within the context of electoral politics*. At the same time, they also issued their quadrennial *Statement on Political Responsibilities in an Election Year*, emphasizing their nonpartisanship and concern with other issues besides abortion.

In 1980, the NCCB issued another election-year *Statement on Political Responsibilities* urging Catholics to consider a broad range of issues in evaluating political candidates. However, some prelates could not resist the lure of partisan politics. A week before the Massachusetts state primary, Cardinal Humberto Medeiros of Boston wrote an open letter to Catholics asking them to vote against candidates who supported legalized abortion. His letter was targeted at candidates in two congressional races: Representative James Shannon, a pro-choice Democrat and a Catholic, in the Fifth District, and State Representative Barney Frank, Jewish, liberal, and pro-choice, in the Fourth District. Despite the cardinal's letter, Shannon and Frank both won their primary battles and went on to win the general election as well.[33]

Cardinal Medeiros' electoral intervention was a harbinger of things to come, principally the actions of bishops and cardinals against pro-choice Catholic candidates in the 1984 election. During the 1984 campaign, Cardinal John O'Connor of New York and Cardinal Bernard Law of Boston attacked Democratic vice-presidential candidate Geraldine Ferraro and New York governor Mario Cuomo for not automatically translating moral opposition to abortion into legal restrictions on abortion rights. The resulting controversy led 97 Catholics leaders to place their signatures in a *New York Times* advertisement protesting the treatment of Ferraro. It also caused divisions among the bishops themselves, who debated whether the church was being true to its own broad-based, respect-life agenda or was giving highest priority to its anti-abortion position.[34]

In 1988, the bishops issued their fourth election-year *Statement on Political Responsibilities*, which again addressed a wide range of issues and stressed non-partisanship. However, they were determined to avoid the controversy generated by the treatment of vice-presidential candidate Ferraro in the previous presidential election. In addition, the continuing ARM lawsuit challenging the church's tax-exempt status led the NCCB's general counsel to issue detailed, explicit instructions regarding permissible activity during election campaigns. Perhaps as a result of these cautionary warnings, the NCCB kept a relatively low profile during the 1988 Bush-Dukakis presidential race.

This low visibility continued in the 1992 presidential campaign between President George Bush and Governor Bill Clinton. The bishops limited their activities to publication of their traditional *Statement on Political Responsibility* and to testimony on key issues before the major parties' platform committees. They also sent candidates Bush and Clinton a questionnaire asking their positions on the issues emphasized by the bishops in their *Statement*. The candidates' responses were then sent to all U.S. bishops and heads of state Catholic conferences. Governor Clinton's responses showed agreement with the bishops' policy views on civil rights, physician-assisted suicide, poverty and hunger, family and medical leave, health care reform, job creation policies, and immigration and refugee policy. However, he disagreed with the bishops' policy positions on abortion, the death penalty, and government assistance for parochial schools.[35]

For his part, Clinton sought to cultivate Catholic voters in an effort to win back "Reagan Democrats" to the Democratic Party. Although Clinton is a Southern Baptist, he is the first U.S. president to have graduated from a Catholic university (Georgetown, Class of 1968). He has always pointed proudly to his Catholic education and emphasized his ties with American Catholics. However, because of his position on the abortion issue, the Catholic bishops sat out the 1992 presidential campaign. They remained studiously neutral and kept an extremely low profile. After Clinton won the election--and won the Catholic vote, despite his support for abortion rights--the bishops met for their annual November meeting and discussed in executive session their relations with the new Clinton administration. Many prelates expressed consternation over Catholics who had voted for pro-choice candidates and referenda. Cardinal James Hickey of Washington, D.C., asked for advice about appearing in public with pro-choice politicians. Common sense and political realism prevailed; two months later Cardinal Hickey, the cardinal-archbishop of the nation's capital, participated fully in all the festivities of Inauguration Day with President Clinton.[36]

While the NCCB/USCC and individual bishops have made their views known in national elections, other bishops have intervened in state elections. The most conspicuous example of such intervention came in

November 1989, the first election after the *Webster* decision permitting states to regulate and restrict abortion. Bishop Leo Maher of San Diego, California, denied the Eucharist to Lucy Killea, a Catholic Democrat running for a seat in the State Senate, because of her pro-choice position on abortion policy.[37] Bishop Maher's criticism of Mrs. Killea apparently helped this Democratic candidate win election in a heavily Republican district. The bishop's action brought national attention to Killea's candidacy, elicited campaign contributions and support from pro-choice groups throughout the country, and arguably triggered a sympathy vote for Killea as a way of protesting intervention by Catholic clergy in the electoral process. Mrs. Killea's victory was decisive in tipping a previously deadlocked California State Senate in favor of continued access to abortion. In other words, the bishop's intervention was counterproductive as a step toward restricting abortion in California.

In light of IRS restrictions on the tax-exempt status of churches that engage in electioneering, the NCCB's general counsel has encouraged the bishops to adopt a lower profile in terms of *electoral* politics. However, this has not prevented individual bishops from involving themselves indirectly in the political process. Some have posed for friendly "photo-ops" with anti-abortion candidates; others have used the pulpit to urge Catholics to vote for candidates who uphold Catholic moral values. Moreover, the fact that the bishops' conference ultimately prevailed in the decade-long suit challenging the church's tax-exemption brought by Abortion Rights Mobilization means, I think, that individual bishops have little to fear legally if they continue their efforts to influence electoral politics.

To summarize, the record shows that the Catholic Church is a lobby that uses all the strategies and techniques we associate with interest groups to protect *both* its institutional interest and what it perceives to be the public interest. The bishops are uniquely positioned to lobby effectively on abortion policy because of the church's quasi-federal organizational structure (which enables it to exert pressure at national, state, and local levels) and because the church is a hierarchical institution that commands tremendous institutional resources and is not obligated to consult its members. It is perhaps a cliche to say that the church is not a democracy and is therefore not obligated to consult its members. However, those members (American Catholics) live in a constitutional democracy in a religiously diverse society. As citizens of a secular state, they are committed to religious freedom and tolerance.

As voters and officeholders, American Catholics have sometimes conflicting obligations to conscience, constituents, the Constitution and the common good. It is not always easy, as Bishop Carroll understood, to reconcile these potentially conflicting duties.

AN EVALUATION OF THE ROLE OF THE CATHOLIC CHURCH AS A POLITICAL LOBBY ON ABORTION

From the perspective of political science, how might we evaluate the political activity of the Catholic Church on the abortion issue? A political scientist might want to know how *effective* the church has been in denying access to abortion and in reinstating restrictive abortion laws. He or she would ask whose interests the church represents and whether the church is accountable to those interests. A scholar in constitutional law would wonder whether the church's political activism on abortion is consonant with First Amendment religion clauses. A political scientist might want to know how church activism on abortion policy compares with its activity on other political issues. Students of political leadership would wonder about the implications of the bishops' political activity for Catholic politicians and voters. Finally, a political scientist might ask whether the church's lobbying activities have contributed to or detracted from the democratic process in the United States--that is, whether they have reinforced existing elitist tendencies in American politics or whether they have advanced greater democratic participation in the United States.

I cannot pretend to answer all these questions here, but I can offer reflections on some of these issues.

Effectiveness

It is very difficult for political scientists to gauge how effective interest groups actually are in the policy process. We can describe all the "inputs" (the measures lobbies take to influence policy), but it is much harder to say with any confidence whether a particular interest group has had decisive influence on "policy outcomes." in my view, the Catholic Church's anti-abortion campaign has had mixed success. Using the technique of elite lobbying, the bishops' conference was able to shape the wording of a congressional rider such as the 1976 Hyde

Amendment and to effectively block abortion-friendly clauses in the 1988 Civil Rights Restoration Act and in the 1993 Religious Freedom Restoration Act. In the wake of the Supreme Court's 1989 *Webster* decision, the church's success in lobbying for passage of restrictive state laws is also mixed, given pro-life policy achievements in Pennsylvania and Louisiana and pro-choice outcomes in Maryland, Connecticut, Florida and California.

However, the real question for political scientists is whether the bishops' lobby actually *represents* 55 million American Catholics. Judging by the results of the 1992 presidential election, for example, it is questionable whether the bishops can "deliver the Catholic vote" to pro-life candidates for high office. Faced with a clear choice between Clinton (pro-choice) and Bush (pro-life), 44 percent of Catholics voted for Clinton, 20 percent voted for Perot (also pro-choice), and 36 percent voted for Bush. (Taking the combined votes for Clinton and Perot, almost two-thirds of Catholics voted for a pro-choice candidate in the 1992 presidential election).[38] In state elections such as the 1989 New Jersey gubernatorial race and the 1990 New York gubernatorial race, individual bishops and state Catholic conferences have been unable to convince Catholic citizens to vote against pro-choice Catholic candidates such as Jim Florio and Mario Cuomo. Of course, this may simply mean that Catholics are multi-issue rather than single-issue voters and bring a certain amount of sophistication to the task of voting.

Obviously, the bishops have paid a price for their partial successes on abortion policy. They have alienated groups of churchmembers who disagree with their policy priorities. Catholic feminists, for example, are not at all pleased with the political tradeoffs the NCCB has made. On an issue of signal importance to women's rights advocates, the bishops failed to endorse the Equal Rights Amendment (ERA) in the late 1970s and early 1980s, because they feared that ERA approval would constitutionally legitimize abortion. The NCCB refused to support other legislation of importance to women's rights groups--the Pregnancy Discrimination Act of 1978 and the Civil Rights Restoration Act of 1988--unless antiabortion riders were attached to these bills.

Catholic lawmakers are also not pleased at the failure of some bishops to distinguish between general moral principles and particular applications in complex, concrete political contexts. Several political leaders have sought to explain to the bishops the undesirability and unfeasibility of using law and policy to enforce the church's ban against abortion; these include Congresswoman Nancy Pelosi (D-CA), Congresswoman Susan Molinari (R-NY), former cabinet cecretary Joseph Califano, and, of course, former New York governor Mario Cuomo in his well-known 1984 speech at the University of Notre Dame.

Thus, in terms of effectiveness the Catholic Church has had some political success in restricting access to abortion, but it has paid a high price for this success in terms of alienating many Catholic feminists and political leaders.

Representation

Questions of representation and accountability are central to the examination of any interest group and apply no less to the Catholic Church viewed as a political actor. Political scientist Mary Hanna has suggested that "the accountability criterion poses problems for any religious-political leadership, but perhaps especially for Catholic bishops, given the hierarchical, supranational nature of the Catholic Church."[39] American Catholic bishops are appointed by the pope, not elected by the American people or even by ordinary clerical or lay Catholics. Thus it would appear that the American bishops are accountable individually and collectively to Rome and, of course, to God. To be sure, the old cliche is relevant: the Catholic Church does not pretend to be a democracy. But when a particular national church in a democratic society becomes as involved in public policy debate and formation as the American church has been on the abortion issue, questions of accountability cannot be evaded.

The bishops try to cope with questions of public accountability and representation in three ways: First, as stated earlier, they deny that the Catholic Church is a democracy and insist upon the hierarchical authority structure of the church. Second, they aver a "prophetic" responsibility to give witness to transcendent moral values; it is in the very nature of the prophetic role *not* to consult the people. Finally, the National Conference of Catholic Bishops appeals to a doctrine of co-responsibility for public statements. In accordance with this notion, the NCCB does in fact consult ethicists and public policy experts when writing pastoral letters on, for example, economic justice (1986) or nuclear war (1983). The bishops in these cases tried to combine the prophetic witness approach with a consultative approach partly because they realized that they had no special expertise in economics or nuclear strategy and partly in order to lend credibility to their statements. However, they have not adopted a collegial, consultative approach in fashioning their policy recommendations on abortion. In fact, the church's uneven treatment of public policy on issues such as abortion, economic justice, and nuclear war is somewhat disturbing.

Uneven Treatment of Policy Issues

One significant difference between the NCCB's development of public policy recommendations on nuclear war and the economy, on one hand, and on abortion, on the other, is that the peace and economic pastorals were written only after consultation with specialists who in many cases *opposed* church views, whereas the development of policy recommendations on abortion has not, for the most part, involved formal consultation with demographers, family planners, feminists, and legal and medical experts who do not accept the church's moral teachings on abortion. A second major difference between the NCCB's strategy on abortion and its approach to the economic and peace pastorals concerns the *absolutism* of the church's position on abortion. Catholic moral teaching holds that the direct killing of innocent unborn human life is never permissible. The bishops argue that Catholic citizens and lawmakers must make vigorous efforts to translate this moral conviction into public policy. However, on other "life" issues such as nuclear warfare, the church's policy position is more subtle and nuanced, and little pressure is applied to Catholic politicians to adopt the church's policy views.

It was Benedictine Sister Joan Chittister who forcefully drew attention to this inconsistency between the bishops's qualified acceptance of some aspects of nuclear war and deterrence and their moral absolutism in opposing abortion. Writing about the first draft of the bishops' pastoral letter on war and peace, she declared:

> The document undermines the credibility of other episcopal statements. The bishops claim that nuclear destruction and policy are repugnant to them but say it is impossible to be morally absolute in their repudiation of the manufacture or use of nuclear weapons because there is enough need for deterrence and enough doubt about their effects to command their toleration.
>
> It is troublesome to note that the bishops show no such hesitation or ambivalence about abortion. In that case from a given principle they draw

universal and absolute implications with ease. Catholic hospitals may not permit abortions; Catholic doctors may not perform them; Catholic nurses may not assist at them; Catholic monies may not be used to sponsor abortion clinics. Nevertheless, the arguments for abortion are the same: the promotion of a greater good and the deterrence of evil for the parents or a handicapped child itself, for instance. What is a woman to think? That when life is in the hands of a woman, then to destroy it is always morally wrong, never to be condoned, always a grave and universal evil? But when life is in the hands of men, millions of lives at one time, all life at one time, then destruction can be theologized and some people's needs and lives can be made more important than other people's needs and lives? It is a theological imperative that we confront this dichotomy.[40]

Chittister left little doubt about how this inconsistency might be resolved. She urged the bishops to "say a clear no to nuclear war and the possession and manufacture of nuclear weapons as well." That is, she argued that the church's absolute prohibition of the violence of direct abortion should be paralleled by total opposition to nuclear war and deterrence. However, I would press for consistency in a different direction from Joan Chittister. What I find striking about the bishops' uneven treatment of these policy issues is the inconsistency between the qualified approach to public policy characteristic of the peace pastoral and the bishops' more simplistic, absolutist approach to abortion policy. In the peace pastoral, the bishops wrote:

The Church's teaching authority does not carry the same force when it deals with technical solutions involving particular means as it does when it speaks of principles or ends. People may agree in abhorring an injustice, for instance, yet sincerely disagree as to what practical approach will achieve justice. Religious groups are entitled as others to their opinion in such cases, but they should not claim that their opinions are the only ones that people of good will may hold.[41]

It seems to me that in complex matters of war and peace, the bishops clearly recognize the contextual nature and prudential character of practical judgments about the relation between morality and public policy. They acknowledge that people of good will can disagree about which public policies will best realize desired moral goals or objectives. Now if loyal Catholics can differ about appropriate nuclear policy, they can also reach different conclusions about sound abortion policy. I am somewhat puzzled as to why the church does not recognize that issues of fertility control and reproductive freedom are similarly complex and require the same kind of subtle, balanced, contextual approach as do questions of economic or defense policy.

This is especially so because the church's moral teaching on abortion is not as rigid, un-nuanced or iron-clad as we are sometimes led to believe. It is worth noting that the church has not pronounced definitively that the fetus is a human being from the moment of conception. Rather, the church holds that since we cannot say with certainty when human life actually begins, we should err on the side of never killing what could well be an actual human being. Christopher Mooney describes the church's reasoning as follows:

> The argument [is] that since there is no way, scientific or otherwise, to ascertain at what point exactly the human fetus becomes a human person (or, in more traditional religious language, when the human soul becomes present in the human body), abortion at any point after conception may in fact be taking the life of an innocent human person; but to risk actually doing such a thing can never be morally justified for any reason in any circumstances; therefore in practice the human fetus must always be treated as if it were in fact a human person at every moment of its existence.[42]

I believe that this construction of the church's position on the morality of abortion is much "softer" and more nuanced that the absolutist view we customarily hear. If the ethics of abortion revolves around risk-taking and questions of acceptable risk, then the type of reasoning associated with calculations of risk is very much like the consequentialist considerations and prudent balancing of competing claims that is the hallmark of American public policymaking. What this suggests is that the same subtlety that characterizes the NCCB's policy recommendations on war and economic justice should also characterize the church's policy recommendations on abortion. Were this the case, the bishops would have little warrant to pressure Catholic politicians to automatically translate the church's moral teaching into public policy.

The Effect of the Church's Political Activity on the American Political Process

Viewing the Catholic Church as an interest group perhaps offers a chilling possibility regarding general trends in American politics. As stated earlier, because of its own quasi-federal internal structure the Catholic Church is one of the few institutions in American life that is well-organized at national, state, and local levels. This means the church can shift rather easily from one level to another as the locus of contention over abortion policy shifts from Washington back to the states. But its hierarchical character gives the Catholic Church a second advantage in interest group politics. Hierarchical institutions such as corporations, universities, and of course the Catholic Church have longevity, resources, and a fundamental freedom of action that member-based or issue-based groups generally lack. As Salisbury has suggested, hierarchical or institutional interest groups have come to dominate interest representation in Washington. Moreover, institutional domination of interest representation magnifies the bias in the American political and policymaking system in favor of those with more resources.

The Catholic Church has the structural advantages of institutional interest groups: (1) tremendous organizational and financial resources, (2) longevity or staying power--the church was around long before the current abortion controversy and will be around long after it has died away--and (3) a fundamental freedom of action that member-based interest groups simply do not have. Moreover, the church has this freedom of action *theologically* as well as *politically*. Theologically, the bishops define themselves as teachers and sources of authoritative doctrine in the church. Politically, as an institutional interest group unresponsive to members, the church has a freedom of action that trade unions and other member-based interest groups simply do not have.

These institutional and structural advantages have enabled the church to take advantage of the opportunities offered by the American political process. They help explain why the church has been an effective pro-life lobbyist, winning victories at the federal level (e.g., the Hyde Amendment) and also at the state level (the Pennsylvania Catholic Conference was a key player in the passage of the 1989 Pennsylvania Abortion Control Act, later upheld by the U.S. Supreme Court in *Planned Parenthood v. Casey*). The Catholic Church has, in other words, adjusted rather nicely to the rules of the game of American politics. It fits right in. Its mode of political participation is perfectly congruent with an interest group system that is elitist, undemocratic, and hierarchical, and that gives the edge to moneyed lobbies.

Thus, the answer to the question whether the NCCB's political activity has enhanced democracy or reinforced elitist tendencies in

American politics may be that the bishops' conference is part of the problem rather than the solution. Because of its organizational structure and the generally elitist character of the church's lobbying on abortion, it has reinforced those tendencies in the American political process that are negative and less desirable from a democratic perspective.

This conclusion about the political behavior of the Catholic Church would seem to contradict the thesis of political scientist Allen Hertzke, who argued in his book, *Representing God in Washington* that "the national religious lobbies, collectively, enhance the representativeness of the modern American polity."[43] According to Hertzke, religious lobbies (church interest groups) provide a significant corrective to the American pluralist system through their role in representing non-elites and unpopular attitudes. Hertzke was thinking particularly of the Religious Right and other evangelical and fundamentalist church groups, whose concerns would probably not be represented by mainstream denominations and who need lobbies such as the Christian Action Coalition to articulate their views. However, in the case of the National Conference of Catholic Bishops, church lobbying has the effect of reinforcing elitist rather than democratic trends within the body politic.

Hertzke and Byrnes both suggest that influence is a two-way street in American politics and that the organization and norms of Congress and the American political system influence religious lobbies and the churches fully as much as they in turn influence politics. Hertzke further suggests that religious groups are most successful in politics when they are least "religious." By this he means that religious interest groups are most likely to achieve their legislative goals when they lose their narrowly religious focus, when they can frame their goals not in narrowly sectarian or grandly prophetic terms but in the more widely accepted, secular terms of normal U.S. politics (e.g., civil rights rather than religious rights). These two points suggest how the bishops' lobby in Washington has managed to be successful on Capitol Hill--by conforming to the norms of American politics and playing hardball just like all the other special interests. Lost in the din of all this politicking is the prophetic voice.

THE CATHOLIC CHURCH AS A POLITICAL LOBBY: THE INTERNAL VIEWPOINT

Studying the church as a religious lobby from the perspective of a political scientist obviously raises a fundamental question: Should the church be a political actor, using the political process to advance its interests and articulate its considered moral judgments on the great questions of the day? More particularly for our purposes, should the church be so deeply involved in the *political* campaign in the United States to reinstate restrictive abortion laws? Are the risks and consequences of political immersion worth the price for the American Catholic Church? What has the church gained and what has it lost through its involvement in abortion politics?

I realize these are age-old questions about the church's spiritual and temporal power, about this-worldly versus other-worldly concerns. The church, of course, has a right to participate in the American political process. Moreover, the message of the Second Vatican Council was that Catholics and the Church should be more active in addressing social and economic problems. But *how* the Church does this in a religiously diverse, pluralist society committed to religious liberty and church-state separation is the central question.

In the final section of this chapter, I want to examine the church's involvement in abortion politics from the internal vantage point of the believer, of the committed Catholic. To me as a Catholic, of course, the church is more than just another special interest in American politics; it is in a category different from, say, the National Rifle Association, the American Medical Association, or People for the American Way. The Catholic Church is not merely one more interest group in the world of Washington lobbies. To the believer, the church is (as the Quakers put it) a "beloved community," a society of friends, a religious and Christian community, "the People of God" (to use the language of Vatican II). Churches are sacred communities that have a special duty to attend to the common good and to universal values of peace and justice. They also have a special obligation to avoid sectarian strife. This, after all, was one of the American Founding Fathers' chief concerns that led them to promote religious freedom and nonestablishment. The Framers advocated church-state separation partly because they feared the religious wars that afflicted Europe throughout the early modern period.

From a believer's perspective, the task is to evaluate the church's political activity in terms of a key principle: whether the bishops' political activities have advanced Gospel norms of justice and charity. We can draw up a balance sheet on the benefits and costs, the pluses and minuses of the Catholic political campaign to ban abortion. On the plus side, it is clear that the Catholic Church has kept the abortion issue alive through its social and political activity. It has given the issue top priority and has thereby refused to allow abortion to become routine, an accepted or standard practice, a matter of conventional wisdom. It has managed through its political lobbying to protect Catholic institutions from being required to perform or condone abortions in violation of their conscience rights. It has also restricted access to abortion more generally through passage of such measures as the Hyde Amendment.

The NCCB has also cut its political teeth on the abortion issue. Over the last 20 years, the institutional church has learned some hard lessons about its mode and style of political participation. As a result of their political activism on the abortion issue, the bishops have learned the importance of not being partisan, the necessity of a multi-issue approach to American politics, and the necessity of presenting a rational and convincing case for their position rather than appealing to scriptural or papal authority for justification. As Bishop James Malone, then NCCB president, noted after the 1984 election, "In the public arena of a pluralistic democracy, religious leaders face the same tests of rational argument as any other individuals or institutions. Our impact on the public will be directly proportionate to the persuasiveness of our positions. We seek no special status and we should not be accorded one."[44]

Nevertheless, while the church has been a major force in the anti-abortion movement and has learned valuable lessons about political participation, it has paid a high price for this knowledge. Many of the church's mistakes here stem from a failure to fully appreciate the importance of political freedom in a liberal democracy. First, the bishops' coercive treatment of pro-choice Catholic officeholders indicates a failure to understand the dilemma of being a lawmaker in a pluralist society with traditions of religious freedom and church-state separation. The abortion issue challenges Catholic politicians to reconcile sometimes conflicting duties to conscience, Constitution, constituents, and the common good. Such a challenge invites subtle balancing rather than easy, simplistic, one-dimensional answers.

Second, with a few exceptions, the bishops have not consulted Catholic feminists about proper abortion policy in any serious, systematic way. Moreover, the church has been willing to sacrifice its support for women's rights legislation--the ERA, the 1978 Pregnancy Disability Act, and the 1988 Civil Rights Restoration Act--to the anti-abortion cause. Add to this the critique voiced by many Catholic women that historically the church's moral theology on abortion has not been informed by the voices and perspectives of women, and it is not difficult to understand how and why the church's anti-abortion campaign has alienated many Catholic women.

Third, while the church trumpets its pro-life call, the NCCB has emphasized the abortion issue to the comparative neglect of other significant "life" issues. For example, despite important pastoral letters about economic justice or war and peace in the mid-1980s, the bishops have not conducted the grassroots mobilization or parish-based educational campaigns on these issues that they have pursued on the abortion issue. This uneven treatment of policy issues undermines the church's commitment to a consistent life ethic. The bishops' annual "Respect Life Sunday" observance focuses on the abortion issue to the neglect of these other social justice issues. This tepid commitment to protect life was reflected in some bishops' reluctance to distance themselves from Operation Rescue efforts in the 1980s and early 1990s. In other words, despite determined efforts by some bishops (e.g., Joseph Cardinal Bernardin of Chicago, Walter Sullivan of Richmond, Rembert Weakland of Milwaukee, Joseph Sullivan of Brooklyn, Thomas Gumbleton of Detroit) to promote a consistent approach to human rights issues, the NCCB's actions and priorities still demonstrate a narrow, single-issue focus on abortion. Finally, the church's political campaign against abortion has tended to reinforce the elitist tenor of American politics and the undemocratic nature of the American interest group system. The USCC and various state Catholic conferences (e.g., those in Pennsylvania and California) have earned the respect of other politicians and lobbyists for their skill in playing the influence game. However, the church is more than an interest group. Whether the American Catholic Church wants to be known and remembered primarily as a powerful lobby and a major player in abortion politics is a compelling question.

As a political scientist, I might congratulate the church for having become a powerful political force on selected policy issues such as abortion. But as an American Catholic, I view with some concern the bishops' intense, long-standing campaign to reinstate coercive abortion laws. Is it a source of pride to American Catholics that their church is indistinguishable from the numerous political lobbies with offices on the K Street corridor in Washington? Catholics may have "arrived" politically, economically, and socially in American society, but the price may have been conformity to the political status quo and loss of the church's prophetic voice. Is it possible that the Catholic Church in the United States has become *too* acculturated to American politics?

Another way of stating this is to say that the Catholic Church should be *more church and less political actor*. By this I mean that a sacred community of Catholic Christians should be more a sign of God's graceful presence in the world than an instrument of intimidation and political-legal coercion. Perhaps the church would be more effective in communicating its message about the wrongs of abortion through primarily *social* rather than *political* efforts. After all, supporting coercive laws restricting abortion tells the world that the church is a powerful political institution. In this image, the church appears frightening and potentially overbearing to non-Catholic Americans, most of whom do not share its moral views. On the other hand, helping involuntarily pregnant women conveys a different message--that the church is a caring community that tries to live up to the ideal of charity in the Christian Gospels.

From a Catholic religious perspective, it is proper to question the impact of the bishops' anti-abortion activities upon internal church relations. Have the bishops' activities strengthened the beloved community that is the church? Or have they proved unnecessarily divisive, setting clergy against lay Catholics, dividing lay Catholics among themselves, and politicizing the church's worship and liturgy?

As a Catholic and a political scientist, I have a tripartite critique of the church's political campaign to reinstate restrictive abortion laws. First, I argue that the church is wrong to sanction Catholic lawmakers who disagree with the church's recommendations on abortion policy. Second, I contend that bishops and clergy should not use church services to issue voting instructions from the pulpit and to otherwise exert coercive pressure on Catholic voters. Both of these tactics, I think, reveal a fundamental misunderstanding by church officials of the nature of political leadership and democratic citizenship in a pluralistic, religiously diverse society. Finally, I maintain that the American church does indeed have alternatives to interest group lobbying and politics-as-usual.

Instead of focusing on abortion law and policy, which inevitably entails winning and losing in the zero-sum game of politics, the church's anti-abortion effort should be focused on social measures to reduce the incidence of abortion without coercing women. Such a church campaign would, I suspect, be both prophetic and more persuasive to non-Catholic Americans than the current political efforts of clergy and hierarchy.

Bishops and Catholic Lawmakers: Elite Lobbying and Electoral Politics

The first section of this chapter reviewed the treatment of pro-choice Catholic lawmakers by bishops and clergy. The sanctioning of politicians has not been one of the church's finer moments. The bishops have demonstrated a baffling failure to understand the dilemma of living in a pluralistic society--a failure to appreciate the complex demands of being a lawmaker with duties to conscience, the Constitution, constituents, and the common good. The case of Joseph Califano, former Secretary of Health, Education and Welfare (HEW) in President Jimmy Carter's cabinet, illustrates this complexity.

As HEW Secretary, Califano had to oversee the administration of the Medicaid health care program for poor people at the time the Hyde Amendment was first passed in the late 1970s. The Hyde Amendment presented him with a major dilemma: reconciling his private beliefs as a Roman Catholic with his public duties as HEW secretary. Califano phrased his dilemma succinctly: "As Secretary of HEW, would I be able, in good conscience, to carry out the law of the land, even if that law provided for federal funding of all abortions?"[45]

Califano's resolution of this dilemma is instructive. In public hearings and in private meetings, Califano stated clearly his opposition to abortion and to public funding of abortions. Nevertheless, once Congress had authorized public funding of abortions in certain instances and Califano had to write specific regulations for administering the law, he correctly perceived his public duty to be paramount and to take precedence over his private religious convictions.

Reflecting on his experience as a Catholic and as a Cabinet executive, Califano noted that the abortion issue was complex and that he "found no automatic answers in Christian theology and the teachings of my church to the vexing questions of public policy it raised." Moreover, he discovered that religious belief could not be decisive, that there were a variety of factors to be weighed and values to be balanced in making public policy. He summarized the competing values and obligations every public servant must consider in exercising political judgment and executing constitutional responsibilities.

> Throughout the abortion debate, I did--as I believe I should have--espouse a position I deeply held. I tried to recognize that to have and be guided by convictions of conscience is not a license to impose them indiscriminately on others by one-dimensionally translating them into public policy. Public policy, if it is to serve the common good of a fundamentally just and free pluralistic society, must balance competing values, such as freedom, order, equity, and justice. If I failed to weigh those competing values--or to fulfill my public obligations to be firm without being provocative, or to recognize my public duty once the Congress had acted--I would have served neither my private conscience nor the public morality. I tried to do credit to both.

I think Secretary Califano's experience makes the point. There are no automatic answers in Catholic theology or church teaching to the vexing public policy questions facing conscientious public officials. Whether the limitations are *constitutional* (as in the case of a Cabinet executive such as Califano) or *democratic* (as in the case of an elected official such as Cuomo or Killea), there are limiting factors on what a political leader can do with respect to public policy on abortion. Public officials take an oath of office to uphold the constitutional democracy that is our government. The norms and rules of that system cannot be treated lightly by any government official.

In view of this, the propriety and effectiveness of church sanctions against prochoice Catholic lawmakers seems questionable. Catholic public officials such as former House Speaker Tom Foley, former New York governor Mario Cuomo, California state senator Lucy Killea, California congresswoman Nancy Pelosi, former Senate Majority Leader George Mitchell, Rhode Island congresswoman Claudine Schneider, and Connecticut congresswoman Barbara Kennelly[46] have a duty to represent Catholics and non-Catholics alike. In a religiously diverse democracy, they must make public policy for believers and nonbelievers. If the church's moral teaching against abortion is not persuasive to a majority of the citizenry, there is little warrant for using the coercive sanctions of public law to ban or restrict abortion.

Moreover, a secular audience in a democratic society is probably not going to be enlightened, much less persuaded, by the spectacle of church authorities resorting to ecclesiastical sanctions to keep Catholic lawmakers in line. In this sense, the bishops' sanctioning of public officials is counterproductive and self-defeating. The church insists that abortion is a *moral*, not a *religious,* issue, an action that all women and men can agree is wrong. However, by publicly threatening Catholic citizens and lawmakers with canonical penalties, the bishops only confirm that abortion is a sectarian issue, a Catholic problem, a matter of church law rather than of public policy.

Ultimately, Catholic lawmakers must enact public policy that respects the conscience rights of non-Catholic Americans. This means that they must search for consensus and make prudent judgments about the possible and probable consequences of policies they enact. Above all, they have a constitutional duty to respect the First Amendment freedoms of all citizens in a religiously diverse society. Although the church says abortion is not a religious issue but an ethical matter about which people can agree despite religious differences, Catholics must face the fact that people from other major religions do indeed reach different policy conclusions. Churchmen may think these conclusions erroneous, but it is the genius of the American constitutional experiment to recognize that "error has rights." Public officials have a moral and constitutional duty to uphold those rights. Bishops and clergy who fail to recognize this obligation of Catholic lawmakers do them a great disservice.

Finally, all Catholics--clergy, citizens, lawmakers--are committed as Catholics and as Americans to the concept of religious liberty. As members of a minority religion in a Protestant country, American Catholics have always valued the religious freedom and tolerance that made it possible for them to thrive. In twentieth-century Europe, Polish Catholics discovered the value of religious liberty under communist rule. More recently, Pope John Paul II has warned Sudanese leaders that Islamic law should not be imposed on those of other faiths, including Christians in the southern part of the Sudan. In the Sudan the Pope promised that the leadership of the Roman Catholic church will "remind leaders of Muslim countries that Islamic law can be applied only to the Muslim faithful." Shortly after publication of the Pope's remarks, a shrewd commentator concluded, in a letter to *The New York Times*, that "the Pope must believe that such actions by Muslims would be as wrong as the Catholic hierarchy's seeking to enact laws in Western countries that would force non-Catholics to obey church teachings on divorce, birth control, and abortion."[47] In short, if the church is to take seriously its commitment to religious liberty enunciated at the Second Vatican Council, then it must accept the corollary principle of respect for the rights of non-Catholics who disagree with church teachings and who do not want the American Catholic Church to use the political process to impose its views upon them.

Politicization of Church Services and Mobilization of Catholic Voters

If Catholic churchmen should respect the constitutional obligations of Catholic lawmakers, they should also respect the citizen rights of Catholic voters. Concretely, this means that bishops and clergy should not use the pulpit to issue voting instructions or otherwise exert coercive pressure on Catholic voters. Catholics do not go to Mass in order to be politically mobilized. Using church services as centers for grassroots mobilization and using sermon time as an occasion for distributing postcards to mail to Congress is erroneous from the perspective of a believer. Tactics of this sort amount to politicization of the liturgy.

An example of such political mobilization occurred during the 1989 gubernatorial election campaign in New Jersey. On Respect Life Sunday (October 1, 1989), Catholics in three New Jersey dioceses were asked during Mass to sign pledge cards authorizing pro-life commissions to use the resulting list of names (called a "Life Roll") to lobby for pro-life legislation.[48] Again in 1993 and 1994, as mentioned above, postcards were distributed nationwide to parishioners during Mass, urging them to lobby Congress in opposition to the Freedom of Choice Act and to the inclusion of abortion coverage in a national health plan.

Politicizing the liturgy in this manner is questionable from an ecclesiological perspective. The Catholic Mass is an inappropriate forum for conducting political mobilization campaigns. It could be argued that using sermon time to exhort a captive audience of congregants to sign political pledge cards is coercive of conscience and disrespectful to Catholic citizens, who have a right and a duty to make their own judgments about sound public policy. Within the church bishops are moral teachers, but in a pluralist democracy members of the hierarchy do not necessarily have either the competence or the right to tell citizens how to vote or what policies to support.

Furthermore, such political mobilizations are imprudent and improper because they suggest that there is a single policy position that all Catholics should adopt. As Califano noted, there are no automatic answers in Christian theology and Catholic teaching to the vexing questions of public policy raised by the abortion issue. Abortion policy must balance the conflicting claims of different interests (believers, agnostics, atheists) as well as the competing values of freedom, order, equity, justice, and privacy. There is no single Catholic solution to this *policy* dilemma just as there is no single Jewish or no single Methodist answer.

Moreover, evidence suggests that issuing voting instructions to Catholics from the pulpit is not effective. A 1993 Gallup survey of Catholic opinion showed that "Catholics are firm in rejecting admonitions from the hierarchy about how to vote based on a candidate's view of abortion. Seventy percent believe they can make their own voting decisions in good conscience."[49]

Bishops are religious and moral teachers, but they do not have, by virtue of their office, any special expertise in public policy. They must therefore recognize that they have no special competence in the politics of a liberal democratic society. They may be good managers and diocesan administrators, and they may be experts in internal church politics. But little in their seminary training or clerical experience in a hierarchically structured, authoritative teaching institution has prepared them for civic participation in a democratic polity. As citizens, clerical and lay Catholics are equals. The bishops therefore have no special expertise in public policymaking that gives them the authority to tell Catholic lawmakers how to do their jobs. Nor do the clergy have any special knowledge or insight that confers upon them the right to tell Catholic citizens how to vote. On those occasions when bishops have taken Catholic politicians to task over the abortion issue or used the pulpit to issue voting instructions, they have exceeded their legitimate authority as church leaders. Such clerical intervention is inappropriate in a democratic society. Not only do the bishops risk losing their tax exemption by such partisan actions; they also betray insufficient awareness of the meaning of church-state separation and of the tension American Catholics feel between a hierarchical church and a democratic government.

Alternatives to Church Lobbying for Restrictive Abortion Laws

Fortunately, the American bishops do have alternatives to lobbying for laws restricting abortion and otherwise coercing or harassing women. These alternative methods emphasize assisting women rather than intimidating them. The idea is to promote measures and policies that will reduce the incidence of abortion without coercing women. In pursuit of this goal, the bishops' conference should support social programs designed to help women, families, and children and which promise to lessen the economic and social pressures on women that drive them to solve their problems through abortion. Such programs include disability rights for pregnant employees, childcare benefits, increased welfare benefits, family-planning funding, and employment training programs. Ideally, the American Catholic Church should support such policies as a means to social justice as well as a way of making unwanted pregnancies less likely. There is a real need for the church to view abortion comprehensively in terms of root causes and the need for social equality and justice.

In other words, I am suggesting that the bishops may be going about their anti-abortion crusade in the wrong way. The preferable approach is to work to change society and people's minds through examples of love and assistance to involuntarily pregnant women. The right way is through moral education of Catholics and others, coupled with strong support of measures to assist women. Instead of spending $5 million to hire a public relations firm to get the church's anti-abortion message across, the church might better spend its time, energy, and money on training the clergy in homiletics, teaching them to give better sermons to parishioners in need of substantive spiritual nourishment. Moreover, in my judgment, the bishops' full institutional support of measures to assist women and children will be far more effective as a sign of God's grace and a positive example to Catholics and non-Catholics alike than any slick public relations campaign. By stressing assistance to women, the church will be giving prophetic witness to Gospel norms of charity and justice. Such an approach would be exemplary and persuasive to non-Catholic Americans.

I am not reiterating here the rigid separationist idea that churches should stay out of politics completely. Such a severe dichotomy between church and state is impossible, impractical, undesirable, and unworkable. Rather, I am questioning the substance and style of the Catholic Church's participation in abortion politics in the United States. I am suggesting that the goal of its political participation should be to reduce the incidence of abortion without coercing women. This means the bishops should continue to support public policies that will assist women. However, it also means that, because the church, unlike other interest groups, is an institutional community engaged in pastoral care and social service, it should concentrate its anti-abortion efforts chiefly in those non-political areas of pastoral counseling and social welfare. By emphasizing these nonpolitical approaches, the bishops' conference would accomplish several goals simultaneously: concretely assisting involuntarily pregnant women; exemplifying compassionate care and demonstrating that the church supports women's rights and recognizes their needs; possibly reducing the incidence of abortion as women realize there are alternatives; and implementing the first two parts of the 1975 Pastoral Plan for Pro-Life Activities which calls for an educational campaign and a pastoral effort to assist women with problem pregnancies. Most important, the example of pastoral care and social service to women can be instructive to Catholics and non-Catholics alike. In exemplifying Gospel norms of charity and nonviolence, the church can best demonstrate its critique of existing cultural values and its determination not to let abortion become the accepted, "first-resort" solution to problem pregnancies.

I believe the Catholic bishops' political campaign to reinstate restrictive abortion laws is misguided and mistaken, and that the church would do better to focus its tremendous resources on moral suasion and assistance to involuntarily pregnant women. Clerical intervention in American politics is always risky. This was recognized by no less important an American Catholic than Bishop John Carroll. This first American bishop had practical misgivings about priests in politics. "I have observed," he wrote, "that when the ministers of Religion leave the duties of their profession to take a busy part in political matters, they generally fall into contempt; and sometimes even bring discredit to the cause, in whose service they are engaged."[50] Perhaps American Catholic Church leaders should heed Bishop Carroll's warning.

NOTES

1. James Hennesey, *American Catholics: A History of the Roman Catholic Community in the United States* (New York: Oxford University Press, 1981), pp. 71-72, 87-88.

2. For a general discussion of the NCCB and USCC, see Thomas Reese, S.J., *A Flock of Shepherds: The National Conference of Catholic Bishops* (Kansas City, MO: Sheed & Ward, 1992), and Timothy A. Byrnes, *Catholic Bishops in American Politics* (Princeton: Princeton University Press, 1991).

3. See Thomas J. O'Hara, C.S.C., "The Multifaceted Catholic Lobby," in Charles W. Dunn, ed., *Religion in American Politics* (Washington, D.C.: CQ Press, 1989), pp. 137-144; see also Thomas J. O'Hara, "The Catholic Lobby in Washington: Pluralism and Diversity among U.S. Catholics," in Mary Segers, ed., *Church Polity and American Politics: Issues in Contemporary American Catholicism* (New York: Garland Publishing, 1990), pp. 143-156.

4. The best recent treatment of religious lobbying is Alan Hertzke, *Representing God in Washington: The Role of Religious Lobbies in Washington* (Nashville, TN: University of Tennessee Press, 1988). See also Timothy A. Byrnes, "Membership Institutions: Group Theory and the Political Role of America's Churches," unpublished paper presented at the annual meeting of the American Political Science Association, Washington, D. C., September 1-5, 1993. Byrnes argues that the usual categories of interest group theory only partly describe the role played by churches in American politics. Neither wholly "institutional interests" nor wholly "membership organizations," churches are a hybrid he calls "membership institutions." For additional political science literature on interest groups, see Kay Lehman Schlozman and John T. Tierney, *Organized Interests and American Democracy* (New York: Harper & Row, 1986); Jeffrey M. Berry, *The Interest Group Society*, 2nd ed. (Glenview, IL: Scott Foresman/Little, Brown, 1989); and Alan Cigler and Burdett Loomis, eds., *Interest Group Politics*, 3rd ed. (Washington, D. C.: CQ Press, 1991).

5. Hertzke, *Representing God in Washington*, p. 100.

6. Robert H. Salisbury, "Interest Representation: The Dominance of Institutions," *American Political Science Review* 78 (1984): 64-76; reprinted in Randall B. Ripley and Elliott E. Slotnick, eds., *Readings in American Government and Politics*, 2nd ed. (New York: McGraw Hill, 1993), pp. 296-302.

7. David Truman, *The Governmental Process* (New York: Columbia University Press, 1950).

8. See James Kelly, "Toward Complexity: The Right to Life Movement," in *Research in the Social Scientific Study of Religion*, Vol. 1 (New York: JAI Press, 1989).

9. In order not to jeopardize its tax-exempt status, the NCCB does not provide funding; instead, the assessment is paid by individual bishops directly to NCHLA without going through the bishops' conference. See Reese, *A Flock*

of Shepherds: The National Conference of Catholic Bishops, pp. 95-97, 178, and 221.

10. See Byron Daynes and Raymond Tatalovich, *The Politics of Abortion: A Study of Community Conflict in Public Policymaking* (New York: Praeger, 1981); Lawrence Lader, *Abortion II: Making the Revolution* (Boston: Beacon Press, 1973); Marian Faux, *Roe v. Wade* (New York: MacMillan, 1988); Kristin Luker, *Abortion and the Politics of Motherhood* (Berkeley: University of California Press, 1984); Laurence Tribe, *Abortion: The Clash of Absolutes* (New York: W.W. Norton, 1990); and Daniel J. O'Neil, *Church Lobbying in a Western State: A Case Study on Abortion Legislation*, Arizona Government Studies 7 (Tucson: University of Arizona Press, 1970).

11. This account relies on Daynes and Tatalovich, *The Politics of Abortion*; also Patricia Steinhoff and Milton Diamond, *Abortion Politics: The Hawaii Experience* (Honolulu: University Press of Hawaii, 1977); also R. J. Pion, Roy G. Smith, and R. W. Hale, "The Hawaii Experience," in H. J. Osofsky and J.D. Osofsky, eds., *The Abortion Experience* (New York: Harper & Row , 1973), pp. 177-187.

12. Steinhoff and Diamond, *Abortion Politics: The Hawaii Experience*, p. 33.

13. Robert F. Drinan, S.J., "Strategy on Abortion," *America*, February 4, 1967, p. 178.

14. Robert F. Drinan, S.J., "The State of the Abortion Question," *Commonweal* 92 (April 17, 1970): 108-109. See also Robert F. Drinan, "The Right of the Foetus to be Born," *Dublin Review* 514 (Winter 1967): 365-381; Steinhoff and Diamond, *Abortion Politics: The Hawaii Experience*, pp. 23-24, 32, 126.

15. Steinhoff and Diamond, *Abortion Politics*, p. 27.

16. For examples, see Timothy A. Byrnes and Mary C. Segers, eds., *The Catholic Church and the Politics of Abortion: A View from the States* (Boulder, CO: Westview Press, 1992). See also Nancy H. Evans and Denise Shannon, "BishopSpeak: A Chronology of the U.S. Catholic Clergy's Involvement in Abortion Politics, November 1989--June 1990," *Guide for Prochoice Catholics* (Washington, D.C.: Catholics for a Free Choice, 1990), pp. 30-36.

17. This testimony is reproduced in *Documentation on the Right to Life and Abortion* (Washington, D. C.: United States Catholic Conference, 1974), pp. 1-44.

18. This testimony is reproduced in *Documentation on Abortion and the Right to Life II* (Washington, D. C.: United States Catholic Conference, 1976), pp. 1-44.

19. *Congressional Record*, June 5, 1973, pp. 18068-18069. The legislation enacted was the Public Health Service Act of 1973. The bishops' statement is contained in "Pastoral Guidelines for the Catholic Hospital and Catholic Health Care Personnel," in Hugh J. Nolan, ed., *The Pastoral Letters of the United States Bishops*, Vol. III (Washington, D. C.: United States Catholic Conference, 1983), p. 366.

20. The NCHLA's lobbyist, Mark Gallagher, was a prominent participant in the arguments, negotiations, and legislative maneuvering surrounding the various Hyde Amendments in the late 1970s. The *New York Times* reported that "every time the Senate conferees make a compromise offer, Mr. Gallagher quietly walks to the conference table to tell a staff aide to the eleven House conferees whether the proposal is acceptable to the bishops. His recommendations invariably are followed." *New York Times*, November 27, 1977, IV, 4.

21. For discussion of the Civil Rights Restoration Act and of the USCC's role in amending it, see Thomas J. O'Hara, "The Civil Rights Restoration Act: The Role of the Religious Lobbies," paper delivered at the 1989 meeting of the American Political Science Association, Atlanta, Georgia.

22. See "Religious Freedom Bill Introduced in Congress," *Christian Century*, 110, 10 (March 24-31, 1993): 313. The Religious Freedom Restoration Act (RFRA) was designed to restore religious freedom, which was thought to be in jeopardy after the Supreme Court ruling in *Oregon Employment Division v. Smith* (1991). In *Smith*, the justices voted 5 to 4 that the government no longer had to prove a compelling state interest before restricting religious freedom. They ruled that government could burden religion as long as the laws that did so were neutral toward religion and had general applicability. The RFRA proposes to put the compelling interest test back into the laws of the nation under the authority vested in Congress by the Fourteenth Amendment to the Constitution. This legislation passed both houses of Congress by overwhelming majorities and has been signed into law by President Clinton. See Rosalie Beck and D.W. Hendon, "Notes on Church-State Affairs," *Journal of Church and State* 35, 4 (Autumn 1993): 936-937.

23. Bishop John Ricard, "Letter to Mrs. Clinton: Reforming Health Care," *Origins* 22, no. 46 (April 29, 1993): 783-785; and U.S. Bishops, "Resolution on Health Care Reform," *Origins* 23, no. 7 (July 1, 1993): 97-102. See also *Christian Century* 110, no. 16 (May 12, 1993): 513.

24. *Abortion Rights Mobilization, Inc. v. United States Catholic Conference* 110 S.Ct. 946 (1990); see also *New York Times*, May 1, 1990, p. A18. The U.S. tax code, in section 501 (c) (3), makes tax exempt nonprofit organizations that do not participate in or intervene in political campaigns.

25. "Pastoral Plan for Pro-Life Activities," in Hugh Nolan, ed., *Pastoral Letters of the United States Catholic Bishops*, Vol. IV (Washington, D. C.: United States Catholic Conference, 1983), pp. 82-89.

26. Timothy A. Byrnes and Mary C. Segers, "Federalism and the Catholic Church's Antiabortion Campaign," unpublished paper.1993.

27. See Mary Meehan, "Prolifers Eye Battlefield," *National Catholic Register*, January 16, 1994; Mimi Hall, "Church Fights Abortion Coverage," *USA Today*, January 28, 1994; and Dan Balz, "Christian Coalition Launches Effort against Clinton Plan," *Washington Post*, February 16, 1994.

28. The first quote is from Archbishop Theodore E. McCarrick's Letter to Archdiocesan Catholics, printed in *Catholic Advocate* (Newark archdiocesan newspaper), November 1, 1989, pp. 1 and 4. The second quote is from Bishop James McHugh, bishop of Camden, during the 1989 New Jersey gubernatorial election. See *Origins*, December 14, 1989, p. 461.

29. Bishop John J. Meyers of Peoria, Illinois, in a pastoral letter to his flock; see *Origins*, May 31, 1990, p. 43.

30. *New York Times*, June 25, 1984, p. D13. See also Mary C. Segers, "Ferraro, the Bishops, and the 1984 Election," in C. W. Atkinson, C. H. Buchanan, and M. R. Miles. eds. *Shaping New Vision: Gender and Values in American Culture* (Ann Arbor: UMI Research Press, 1987), pp. 143-167.

31. On Ferraro, see *New York Times*, September 9, 1984, p. 34. On excommunication, see Cardinal John O'Connor's column in *Catholic New York*, June 14, 1990.

32. For a discussion of the controversies in 1976, see Timothy A. Byrnes, "The Bishops and Electoral Politics: A Case Study," in Mary C. Segers, ed.,

Church Polity and American Politics: Issues in Contemporary Catholicism (New York: Garland, 1990), pp. 121-141.

33. For Cardinal Medeiros' actions during the 1980 Massachusetts primary, see Andrew H. Merton, *Enemies of Choice: The Right to Life Movement and Its Threat to Abortion* (Boston: Beacon Press, 1981), pp. 115-116. For an example of the bishops' quadrennial statements on political responsibility during a presidential election, see USCC Administrative Board, "Political Responsibility: Revitalizing American Democracy," *Origins* 21, no. 20 (October 24, 1991): 313.

34. See Mary C. Segers, "Ferraro, The Bishops, and the 1984 Election," in Atkinson, Buchanan, and Miles, eds. *Shaping New Vision.* Also see Mary E. Hunt and Frances Kissling, "The *New York Times* Ad: A Case Study in Religious Feminism," *Journal of Feminist Studies in Religion*, 3, 1 (Spring 1987): 115-127.

35. *Origins*, 22, no. 20 (October 29, 1992): 341-352.

36. Thomas J. Reese, S. J., "Women's Pastoral Fails," *America*, December 5, 1992, pp. 443-444. See also Peter Steinfels, "Beliefs," *New York Times*, January 23, 1993, p. 7.

37. For Bishop Leo Maher's letter to Lucy Killea, see *Origins*, December 14, 1989, p. 457.

38. Gerald M. Pomper et al., *The Election of 1992* (Chatham, NJ: Chatham House Publishers, 1993), p. 139.

39. Mary Hanna, "Bishops as Political Leaders," in Charles W. Dunn, ed., *Religion in American Politics* (Washington, D. C.: CQ Press, 1989), p. 83.

40. Sr. Joan Chittister, O.S.B., "Stepping Tentatively between Prophetism and Nationalism," *Commonweal* 109 (August 13, 1982), p. 428.

41. National Conference of Catholic Bishops, "The Challenge of Peace: God's Promise and Our Response" (1983), sections 9 and 10, reprinted in Philip J. Murnion, ed., *Catholics and Nuclear War* (New York: Crossroad, 1983), p. 258.

42. Christopher F. Mooney, *Public Virtue: Law and the Social Character of Religion* (Notre Dame: University of Notre Dame Press, 1986), p. 154.

43. Allen D. Hertzke, *Representing God in Washington: The Role of Religious Lobbies in the American Polity* (Knoxville: University of Tennessee Press, 1988).

44. Address of Bishop James W. Malone, President, to the General Meeting of the NCCB, excerpted in *New York Times*, November 13, 1984, p. A22. Also in *Origins* 14, no. 24 (November 29, 1984): 384-390.

45. Joseph A. Califano, Jr., *Governing America: An Insider's Report from the White House and the Cabinet* (New York: Simon & Schuster, 1981). This and the following quotations are taken from Califano's account in Chapter 2, "Abortion," pp. 49-87. See also Mary C. Segers, "Moral Consistency and Public Policy: Cuomo and Califano on Abortion," in M. C. Segers, ed., *Church Polity and American Politics: Issues in Contemporary American Catholicism* (New York: Garland Publishing, 1990), pp. 157-173.

46. For a recent example of the tension between prominent Catholic politicians who support abortion rights and Roman Catholic leaders in their home districts, see Daniel Haar, "Archbishop Criticizes Kennelly's Leadership on Abortion," *Hartford Courant*, February 17, 1994. The article describes Archbishop Daniel A. Cronin of Hartford's objections to Congresswoman Barbara Kennelly's support for the Freedom of Choice Act in the House of Representatives.

47. Bruce E. Altschuler, "Only to the Faithful," Letter to the Editor of *New York Times*, March 6, 1993, p. 20. See also "Pope Warns Sudan on Imposing Islamic Law," *New York Times*, February 4, 1993, p. A3.

48. Mary C. Segers, "Abortion Politics Post-*Webster*: The New Jersey Bishops," in Timothy A. Byrnes and Mary C. Segers, eds., *The Catholic Church and the Politics of Abortion: A View from the States* (Boulder, CO: Westview Press, 1992), pp. 27-47.

49. Report on the Gallup Survey of Catholic Opinion, prepared by Catholics Speak Out, a Project of the Quixote Center, Hyattsville, MD, 1993.

50. Hennesey, *American Catholics: A History of the Roman Catholic Community in the United States*, p. 65, quoting the John Carroll Papers I:46.

5

The Constitutional Underpinnings of the Abortion Debate

L. Kent Sezer

Philosophical rationalizing of the attempt to avoid the overpersonal administration of justice . . . . reinforced the assumption that judicial application of law was a mechanical process and was but a phase of interpretation. In the eighteenth century it was given scientific form in the theory of separation of powers. The legislative organ made laws. The executive administered them. The judiciary applied them to the decision of controversies. It was admitted in Anglo-American legal thinking that courts must interpret in order to apply. But the interpretation was taken not to be in any wise a lawmaking and the application was taken not to involve any administrative element and to be wholly mechanical.

Roscoe Pound[1]

Nobody wants justice.

Alan Dershowitz[2]

There is a duality with respect to the concept of "justice." Under our system of jurisprudence, judges are appointed to interpret the law based on the intent of the drafters. In theory, a judge will have given parties "justice" by interpreting a law in a way which is consistent with the intent of the drafter. In many instances, however, a judicial decision will be criticized as "unjust" because the result is not one that benefits the person making the criticism. In other instances a judicial decision will be characterized as unjust because it does not conform to someone's "innate" sense of what is good for society. Thus, for example, a person who misuses a product and is injured may feel that justice is not done unless the manufacturer pays for the injuries caused by its product. A victim of a crime may feel that justice is not done if the defendant is acquitted on the grounds that the evidence against him is not admissible in court. At the same time, others in our society may criticize judicial decisions precisely because they believe they are based on the judges' personal moral values, and not on the law in question.

This duality with respect to the concept of justice is nowhere stronger than in the area of abortion rights. Individuals who believe that abortion is morally wrong are inclined to see Supreme Court decisions that prevent states from enacting anti-abortion laws as unjust. Similarly, those in favor of the right to choose an abortion tend to see Supreme Court decisions that allow abortions as just.

Yet, in theory, Supreme Court justices are not being asked to vote in favor of or against abortion in the abstract. Rather, they are being asked to decide whether state laws that restrict abortions violate a provision of the Constitution. The Court has been criticized for going beyond this role and deciding abortion cases based on a vague sense of "justice" found nowhere in the Constitution. As will be seen, there is absolutely nothing in the Constitution that explicitly guarantees a right to choose an abortion, or even some measure of privacy with respect to reproduction.

This chapter explores the question whether there is a constitutional underpinning to the declared right to choose an abortion. In other words, does this "right" depend on the collective sense of justice of the individual members of the Court, or is there something more "objective" in the Constitution which supports Supreme Court precedent in this area. To answer this question, it is necessary to examine the nature of judicial review and the substantive provisions of the Constitution that have been used to attack restrictive abortion laws.

JUDICIAL REVIEW

Marbury v. Madison

Nothing in the United States Constitution states that the U.S. Supreme Court has the power to invalidate federal and state statutes. The justification for such power came in the case of *Marbury v. Madison.*[3] Two weeks before the end of John Adams' term as president, Congress passed a law creating a number of justice of the peace positions for the District of Columbia. William Marbury had been appointed by Adams to be a justice of the peace, and the Senate had confirmed the appointment on March 3, 1801, Adams' last day in office. The signed and sealed commissions had been put into the hands of the acting Secretary of State, John Marshall, who was also Chief Justice of the United States.[4] Marshall neglected to deliver the commissions. The new president, Jefferson, chose to ignore Marbury's commission. Marbury filed a lawsuit directly with the Supreme Court. Marbury's suit was an attempt to force Jefferson's Secretary of State, James Madison, to deliver the commission.[5]

In 1789 Congress had passed a law that granted the Supreme Court the power to issue writs of mandamus. These are orders from a court to a public official to compel that official to do something that it is his or her duty to do and that do not require the use of discretion to accomplish. Marshall found that this was an authorization by the Congress to entertain actions such as the one brought by Marbury.[6] If the Supreme Court did not have the power of judicial review, the analysis would have stopped there. Marbury was entitled to his commission, and Congress had authorized the Supreme Court to issue the proper order to see that he received it.

The opinion does not, however, stop at this point. There is a distinction in the law between original and appellate jurisdiction. A court has original jurisdiction if the parties come to that court for the initial decision of the controversy between them. A court has appellate jurisdiction if it hears cases in which the parties are appealing a lower court ruling. The Constitution gives the Supreme Court original jurisdiction over cases involving ambassadors, other public ministers and consuls, and those in which a state is a party.[7] In all other cases the Supreme Court is given appellate jurisdiction. Chief Justice Marshall's opinion points out that an action initiated in the Supreme Court asking for a writ of mandamus is not a call for the exercise of appellate jurisdiction.[8] According to Marshall, this leaves the Court with the question, "whether an act, repugnant to the Constitution, can become the law of the land"[9]

To answer this question, Marshall first examines the nature of a written constitution. He equates the U. S. Constitution with the original and supreme will of the people.[10] The government of the United States is seen as a product of that supreme will. The written constitution specifies precisely what powers have been given to the government and what limitations have been placed on those powers.

Marshall argues that if governmental officials are allowed to go beyond the limits set in the Constitution, the will of the people, which is to have a limited government, will have been thwarted. Therefore, either the unconstitutional law is null and void or there is no purpose in a written constitution. Of course, Marshall finds that the law (in this case the Judiciary Act of 1789) must be void.

The next step in the analysis is to decide whether a void law should, nevertheless, bind the judiciary. In answer to this question, Marshall sets forth the essence of his justification for judicial review. He says:

> It is emphatically the province and duty of the judicial department to say what the law is. Those who apply the rule to particular cases, must of necessity expound and interpret that rule. If two laws conflict with each other, the court must decide on the operation of each. So if a law be in opposition to the Constitution; if both the law and the Constitution apply to a particular case, so that the court must either decide that case conformably to the law, disregarding the Constitution; or conformably to the Constitution, disregarding the law; the court must determine which of these conflicting rules governs the case. This is the very essence of judicial duty.[11]

Based on this reasoning, the Court held the Judiciary Act of 1789 unconstitutional and refused to give Marbury his commission.

There have been many criticisms of *Marbury v. Madison*. The question has been raised whether Marshall should have disqualified himself in light of his participation in the events that led up to the case.[12] It has also been argued that the Judiciary Act of 1789 did not in fact authorize original actions for mandamus in the Supreme Court and that Marshall distorted the statute in order to declare it unconstitutional.[13] What is important for our purposes, however, is not the manipulation that went into the opinion, but rather the reasoning upon which it is based.

Marshall makes judicial review appear to be nothing more than choosing between two clearly defined alternatives: a statute or the Constitution. As a judge, he was bound to uphold the superior law, which is the Constitution. Because Marbury was so clearly in the wrong court, the Supreme Court was almost compelled to void the congressional grant of power to hear the case.

It has been argued that Marshall obscured the true scope of the power he was declaring for the Court by using a statute that purported to give power to the judiciary. Thus, in considering whether to give Marbury his writ, the Court necessarily had to examine its own power to act under the Constitution. This is a far cry from accepting constitutional challenges in which the judiciary's own power is not at issue.[14]

McCulloch v. Maryland

Sixteen years after *Marbury*, the true nature of the Supreme Court's power of judicial review was evidenced by the Court's decision in *McCulloch v. Maryland*.[15] The State of Maryland had passed a tax which purported to apply to all banks or branches doing business in the state and not chartered by the legislature. The Bank of the United States had been chartered by the U.S. Congress. It had a branch in Maryland that refused to pay the tax. The question before the Court was whether the U.S. Constitution permitted Maryland to collect the tax. Unlike *Marbury*, there was no obvious answer to the constitutional question presented. Not only was there no constitutional provision dealing with the power of the states to tax banks established by the federal government, there was not even a constitutional provision that authorized Congress to create a bank.

Thus, the underlying rationale of *Marbury* could not be applied in unaltered form. Marshall could not look at what the U.S. Constitution said about the ability of states to tax banks of the United States and then void the law to the extent that it conflicted with the Constitution. Instead, he looked to the nature of the Constitution and the philosophy behind it. Once again, Marshall explained that the power of the government of the United States came from all of the people in all of the states. Maryland's power to tax came only from the people of Maryland. The bank, as a product of federal power, was an expression of the sovereignty of all the people. Since the Constitution makes laws enacted thereunder supreme, it was clear to Marshall that the bank, as an expression of the sovereignty of all of the people, could not be subject to the sovereignty of the people of Maryland. Taxing is an assertion of sovereignty, and thus the Maryland law was unconstitutional to the extent that it applied to the Bank of the United States.

Marshall recognized that there was no provision in the Constitution that mandated this result. He said, however, that the supremacy of the federal Constitution vis-a-vis the states was such an important part of the constitutional scheme that it followed that the Constitution would not permit the federal sovereignty (i.e. the bank) to yield to an authority over which it is supreme (i.e., the State of Maryland).[16]

Similarly, Marshall acknowledged that there was no explicit provision in the Constitution that authorized the creation of a bank. He said, however, that for a constitution to contain an accurate detail of all the subdivisions of its great powers and of all the means by which they may be carried into execution, it would be as long and complex as a legal code and could scarcely be embraced by the human mind.[17] In Marshall's view, a constitution must only set out in outline form its objects. The minor ingredients that compose these objects can be deduced from the nature of the objects themselves.[18] He concluded, "... we must never forget that it is a *constitution* we are expounding."[19] Based on these principles, he found that Congress had the authority to create the bank.

Thus, as early as 1819 the Supreme Court acknowledged that the process of judicial review was not just a matter of following clearly defined Constitutional prohibitions, but was an attempt to give meaning to the larger aims of the Constitution.[20]

CONSTITUTIONAL RESTRICTIONS ON STATE ACTIONS

Having explored the nature of judicial review, it becomes necessary to examine the substantive provisions of the Constitution that are at issue when a state anti-abortion statute is challenged as unconstitutional.

Pre-Civil War

Prior to the Civil War, the U.S. Constitution imposed very few restrictions on states. The body of the Constitution is mainly concerned with the granting of power to the three branches of the federal government. In *Barron v. Baltimore*,[21] the Supreme Court declared that the Bill of Rights constituted a restriction on the federal government, not the states. With limited exceptions not relevant here, the U.S. Constitution did not speak to the nature of the relationship between a state and its residents.

The limited nature of the Constitution drafted in 1787 can be seen in the debate over the necessity of a bill of rights. In *Federalist* No. 84,[22]

Alexander Hamilton said that the federal Constitution was not intended to govern every species of personal and private concern. It was intended to regulate the general political interests of the nation.[23] Hamilton thought it would be dangerous to include a bill of rights because the Constitution was set up to grant only limited powers to the federal government. It was clear that the government could not go beyond the grants of authority contained in the Constitution. It made no sense to put in specific restrictions in areas where there had never been a grant of power. For example, Hamilton could not see why there was a need to put in a restriction on the power to regulate the press when the body of the Constitution never gave Congress the power to regulate the press in the first place.[24]

To allay fears such as this, the Ninth Amendment was added to the Bill of Rights. It reads as follows: "The enumeration in the Constitution, of certain rights, shall not be construed to deny or disparage others retained by the people."[25] The Bill of Rights was adopted in 1791.

The Fourteenth Amendment

After the Civil War, the Fourteenth Amendment was adopted. The first section reads as follows:

> All persons born or naturalized in the United States, and subject to the jurisdiction thereof, are citizens of the United States and of the State wherein they reside. No State shall make or enforce any law which shall abridge the privileges or immunities of citizens of the United States; nor shall any State deprive any person of life, liberty, or property, without due process of law; nor deny to any person within its jurisdiction the equal protection of the laws.

The Slaughter-House Cases. The meaning of these provisions was first explored by the Supreme Court in a consolidated matter known as the *Slaughter-House Cases*.[26] It is possible to read the privileges and immunities clause to make the federal Constitution the guarantor against infringement by states of what can broadly be described as "civil rights." In the *Slaughter-House Cases* a divided Court rejected that interpretation. The Court applied the clause to a very limited range of "national" or "federal" rights, such as the right to go through states to Washington to deal with the federal government free from state interference.[27] This restrictive interpretation of the privileges and

Figure 5.1
Procedural Due Process

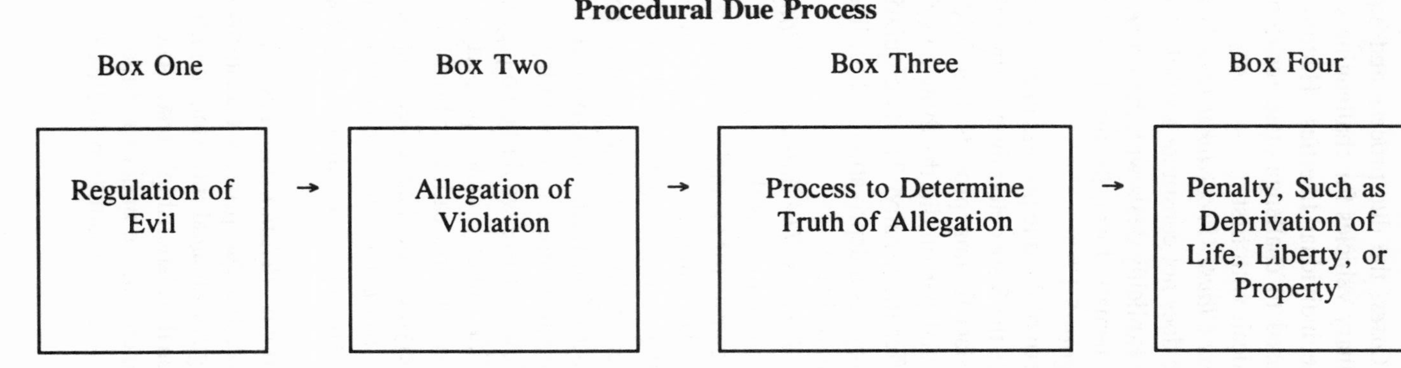

immunities clause has never been successfully challenged. Since the *Slaughter-House Cases*, the due process and equal protection clauses have been the primary vehicles for challenging state regulation of what are asserted to be individual liberties. Historically, the due process clause has been used to challenge state restrictions on abortions and therefore will be dealt with first.

The Due Process Clause: Procedural Due Process. On its face, the due process clause does not constitute a substantive restriction on states rights. The clause explicitly deals with the *process* by which liberty can be restricted. In schematic form, the usual operation of the amendment can be seen in Figure 5.1.

The usual concern of the due process clause is with Box Three shown in Figure 5.1. Once the State determines to impose a penalty, there must be some sort of fact-finding process that is designed to determine whether the particular person did the thing he or she is accused of and therefore must suffer the penalty. The two questions usually asked are whether the "penalty" is a deprivation of life, liberty or property, and, if so, what process is due.[28]

Substantive Due Process: The Rational Relationship Test. There is a form of substantive due process that is not controversial. A legislature might pass a law against, for example, wearing a striped tie and a plaid suit together. The law might provide for an elaborate trial on the question whether the tie was in fact striped and allow for the calling of expert witnesses on plaid. Although such a law might provide for sufficient "due process" in form, in substance it does not because the State has no legitimate interest in preventing bad taste in clothing. If such laws were allowed, there would be no protection against arbitrary deprivations of life, liberty, and property. A legislature could conceivably pass laws against eating or breathing. Everyone would be guilty, and thus everyone would be subject to penalty. Accordingly, the due process clause has been seen as protecting against the passage of laws that bear no rational relationship to any legitimate governmental function.[29]

Beyond the Rational Relationship Test. The next question to be answered is whether the due process clause provides any substantive protection against governmental intrusions on life, liberty, and property beyond the "rational relationship" test. The argument for such a substantive component can be understood most clearly by reference to Figure 5.1. There was an assumption in Box One of an "evil" that the legislature wanted to regulate. The deprivation of liberty in Box Four was the "penalty" for the violation of the law. As long as everyone agrees that the "evil" that is the subject of the regulation is really "evil," then the focus must be on whether the person who has been charged actually engaged in the prohibited activity. Here the emphasis is on the *procedure* that is used.

What happens where there is no agreement on whether the thing being regulated is, in fact, evil? It can be argued that under these circumstances the deprivation of liberty does not occur in Box Four as a "penalty" for noncompliance with the regulation. Instead, the fact that the individual must comply with the regulation is seen as the deprivation of liberty. In such situations there is no "due process." Either the individual complies with the regulation (in which case there is no trial), or the person violates the regulation and has a trial, but the trial is limited to the question of whether the person attempted to exercise his or her "liberty" by violating the regulation. In either case, the "process" in Box Three is meaningless. There is nothing which can happen in Box Three that can restore liberty.

An extreme example will help to clarify this proposition. In a short story, the noted science fiction writer Philip K. Dick hypothesized a future world in which it was possible to predict with great certainty when a crime would occur and who would commit the crime.[30] A society having this power might pass a law such that if it was predicted that a person would commit a crime on a given day, that person would have to stay in his or her house all day. If the person left the house, he or she would be arrested. Let us assume for purposes of this hypothetical situation that this "regulation" is effective. If the person stays inside, the crime does not occur. If the person is allowed unrestricted movement, the crime does occur. This is not a situation in which the person is already engaged in a conspiracy to commit a crime. This hypothetical society has the power to predict that a person will decide to commit a crime on a day in the future if he or she goes out of the house.

It is apparent that such a scheme would not violate the rational relationship test. Preventing murders, robberies, and other crimes of the same sort is obviously a legitimate state purpose. The proposed law does not violate any other specific constitutional prohibition. Finally, the proposed law does not violate procedural due process because there would be a criminal trial in which the person would be allowed to prove that he or she was not out of the house or was not the person identified in the prediction.

Thus, the focus is placed back on the first box in Figure 5.1. Here, the "regulation" is confinement to one's house, which is--itself--a deprivation of liberty. Since the passage of the regulation was not accompanied by "due process," confinement to one's house under such a regulatory scheme would be a deprivation of liberty without due process in violation of the Fourteenth Amendment.

For reasons that will become clear, the idea that the due process clause has a substantive component is controversial. Former judge Robert Bork, whose nomination to the U.S. Supreme Court was rejected at least in part over this issue, has said that the due process clause simply will not support judicial efforts to pour substantive rather than procedural meaning into it.[31]

The Dred Scott Decision. It has been argued that the first use of substantive due process to strike down a law came in the infamous case of *Dred Scott v. Sanford.*[32] There is certainly language in the opinion that is consistent with a substantive due process rationale. The case involved a slave, Dred Scott, who had been taken into an area of federal territory in which Congress had banned slavery. One of the arguments made by Scott was that he became free by operation of federal law when his "owner" brought him into a territory where slavery was banned. Speaking for the Court, Chief Justice Taney wrote:

> [A]n Act of Congress which deprives a citizen of the United States of his liberty or property, merely because he came himself or brought his property into a particular Territory of the United States, and who committed no offense against the laws, could hardly be dignified with the name of due process of law.[33]

Although the focus in *Dred Scott* was on the Fifth Amendment due process clause instead of the Fourteenth, the analysis is the same. The focus is on the first box in Figure 5.1. The only thing that the owner had done was to travel into a federal territory. Taney said that it was a denial of due process to pass a law that worked to take away someone's property who had done nothing wrong.[34]

Notice, once again, that in this kind of situation, Box Three in the figure is irrelevant. It is not enough for the owner to be able to present evidence at trial whether he did or did not enter the designated area with his slave. It is the very fact of the regulation (in this instance, the no slave rule in certain federal territories) that works the deprivation.

The Lochner Era. Although Chief Justice Taney touched on substantive due process in the *Dred Scott* decision, the case that epitomizes the era of substantive due process is *Lochner v. New York.*[35] Lochner owned a bakery. A New York state law prohibited a bakery owner from requiring his employees to work more than 10 hours per day or 60 hours per week. Lochner was convicted of violating this law. He challenged the conviction on the grounds that the New York law violated the due process clause of the Fourteenth Amendment.

What is interesting about *Lochner* is that the focus in this case is not entirely on the liberty or property of the bakery owner. Rather, Justice Peckham, speaking for the Court, focussed on the loss of liberty experienced by the *employee* because of the state statute.

Peckham stated that liberty could be infringed upon by a regulatory scheme if the "evil" being regulated was part of the traditional "police" powers of the states. The police powers relate to the safety, health, morals, and general welfare of the public. In terms of the analysis we have been using, the question was whether there was something "evil" about working more than 60 hours in a week.

Peckham could see no justification other than health for the legislation. Bakers were capable of contracting for fewer hours if they wanted to do so, and the practice of working more than 60 hours in a week involved neither the safety, the morals, nor the welfare of the public.[36] Turning to the question of health, Peckham acknowledged that working long hours as a baker was not healthy. He found, however, that other professions were not particularly healthy, and that the State of New York had not shown such a direct threat to health as to justify the infringement on the bakers' right to contract for their labors.[37]

Here the focus is again on Box One in Figure 5.1. The regulation itself (i.e., restrictions on working hours) is seen as the deprivation of liberty (here, the liberty to contract for one's labors). The fact that Lochner was entitled to a trial on the question of whether he had violated the law was irrelevant because the law--by its existence--deprived him and his bakers of liberty. According to the *Lochner* Court, once we have this kind of situation the "due process" that justifies the deprivation of liberty is the existence of a traditional police power in the State. In other words, there must be something "wrong" with a baker contracting to work more than 60 hours in a day. Peckham cold see nothing "wrong" from a societal viewpoint.

Justice Holmes dissented from the Court's opinion. He said:

> The liberty of the citizen to do as he likes so long as he does not interfere with the liberty of others to do the same, which has been a shibboleth for some well-known writers, is interfered with by school laws, by the Postoffice, by every state or municipal institution which takes his money for purposes thought desirable, whether he likes it or not. The 14th Amendment does not enact Mr. Herbert Spencer's Social Statics.[38]

Holmes' dissent points out the major problem with putting a substantive component into the due process clause. There is no firm agreement on what "evils" government may legitimately attempt to regulate. Holmes accused the Court of finding the principles of *laissez faire* economics and Social Darwinism in the Constitution. He said that a constitution is not intended to embody a particular economic theory.[39] He concluded that the word "liberty" in the Fourteenth Amendment is perverted when it is held to prevent the natural outcome of a dominant opinion, unless it can be said that a rational and fair man necessarily would admit that the statute proposed would infringe fundamental principles as they have been understood by the traditions of our people and our law.[40]

After *Lochner* it is possible to modify the general due process model in Figure 5.1 to focus on substantive due process. The modification is illustrated in Figure 5.2.

Holmes would focus on Box Two. In his view, the "liberty" protected under the substantive provisions of the due process clause is not the "liberty" contained in the dictionary. The due process clause protects only those "liberties" that are fundamental and traditional. In effect, if the proposed legislation does not impact on a right that has a separate existence outside the due process clause, it is not a protected liberty. The Court's opinion focuses on Box Three. If there is not a strong governmental (police power) justification for the deprivation of liberty, there is a denial of due process. This is true even if the supposed liberty is something with as little value as the right to work long hours for low pay at a dangerous job. The quality or type of "liberty" at issue does not appear to be relevant.

After *Lochner* a substantial number of economic regulations were struck down by an increasingly activist court on substantive due process and other grounds. The Court struck down a number of New Deal

Figure 5.2
Substantive Due Process

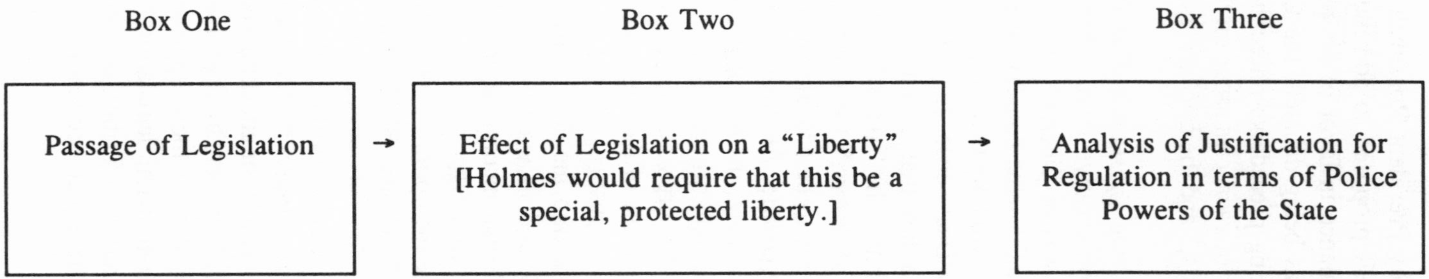

Box One		Box Two		Box Three
Passage of Legislation	→	Effect of Legislation on a "Liberty" [Holmes would require that this be a special, protected liberty.]	→	Analysis of Justification for Regulation in terms of Police Powers of the State

measures designed by President Roosevelt to deal with the economic depression. Roosevelt proposed to add more justices to the Court in order to shift the balance in favor of his programs. While this "court packing" scheme was being debated, the Court issued a decision that reversed some existing precedents on economic regulations.[41] Shortly thereafter, a number of vacancies arose on the Court. These were filled by Roosevelt "liberals," and the *Lochner* era of substantive due process was over.[42]

Social Cases Involving Substantive Due Process. The *Lochner* Court was seen as very conservative from a New Deal liberal perspective. *Lochner* stood in the way of "liberal" causes such as minimum wage and pure food laws. Yet, the same conservative justices used *Lochner* type arguments to strike down laws that, from a modern day perspective, are not liberal in a New Deal sense. In 1923 in *Meyer v. Nebraska*,[43] the Court struck down a law that prohibited the teaching of German to children. Justice Holmes, the "liberal" of *Lochner*, dissented. In 1925, in *Pierce v. Society of Sisters*,[44] the Court struck down an Oregon law which required students to be educated at a public school.

The Incorporation Debate. As noted above, prior to the adoption of the Fourteenth Amendment, the Bill of Rights was not seen as applying to regulation by states. After the passage of the Fourteenth Amendment, there was a move to "incorporate" the provisions of the Bill of Rights into the due process clause of the Fourteenth Amendment. Putting this into the terms used by Justice Holmes in *Lochner*, incorporationists argued that rights put into the Bill of Rights protected "fundamental principles" of American democracy. Concurrent with the *Lochner* line of cases, the Court began incorporating selected amendments into the due process clause. In *Palko v. Connecticut,*[45] the Court said that amendments would be incorporated if they were "implicit in the concept of ordered liberty."[46] Justice Black saw the Bill of Rights as the beginning and the end of substantive due process. Black saw incorporation as a check against the *Lochner* excesses.

The Equal Protection Clause. As noted above, the due process clause has been the primary vehicle for attacking state restrictions on abortions. It has been suggested, however, by Ruth Bader Ginsburg that the equal protection clause might be a more appropriate provision to consider when reviewing anti-abortion legislation.[47] Similarly, Harvard Law School Professor Laurence Tribe has argued that laws restricting abortion implicate the equal protection clause because they burden women's reproductive rights while leaving men with full sexual and reproductive autonomy.[48] Accordingly, it is appropriate to consider the history of that provision before analyzing the abortion cases.

The Slaughter-House Cases Revisited. The first Supreme Court consideration of the equal protection clause came in the *Slaughter-House Cases.*[49] The Court did not interpret it broadly. It posited that the purpose of the clause was to eliminate discrimination against blacks after the end of the Civil War. The Court went on to say:

> We doubt very much whether any action of a State not directed by way of discrimination against the negroes as a class, or on account of their race, will ever be held to come within the purview of this provision. It is so clearly a provision for that race and that emergency, that a strong case would be necessary for its application to any other.[50]

The Rational Relationship Test Revisited. The prediction of the Court in the Slaughter-House Cases did not come true. Although the equal protection clause may have been proposed because of racial discrimination, its words are general. Therefore, all groups have been seen as entitled to its protection. The problem with application of the clause beyond racial discrimination is that its meaning is not clear. Almost all legislation is based on putting people into categories and making distinctions based on those categories. Thus, many state income tax structures discriminate on the basis of financial status. Rich people pay at a higher rate than poor people. Similarly, licensing laws make distinctions based on formal education. Criminal statutes make distinctions between robbers and embezzlers. In each of these cases defined groups are being treated differently by state laws. Yet no one would seriously argue that such distinctions violate the equal protection clause. If they did, government as we know it could not exist.

In most cases the Court will allow states to make distinctions among groups as long as they bear some rational relationship to the governmental objective sought to be achieved. It is only where the classification scheme is totally arbitrary that the Court will declare a denial of equal protection.

A good example of the rational relationship test in action is found in the case of *Railway Express Agency v. New York.*[51] In that case a New York City traffic regulation prohibited trucks from carrying advertising. There was an exemption for advertising related to the business of the owner of the truck. An express delivery business routinely carried advertising for other businesses on its trucks. It argued that there was a denial of equal protection because it was being singled out for regulation. The Court rejected the argument. It stated that the New York authorities could rationally conclude that the owners of trucks *might* choose a different and less distracting kind of advertising with respect to posters on their trucks, as opposed to the kind of advertising that they might allow to be placed on their trucks in exchange for money from other businesses.[52]

The *Railway Express Agency* case epitomizes the Court's use of the rational relationship test. There is an extreme deference to legislative expertise. In most cases, if the rational relationship test is used, the regulation in question will be upheld.

Strict Scrutiny. As noted above, the Court acknowledged that the main purpose of the equal protection clause was to eliminate legal barriers to complete citizenship for blacks erected by states after the Civil War. Because of this clear purpose, the extreme deference of the rational relationship test is inappropriate in cases where states make explicit distinctions based on race. In such cases the Court has applied what has been called "strict scrutiny." This means that racial distinctions will be sustained only if they are tailored to serve a compelling state interest.[53]

The Court will apply strict scrutiny in non-racial cases that are directly analogous. Thus, statutes that make distinctions based on alienage or national origin are also subject to strict scrutiny.[54] This level of review is also applicable where the subject of the regulation is a "fundamental interest." Interests which have been considered fundamental include the right to vote, the right to access to the judicial process and the right to move across state lines.[55]

Although this two-tier system of scrutiny makes some sense, it lacks a logical relationship to the text of the equal protection clause. The Constitution does not talk about fundamental interests, and there is no explicit guide in the Constitution as to how they are to be derived. As will be seen, their use in equal protection analysis raises some of the same questions as the use of principles of substantive due process.

The Equal Protection Clause and Women. The application of the equal protection clause to "women," as a class, has presented unique issues for resolution by the Supreme Court. There is a history of legislation passed by the states and the federal government that treat women differently based upon a supposed need by women for legislative support or protection. Many such laws reflected the social and economic position of women at the time they were enacted, and thus would probably be justified under a rational relationship test. On the other hand, there was and is no "compelling" state interest in such laws. Further, although such laws appeared to be benign, they sometimes worked to prevent women from achieving full equality. Therefore, such laws would not survive strict scrutiny.

In 1973 a plurality of four justices was willing to apply strict scrutiny to such schemes. The case before the Court involved a law which made it easier for women to be declared dependent on members of the armed services. The wife of a serviceman automatically qualified. The husband of a servicewoman had to prove that he was dependent. Eight Justices found the law unconstitutional, but there was not a majority position on the question of whether strict scrutiny should apply.[56]

In 1981 the Court characterized its precedent on the subject by stating that it had found gender-based distinctions unconstitutional absent a showing that the classification was tailored to further an important governmental interest.[57]

In 1982 the Court summed up the State's burden as presenting an exceedingly persuasive justification for the gender-based classification.[58] Thus, although a majority of the Court has never applied strict scrutiny to a gender-based law, it is clear that a heightened level of scrutiny is applied when a legislature passes a law that discriminates either for or against women.

REPRODUCTIVE FREEDOM

Having explored the concept of judicial review and the general contours of the restrictions on State action imposed by the due process and equal protection clauses of the Constitution, it is now appropriate to look at how these doctrines and principles apply in the area of reproductive freedom. However, this analysis cannot start with the question of abortion. As will be discussed, the Supreme Court acts on the principle of *stare decisis*. This means that similar cases have to be decided similarly. Much of the justification for the Court's abortion decisions comes from what were said to be similar questions resolved in favor of reproductive freedom in *Griswold v. Connecticut*.[59]

Griswold v. Connecticut

A Connecticut law made it illegal for anyone to use any drug, medicinal article, or instrument for the purpose of preventing conception.[60] The question presented was whether this law violated the Constitution.

William Douglas wrote the opinion for the Court. Significantly, Douglas was a New Deal liberal and a Roosevelt appointee. The first thing he did was to eschew any implication that the Court was following a *Lochner-style*, substantive due process approach to the question.[61] He also pointed out that whereas *Lochner* had concerned itself with economic and business-type regulation, this law operated on the intimate relations of husbands and wives.[62] Although the Connecticut law made no distinction between single or married people, much of Douglas' opinion was taken up with the importance of marriage. He said:

> We deal with a right of privacy older than the Bill of Rights--older than our political parties, older than our school system. Marriage is a coming together for better or for worse, hopefully enduring, and intimate to the degree of being sacred. It is an association that promotes a way of life, not causes; a harmony in living, not political faiths; a bilateral loyalty, not commercial or social projects. Yet, it is an association for as noble a purpose as any involved in our prior decisions.[63]

Douglas acknowledged, as he had to, that there was no specific provision in either the Bill of Rights or the Civil War amendments that prohibited the banning of the use of contraceptives, either in or outside of marriage. Having eschewed *Lochner*-style substantive due process, it appeared that Douglas would have to uphold the law. This was not the case.

It was Douglas' belief that the specific constitutional guarantees contained in the Bill of Rights carried with them certain ancillary rights that were necessary to give effect to the specified rights. He stated, for example, that even though the right of "association" is nowhere mentioned in the Constitution, such a right had been found by the Court to be necessary to protect the explicit First Amendment freedom of speech.[64] Douglas cited *Pierce v. Society of Sisters* and *Meyer v. Nebraska* for the proposition that there is a First Amendment right regarding the education of one's children. However, those cases were not explicitly First Amendment cases. On their faces, they turned on the concept of substantive due process.

In any event, Douglas saw in those cases a precedent for deciding Constitutional challenges based not only on the language of the Bill of Rights, but also on "penumbras", formed by emanations from those guarantees. The word "penumbra' is not legal in origin. It means the partly lighted areas surrounding the complete shadow of a body.[65] When an object casts a shadow, there is not a sharp distinction between what is covered by the shadow and what is in full light. Douglas saw a similar grey area or penumbra created by explicit Constitutional guarantees.[66]

Douglas found a pattern, or unifying theme, with respect to the Bill of Rights. The specific guarantees do not stand as random prohibitions in a legal code. The unifying theme is "privacy." The Fourth Amendment's protection against search and seizure creates a form of privacy in one's home. The Third Amendment's prohibition against the quartering of soldiers in someone's home has a similar effect. The Fifth Amendment's prohibition against forced self-incrimination creates a zone of privacy with respect to one's thoughts and personal papers. As previously discussed, Douglas thought the First Amendment created a significant zone of privacy with respect to learning, reading and entering into associations.

So far, what Douglas had to say was not controversial. His next step was. He derived from the specific zones of privacy created by the explicit amendments in the Bill of Rights, a generalized right of privacy created by the cited constitutional guarantees. He then found that the marriage relationship could be found within that zone. Finally, because the Connecticut law concentrated on the use of contraceptives in the home, not sale or manufacture, Douglas found that the effect of the law was to enter the zone of privacy unnecessarily and damage the protected marital relationship.[67]

This was a remarkable performance. Douglas found a law unconstitutional, even though there is nothing in the Constitution that explicitly prohibits this type of law. Douglas did this while claiming that he was not using substantive due process as a tool. Two more things should be noted about the majority opinion in *Griswold*. First, the rationale for judicial review given in *Marbury v. Madison* was left in the dust. Marshall stated in *Marbury* that as a judge he had to decide the case either according to the Constitution or according to a challenged law. The two were in such direct conflict that both could not be given effect. By declaring the law void, Marshall was merely bowing to a superior law.

In *Griswold*, there was nothing in the text of the Constitution that mandated the result reached. Douglas was not faced with a law that clearly conflicted with a specific prohibition in the Constitution. He was not "forced" to choose the superior law. The process of judicial review in *Griswold* is a much more subtle process, which will be explored in greater detail below.

The second aspect of the majority opinion worth noting is the nature of the rights created. The precedent relied on by Douglas for the concept of penumbral rights concerned itself with protecting explicit rights. For example, the right to speak is threatened if there are government restrictions on printing presses. Printing presses are not speech. Yet they are instruments used *for* speech, and therefore any law which regulates presses may have an effect on speech. The precedent relied on by Douglas started with the First Amendment and went forward. Douglas' analysis goes backwards. He was not concerned with what prohibitions are necessary to protect the specific guarantees in the Bill of Rights. He was concerned with what "rights" the Bill of Rights was designed to protect. Just as the protection of printing presses is necessary to protect free speech, free speech and the other constitutional prohibitions were put into the Constitution to protect something even more fundamental. That fundamental rights is the "right to privacy."

Justice Goldberg filed a concurring opinion that focused on the Ninth Amendment. It will be remembered that the Ninth Amendment was intended to protect against an assumption on the part of the federal government that what was not prohibited to it in the Bill of Rights was within its powers. As originally enacted, the Ninth Amendment had nothing to do with actions by state governments. But Justice Goldberg saw in the Ninth Amendment not just a rule of construction, but an acknowledgment by the Framers that there were real and fundamental rights that could not be written down in a comprehensive fashion. He found that the right to privacy in the home was one of those rights.[68]

Justices Harlan and White filed concurring opinions.[69] Harlan did not join in the majority opinion specifically because it did not rely on the due process clause. He found that the concept of "penumbras," like the doctrine of incorporation would unreasonably restrict the definition of "liberty" in the due process clause to areas covered by or related to explicit constitutional guarantees.[70] Justice White found that the Connecticut law--as applied to married couples--implicated a liberty interest and Connecticut had not set forth a legitimate and substantial reason for the restriction.[71]

Dissenting opinions were filed by Justices Black and Stewart. Black, the only other Roosevelt appointee, attacked the majority opinion as one further step in the *Lochner* line of cases.[72] The problem that Black saw with the majority opinion was that it left to the courts, not the political institutions (i.e., the legislatures), the power to make decisions based on personal preference. The Court was making an unconstitutional grab for power unless it was acting pursuant to a specific Constitutional provision.[73]

Black's opinion can be traced directly to Marshall's justification for judicial review. Marshall said that the idea of a limited government created by a written constitution would be thwarted if the Court did not have the power to strike down laws that exceeded the written limits. The Connecticut contraceptive law did not exceed any explicit written restriction on state law. The idea of tapping some unseen font of ill-defined "rights" not contained in the text of the Constitution to strike down laws enacted by democratic legislatures appeared to Black to be the use of extra-constitutional power by the Court.

Eisenstadt v. Baird

As noted above, the Supreme Court works on the doctrine of *stare decisis*. *Griswold* was an important case, and similar cases had to be decided in the same way. What exactly did *Griswold* decide? Clearly, it decided that the State could not interfere with the use of contraceptives by a married couple. It was unclear at the time how much more the case stood for. Did it apply to unmarried couples? Did it apply to manufacture and sale? Was the privacy right grounded in marriage, procreation, sex, or the use of one's home? A partial answer to some of those questions came in the case of *Eisenstadt v. Baird*.[74] In that case a man was convicted of giving contraceptive foam to women, which was a crime in Massachusetts. In the course of his opinion for the Court, Justice Brennan made it clear that the right of privacy enunciated in *Griswold* was not limited to the marital relationship. He said:

If the right of privacy means anything, it is the right of the *individual*, married or single, to be free from unwarranted governmental intrusion into matters so fundamentally affecting a person as the decision whether to bear or beget a child.[75]

This characterization of *Griswold* by Brennan illustrates how slippery concepts in this area of the law can be. As noted above, Justice Douglas went out of his way in *Griswold* to cast the Connecticut law as an attack on marital privacy. Nevertheless, after *Eisenstadt*, there existed a generalized right of privacy in the area of reproduction. The stage was now set for a direct assault on abortion laws.

Roe v. Wade

A Texas law made it a crime to have an abortion. The question before the U.S. Supreme Court in *Roe v. Wade*[76] was whether that Texas law was constitutional. The opinion of the Court was delivered by Justice Blackmun. He acknowledged that the Constitution does not mention a right of privacy. He then cited a number of cases that relied on specific constitutional guarantees. Blackmun contended that these cases simultaneously recognized both the specific guarantee and an implicit right of personal privacy.[77] This part of the decision is similar to the *Griswold* idea of penumbral rights. Blackmun then moved beyond the Bill of Rights to discuss the concept of "liberty" in the Fourteenth Amendment.

Blackmun's discussion was not so much an analysis as a listing of cases. He cited *Meyer v. Nebraska*[78] and *Pierce v. Society of Sisters*[79] for the proposition that the right to privacy inherent in liberty has something to do with child rearing and education. *Loving v. Virginia*,[80] which struck down a state law prohibiting inter-racial marriage, was cited for the proposition that the right of privacy had something to do with marriage. *Skinner v. Oklahoma,*[81] which struck down a state law which provided for the forced sterilization of certain criminals, was cited for the proposition that the right to privacy had something to do with procreation. Finally, *Prince v. Massachusetts,*[82] a case in which the Supreme Court upheld the application of a Massachusetts child labor law against the legal custodian and aunt of a little girl who was forced to sell religious magazines, was cited for the proposition that the right to privacy has something to do with family relationships.

Judge Bork, criticizing the *Roe* decision, contends that none of the cases cited bears on the subject of a right to an abortion.[83] This is an extreme viewpoint. It is clear, however, that none of the cited cases can be considered a direct precedent for *Roe*. The primary ground for decision in *Loving* was the equal protection clause. The explicit classification based on race made the statute in that case vulnerable to constitutional attack. There is some language in the decision about due process, but it is tied up with the discussion of the invidious racial discrimination.[84]

Similarly, the decision in *Skinner*, the sterilization case, was explicitly based on the equal protection clause. The Court found that the law was not applied equally to all "similar" crimes.[85] In fact, *Buck v. Bell*,[86] which upheld the forced sterilization of the "feeble-minded" was not reversed. As noted above, the *Prince* decision *upheld* state regulation of the use of family members (children) to sell religious materials. This leaves *Pierce* and *Meyer*. Both of these decisions are liberty interest cases. It is clear, however, that they also could have been decided under the First Amendment. The freedom to learn things and hear opinions not part of an official State curriculum is closely tied to the freedom of speech.

Thus, the only precedent for a right to privacy not tied to the Bill of Rights came from *Griswold* and *Eisenstadt*. Judge Bork is wrong, however, when he says that the other cited cases have nothing to do with the subject of abortion. Their relevance to this subject will be discussed below.

Returning to Blackmun's discussion in *Roe*, the next step in his analysis is remarkable. He holds out three possible bases for the right of privacy: penumbras of the Bill of Rights, the Ninth Amendment, and the due process concept of liberty. The opinion states the Court's belief that the right lies in the Fourteenth Amendment. It acknowledges that the lower court had found the right to privacy in the Ninth Amendment. Blackmun then implies that it does not make any difference where the right lies. Wherever it may come from, it is "...broad enough to encompass a woman's decision whether or not to terminate her pregnancy."[87]

Having found that a right to choose an abortion exists, Blackmun proceeded to determine whether there was any justification for deprivation of that right by the State. In terms of the substantive due process analysis shown in Figure 5.1, having found an impact on a protected liberty, Blackmun moved to Box Three to determine whether the deprivation of liberty was justified. Blackmun found that the only thing that would justify this kind of restriction on liberty would by a "compelling state interest."[88] In other words, it would not be enough to find that the abortion restriction was rationally related to a legitimate State interest. Blackmun required the State to have such a strong and important interest that it would justify the deprivation of liberty.

The Court in *Roe* found two such interests. The first was the fetus. Blackmun said that a pregnant woman cannot be isolated in her privacy. The fetus makes this situation different from marital intimacy, marriage, the right to have the ability to procreate, or education.[89] On the other hand, the unborn had never been recognized in the law as persons in the whole sense.[90] Blackmun then declared that the State's interest in protecting the fetus becomes "compelling" at the point of viability. He said that this is so because the fetus then presumably has the capability of meaningful life outside the mother's body. After viability a state may proscribe abortions, except when it is necessary to preserve the mother's life or health. Blackmun stated that states could regulate abortions from a health perspective after the first trimester because until the end of the first trimester mortality in abortion may be less than mortality in normal childbirth.

The upshot of this analysis was a trimester approach to abortion regulation: first trimester--no regulation; second trimester--regulation directed to the mother's health; and third trimester (viability)--regulation, including the proscription of abortion except to preserve the life or health of the mother.

Justice Douglas filed a concurring opinion. Douglas, the author of *Griswold*, wanted it clear that his vote did not rest on a concept of substantive due process.[91] Once again, he contended that the Bill of Rights created a right of privacy.

Justice Stewart also concurred. He said that he had dissented in *Griswold* because he did not find a right to privacy in the Bill of Rights. Stewart said that it was now clear to him that *Griswold* could be rationally understood only as holding that the anti-contraceptive statute invaded the "liberty" protected by the due process clause.[92] On this basis he concurred in the *Roe* decision.

There were two dissenting justices, White and Rehnquist. It should be remembered that White was with the majority in *Griswold*. Obviously, White believed in a Constitutional right to privacy. He did not believe, however, that it extended to abortion. White did not explain his own concept of the right to privacy. He merely attacked Blackmun for stating that the right to privacy included the right to an abortion. According to White, Blackmun provided no explanation for why such a right existed.[93]

Rehnquist completely rejected the idea that a law such as this had to meet anything other than the rational relationship test.[94] As noted above, the *Lochner* line of decisions held that states had no legitimate interests in regulating certain kinds of commercial transactions. Under *Lochner*, the emphasis in Box Three of Figure 5.2 was whether there was *any* legitimate, "police power" type purpose for the legislation. Thus, in a sense Lochner was using the "rational relationship" test. Rehnquist commented that there was no precedent for using a "compelling state interest" test in the part of the Court's analysis that corresponds to box three.[95] In fact, as noted above, the compelling state interest test had been used in equal protection cases. Rehnquist saw no justification in the history of the Fourteenth Amendment for importing that test into due process cases.

Post-*Roe*

Many cases have attempted to apply the *Roe* decision to a variety of statutory schemes that had impacts on the right to choose an abortion. States have attempted to impose waiting periods, parent and husband consent requirements, and reporting requirements. Laws have required the presence of a second doctor and have attempted to limit the types of abortion techniques used. The federal government and some state governments have cut off money for indigent women seeking an abortion.

Throughout all these challenges, the basic right to choose an abortion outlined in *Roe* has remained essentially unchanged. In 1992, four justices of the Supreme Court took the explicit position that *Roe* should be overturned. In *Planned Parenthood v. Casey*,[96] Justices Scalia, Rehnquist, White, and Thomas voted to reverse *Roe*. Scalia said that he took that position for two reasons: the Constitution says nothing about a right to an abortion, and the longstanding tradition of the American people is to permit abortion to be legally proscribed.[97] According to Scalia, the zone of privacy protected by *Roe* would equally protect homosexual sodomy, polygamy, adult incest, and suicide. He pointed out that Justice O'Connor joined the majority opinion in *Bowers v. Hardwick*,[98] which declared that laws against homosexual sodomy did not violate the constitutional right to privacy. Therefore, there is no principled rationale behind the right to privacy as described in *Roe*.

Justice O'Connor, joined by Justices Kennedy and Souter, issued a joint opinion that refused to reverse *Roe*. The basis for this decision is not completely clear. At one point in her opinion it appears that O'Connor found that *Roe* was not so clearly wrong that it could be overruled. At other points it appears that she found that much of *Roe* was correctly decided.

Justice O'Connor first placed the right to choose an abortion squarely within the due process clause. There was no talk in her opinion of emanations or penumbras. She said, "It is a promise of the Constitution that there is a realm of personal liberty which the government may not enter."[99] She then went on to meet the argument that substantive due process allows judges to impose their own policy preferences on the democratic institutions in this country. According to O'Connor, the fact that there is no simple rule to guide judges does not invalidate the concept of substantive due process protecting liberty. She quoted the following part of Justice Harlan's dissenting opinion in *Poe v. Ullman*.[100]

> Due process has not been reduced to any formula; its content cannot be determined by reference to any code. The best that can be said is that through the course of this court's decisions it has represented the balance which our Nation, built upon postulates of respect for the liberty of the individual, had struck between that liberty and the demands of organized society. If the supplying of content to this Constitutional concept has of necessity been a rational process, it certainly has not been one where judges have felt free to roam where unguided speculation might take them. The balance of which I speak is the balance struck by this country, having regard to what history teaches are the traditions from which it developed as well as the traditions from which it broke. That tradition is a living thing. A decision of this court which radically departs from it could not long survive, while a decision which builds on what has survived is likely to be sound. No formula could serve as a substitute, in this area, for judgment and restraint.[101]

Applying these principles, O'Connor found that State regulations forcing a woman to bear a child implicate the liberty interests protected by the due process clause. She stated that, in light of this, and considering the principles of *stare decisis*, she would not overturn the basic holding of *Roe*.

Almost in the next breath the joint opinion threw out the trimester framework of *Roe*. O'Connor said that this was not part of the essential holding.[102] Only where state regulation imposes an "undue burden" on a woman's ability to make a decision to terminate her pregnancy does the power of the State reach into the heart of the liberty protected by the due process clause.[103] Because four justices would have overturned *Roe*, the "undue burden" test became the law of the land. It appears that it will remain so for some time. As of the time this chapter is being written, there appear to be three solid votes in favor of *Roe*: Breyer, Stevens, and Ginsburg. There are three votes to overturn *Roe* in its entirety: Scalia, Rehnquist, and Thomas. This leaves the "undue burden" faction of O'Connor, Kennedy and Souter firmly in control.

Equal Protection and the Right to Choose an Abortion

The equal protection clause has not been used as a basis for striking down laws that restrict abortions. The major reason for this is the refusal of the Supreme Court to apply the clause to laws that are not explicitly based on gender.

Two types of discrimination are recognized in the law. One type is referred to as "disparate treatment." In this situation someone is treated in a different way explicitly because of gender. For example, in the case of *Mississippi University for Women v. Hogan*,[104] the plaintiff, a man, was not allowed to attend a state-supported school of nursing explicitly and solely because of his gender. The Court has said that the equal protection clause applies to this kind of discrimination. As noted above, where the equal protection clause applies to gender based discrimination, a heightened level of scrutiny is used.

The second type of discrimination is known as "disparate impact." Here, there is a regulation or required procedure that is neutral on its face, but tends to have a disproportionate impact on a particular group. The Supreme Court has recognized that the federal anti-discrimination in employment law protects against discrimination of the disparate impact type.[105] With respect to the equal protection clause of the Constitution, however, the Court has been unwilling to find discrimination unless the legislature enacted the law with the purpose of discriminating against a group.[106]

The consequences of this doctrine were made clear in the case of *Personnel Administrator of Mass. v. Feeney.*[107] The Commonwealth of Massachusetts gave an absolute preference to veterans over other applicants for civil service jobs. Fewer than 2% of the veterans in Massachusetts were female. Women with high test scores were consistently being denied higher level jobs because men with lower scores were being given a veteran's preference. Nevertheless, in a 7:2 decision, the Court held that because there was no proof that the Massachusetts legislature had passed the law in order to benefit men as a class, there was no denial of equal protection.

This leaves the question of whether state regulation of abortion is explicitly a gender-based scheme. Many feminist writers have answered this question in the affirmative. The argument is that discrimination against someone because she orhe is not a veteran is truly neutral. There is no physical reason why a woman could not be a veteran. It is argued that abortion laws are different. For example, University of Chicago Professor Cass Sunstein argues that a statute that invokes a "defining characteristic" of being a woman is the same as a statute explicitly based on gender.[108] It is contended that the phrase "no person shall obtain an abortion" is the same as "no *woman* shall obtain an abortion."[109] This argument has never been accepted by the Court. It has come up in the context of pregnancy and a nonconstitutional case involving abortion.

In *Gedulig v. Aiello*[110] the Court was asked to declare that it was a denial of equal protection for the State of California to pay insurance befits to employees who were disabled by most diseases but to refuse to pay those benefits to women who were disabled because of normal pregnancy. The Court refused to look at the case as invidious discrimination against women. All employees, both men and women, were covered for the same diseases. The fact that only women can become pregnant did not make the failure to include pregnancy a distinction based on gender.

In *Bray v. Alexandria Clinic*[111] a lawsuit was brought against Operation Rescue, which allegedly was part of a conspiracy to block access to abortion clinics and thus prevent women from obtaining abortions. In order to succeed in Federal Court, the plaintiff had to demonstrate that the conspiracy was based on gender. The Court majority said that this point had not been established. Justice Scalia, speaking for the Court, stated that there are reasons for opposition to abortion other than an animus against women as a class. He pointed out that both men and women can be opposed to abortion.[112]

Professor Sunstein has criticized this approach on the ground that it invites discrimination.[113] He argues that abortion laws are not considered "discriminatory" only if one takes as the baseline for the analysis the reproductive capacities of males. Then, because there is no male analogue to a woman's ability to become pregnant, there can be no denial of equality. Professor Sunstein contends, however, that it is precisely where a unique characteristic of one gender is made into a legal disability that questions of discrimination are raised.[114]

Although such arguments can help to frame the debate over women's role in society, they do not address the fundamental question presented to the Court, which is the meaning of the equal protection clause. The natural and normal meaning of the term "unequal treatment" is to treat equal things as if they were unequal. Thus, in most cases where there is a facially discriminatory gender- based law, it is possible to analyze the case by asking whether a similarly situated man would be treated in the same way. In the context of abortion this question makes no sense. Because there are two genders and because equality implies treating the genders in the same way, the traditional concept of equality cannot apply in areas where the two genders cannot be the same. Comparison with men is not done by the Supreme Court because of an anti-female animus, but because the concept of equality implies a comparison and there is no other gender to which the treatment of women can be compared.

This does not mean that the questions asked by Professor Sunstein and others are not important. The value we place on things that are uniquely female says much about our society. There are important social and moral values at stake. There is simply no evidence, however, that the concept of "equality" used in the equal protection clause was ever meant to answer questions regarding the place of the unique reproductive capacities of women.

If it is accepted that restrictions on abortion are not on their faces gender-based regulations, then they are subjected to a higher degree of scrutiny only if they interfere with a "fundamental right." There is nothing in the Constitution that would give rise to a fundamental right to an abortion other than the provisions that have been discussed in connection with the due process clause. Thus, under current Supreme

Court precedent, the equal protection clause does not provide an independent source for the right to an abortion. If an equal protection challenge were to be accepted by the Court, it would have to be analyzed under the rational relationship test. Because restrictions on abortion promote such values as the life of the fetus, the equal protection challenge would fail. In sum, because disparate impact analysis is not allowed under the equal protection clause, and because abortion restrictions are not seen by the Court as explicit, direct discrimination based on gender, the equal protection clause has not been an important vehicle for attacking state restrictions on abortions.

IS THERE A CONSTITUTIONAL UNDERPINNING TO THE DECLARED RIGHT TO CHOOSE AN ABORTION?

Having analyzed the nature of judicial review and the precedents for *Roe v. Wade*, it is appropriate at this point to tackle the question of whether there is a constitutional underpinning to the abortion decisions made by the Supreme Court. In other words, are the votes of the justices in the majority based merely on their personal opinions regarding the propriety of abortion restrictions, or are those votes justified on principles relating to the Constitution and the role of the Court in judicial review? Is there a sound, Constitutional justification for the *Roe* decision?

The Natural Law Solution

As noted above, John Marshall stated that the purpose of a written constitution was to make sure that the powers granted to the government by the people were limited. The Court is in the unique position of being both a part of the government and the guardian against abuse of power by the government. This idea of the Court, as articulated in *Marbury v. Madison* worked for two reasons. First, the constitutional limitation in that case was very specific (i.e., the Court cannot hear a mandamus action as an original action). Second, the federal government had only limited powers to begin with. No one was concerned with whether the Bill of Rights was a complete protection against government tyranny. It was quite clear that the framers of the Constitution contemplated that the structure of the federal Constitution, much more than the Bill of Rights, was the true protection against abuse of power.

Almost immediately after *Marbury*, Marshall was forced to state that there need not be a specific provision in the Constitution to allow the Court to act. In *McCulloch v. Maryland* he struck down a state tax law because it tended to interfere with the constitutional scheme of federal supremacy.

It is appropriate, then, for justices to look at the nature of the Constitution itself, not just its specific prohibitions, in construing its meaning. Further, because the due process clause is concerned with "liberty," it is appropriate to look to the nature of the "liberty" inherent in the Constitutional scheme in deciding questions under the due process clause.

Paradoxically, the idea of liberty held by the framers of the Constitution involved the concept of natural law. As we shall see, the concept of natural law depends on the idea of certain natural rights of people. These rights do not depend for their legitimacy on any written instrument. It can be argued that by placing the concept of "liberty" into the Constitution, the Framers virtually mandated judges to go beyond the written Constitution to find solutions.

An argument for a Constitutional right to choose an abortion based on "natural law" was set forth by Ummuhan Turgut and James Bowers in an article in the University of Dayton Law Review.[115] The theory of natural law hypothesizes individuals in a state of nature. In that state they can do as they see fit, without the leave of anyone else. The political community is an agreement to protect liberty. Theoretically, the only liberty which is regulated by the government is the "liberty" to invade the liberty of others.

As Turgut and Bowers make clear, this concept of government is clearly reflected in the Declaration of Independence.[116] It states:

> We hold these truths to be self-evident, that all men are created equal, that they are endowed by their Creator with certain unalienable Rights, that among these are Life, Liberty and the pursuit of Happiness. That to secure these rights, Governments are instituted among Men, deriving their just powers from the consent of the governed, That whenever any Form of Government becomes destructive of these ends, it is the Right of the People to alter or abolish it, and to institute a new Government.[117]

Even the concept of a "limited" government inherent in the Constitution is a part of natural law doctrine.

Turgut and Bowers state that natural law does not recognize liberty rights in children until they are born. Since the abortion decision does not affect anyone else's liberty, it is beyond the power of government to control. Bowers and Turgut equate the *Roe* definition of viability with the natural law concept of a born child.[118]

There is another way of analyzing this question that is almost directly analogous to Marshall's opinion in *McCulloch v. Maryland.* Just as the superiority of the federal government had implications for the ability of Maryland to tax a federal instrumentality, so too does the superiority of "the people" have implications for the ability of government to act in a way that would fundamentally change the nature of the power relationship. Thus, it could be argued that even without the First Amendment, it would be unconstitutional under *McCulloch* for the government to suppress political speech because such speech is necessary for the formulation of the political will to which the government must be subordinate. Each person contains an aspect of the total sovereignty that, in turn, legitimizes government. Where sovereignty exists, it is absolute.

The next question is whether the freedom of people to form a political will includes a freedom over reproduction. Here is where the precedent cited by the Court in *Roe* becomes relevant. Although the precedent might relate to specific guarantees, focusing on the nature of the Constitution as an aid to interpreting the word "liberty", allows us to ask the question why those particular guarantees were placed in the Constitution. It appears from the cited precedent that it is important in our political system that individuals in our society have the right to marry those whom they wish to marry, learn what they wish to learn, and in general make fundamental choices about who they are and what they will become. If the government can interfere with these aspects of our lives, there is, in effect, no government "by the people."

It is difficult to imagine a decision more fundamental to who we are than the decision to terminate a pregnancy. It must be remembered that what we are talking about is the degree of control over this aspect of our lives, not the particular policy outcome. Professor Tribe has stated that if *Roe* had not been decided in the way it was, there would appear to be nothing preventing *mandated* state abortions.[119] This statement might be a little strong, but there is clearly nothing in the text of the

Constitution other than the liberty provision of the due process clause that would prevent the government from interfering with many fundamental decisions involving reproduction other than abortion. Because our decisions about who we are and what we will become have a powerful political impact, the natural law theory would protect them against intrusion by the government.

The Problem with the Natural Law Solution. Anyone who is completely satisfied with the natural law solution to the abortion question has not properly understood it.[120] History has shown that the Supreme Court is capable of putting into the concept of "liberty" ideas that virtually everyone today would acknowledge have no business being in our Constitution. The Court's use of *Lochner* principles to strike down social and economic welfare legislation stands as a warning that a departure from specific constitutional guarantees is a two-edged sword. Although it can help us prevent government abuse, it can be used to prevent government from changing appalling conditions in the private sector.

Further, as noted by Justice Holmes in the *Lochner* case, a pure version of "natural law" has never been accepted as a part of our Constitution. We have always accepted restrictions on our liberty that go far beyond anything which would be allowed under natural law. For example, laws that restrict gambling, drug use and prostitution are well accepted even though they restrict liberties that do not have a direct impact on the liberties of others. How, then, can one make a rational distinction between what is allowed and what is not?

In *U.S. v. Carolene Products Co.*[121] the Court made a distinction between legislation that is "economic" and legislation that might suppress minorities.[122] Thus, restrictions on liberty that tend to prevent minorities from gaining political influence might be struck down without allowing courts to strike down needed social welfare and economic legislation. This distinction might help to prevent *Lochner* type cases; but with the recognition of commercial free speech, the distinction drawn becomes less clear. Further, the distinction drawn in *Carolene Products* does not even address itself to the regulation of abortion, unless one takes the position that the regulation of abortion is the regulation of women and that women are a minority.

Thus, although "natural law" provides a conceptual justification for abortion rights, it is such a broad and vague concept that it is not an unerring guide for how to vote on abortion cases.

Much the same analysis applies to other proposed justifications for the vote in *Roe*. As specifically noted by Justice Goldberg in *Griswold*, although the Ninth Amendment indicates that there may be other rights beyond those enumerated in the Bill of Rights, the Ninth Amendment is not itself an independent source of such rights. In order to define the rights referred to in the Ninth Amendment, one would have to look at the nature of our governmental structure and the beliefs of the Founders. Similarly, the contours of any "penumbral" rights would have to be defined based upon something more than the mere text of the Bill of Rights. Once again, one would have to look at the nature of the governmental scheme set up by the Founders to help delineate penumbral rights.

Having examined the justification for the pro-*Roe* vote, it is next appropriate to look at the justification for the vote against *Roe*. Is the vote against *Roe* merely an expression of a moral antagonism to abortion, or is there a sound constitutional foundation for the anti-*Roe* vote?

The "Specific Intent" Solution

If one looks only at the words of the Constitution, one finds no right to an abortion. Even if one looks at the specific intent of the framers of the Bill of Rights and the Fourteenth Amendment, there is still no right to an abortion. As noted by Justice Scalia in the *Casey* decision, our tradition is not to prohibit the states from regulating abortion[123]. For many people, the idea that five justices of the Supreme Court can overturn democratically passed legislation is intolerable. The solution reached is to limit the Court to the words of the Constitution or the specific intent of the drafters.

The Problem with the Specific Intent Solution. Paul Brest points out the problem with this line of analysis.[124] As noted by Justice Marshall, a constitution is not like an ordinary legal code. A constitution's framers do not have the time or the ability to specify in detail what is required and what is prohibited. Its drafters have only the ability to set out the great objects of the form of government created. Brest analogized the drafters of the Constitution to parents who are attempting to instill in their children certain core values. When the child grows up, the child may make some decisions with which the parents disagree. The choice made by the child may be exactly the opposite of the choice that the parents would have made. If asked, however, whether the child has adhered to the core values that the parents taught him, the parents might well answer yes.[125]

This analogy is directly applicable to the inclusion of liberty in the Fourteenth Amendment. It may be that the adopters of that amendment had no idea that what they were adopting could by used to create a right to privacy. They might agree, however, that a core value of the amendment was liberty and that privacy is an essential element of liberty.

If it was the intent of the Framers to create certain core values, Scalia, by freezing things as they were at the time of the adoption of the Fourteenth Amendment, would actually be violating the will and the original understanding of the drafters of the due process clause. The reason is this: "core values" are so broad and detached from specific factual situations that may come before the Court that no one is capable of predicting with precision the implications of putting a core value into law.

For example, in 1964 Congress enacted a comprehensive civil rights law. Title VII of the law[126] provided for "equality" in employment. In a country where there were specific jobs set aside for whites, where a person's religion was seen as an insurmountable barrier to certain jobs and where unions were segregated along racial lines, it was not hard to see what the specific intent of Congress was.

However, there arose a situation not explicitly addressed in congressional debate. Certain employers would comply in every respect with what they thought was the letter of the law. They would give minorities the same jobs, the same wages and the same benefits as white employees. They did not, however, do anything to change the prevailing racist and discriminatory attitudes that prevailed in the workplace. Minorities were subjected to numerous derogatory references, excluded from the places where white employees ate lunch, and made to watch while the employer discriminated against minority clients.[127] Eventually, the courts found that it was possible to discriminate against a minority by creating a hostile working environment, even though the person was being treated in an equal manner with respect to hiring, pay, benefits, promotion, and all other "objective" aspects of the job.

In 1982, some 17 years after Title VII went into effect, the Appellate Court for the Eleventh Circuit found that under certain circumstances repeated unwanted sexual advances in the workplace constituted sex discrimination.[128] The Supreme Court has ruled unanimously that this is a correct interpretation of Title VII.[129]

Congress did not enact Title VII to prevent sexual harassment. Expanding the reach of Title VII to sex discrimination was an afterthought, put into the law at the last second on the floor of the House of Representatives without much debate. It would not be surprising to find out that make members of Congress who voted for Title VII have made sexual advances to the women on their staffs and have not seen their behavior as contradictory.

If one were to follow merely the specific intent of the Congress, one would probably not find sexual harassment to be a violation of Title VII. Yet, partially as a result of Title VII, millions of women have now entered the workforce in jobs that were not open to them in 1964. The effects of sexual harassment on women in such jobs could not be known to legislators in 1964. Similarly, when there is a segregated workforce, it is simply not possible to know what the effect of racial slurs will be when the workforce is integrated. Prior to the enactment of Title VII, it was not possible to know how much of a barrier a "hostile working environment" would be to the equality that Title VII sought to achieve.

Thus, a legislator who voted for Title VII in 1964 may not have intended to bar sexual harassment and may himself have engaged in sexual harassment, yet it may be against his intent in voting for Title VII to rule that sexual harassment is not a violation. As sexual harassment emerged as a major barrier to equality in the workplace for women, his vote for Title VII could be seen as an authorization to make sexual harassment illegal. In other words, if his vote for Title VII was for the core value of equality, the failure to eliminate this barrier to equality could be seen as contrary to his legislative intent.

What has been said for Title VII is even more true for constitutional provisions. The Constitution is, by definition, a general document, not a specific answer to the myriad legal questions which may arise under it. This is why Justice Marshall cautioned future justices to never forget that it is a *constitution* that is being interpreted.[130]

Although the incorporation doctrine has appeal, nothing in the due process clause indicates that the drafters intended either to incorporate the Bill of Rights or to limit the scope of the clause to rights previously articulated in the Constitution.

Thus, there is no safe haven. Insisting that concepts that were meant to last for the ages must be read as if the world has not changed since

1868 may be every bit as much an usurpation of power by the Supreme Court as creating a "liberty" that does not exist.

Conclusion

There are sound constitutional underpinnings for the Supreme Court's debate on abortion laws. The majority decision in *Roe v. Wade* is defensible. Unfortunately, because of the legacy of *Lochner*, there is a reluctance to rely on the principle of substantive due process to justify constitutional decisions. Yet, as even Justice Holmes acknowledged in the *Lochner* decision, there are certain principles of liberty that cannot be infringed upon by the State, merely by passing a law. Because our ability to reproduce defines us in a fundamental way, restrictions on reproductive freedom go to the heart of the relationship between the government and the governed that is the essence of our Constitution. Thus, one could be morally opposed to abortion and yet concede that it is important that the Constitution prohibit states from restricting a woman's right to choose an abortion.

On the other hand, it is possible to be in favor of a woman's right to choose an abortion, yet come to the conclusion that the Constitution does not prohibit a state from restricting abortions. As noted above, the concepts of "privacy" and "natural law" are so vague that they do not present a clear and objective guide as to what is constitutional and what is not. Without such a guide, the Court runs the risk of usurping the power that has been granted to the people in the form of state legislatures.

Thus, the argument at the Supreme Court level is not merely about abortion, it is about the role of the Court and the nature of the relationship between the government and the people in a democratic society. There may not be clear answers, but the conclusion one reaches does not necessarily depend on one's view of abortion. For example, someone could vote with the majority in *Roe* yet easily find that state restrictions on abortions do not violate the equal protection clause of the Constitution. Similarly, it is possible to oppose abortion yet find no reason to overturn *Roe* as acceptable Supreme Court precedent.

Part of the problem in terms of the public's perception of *Roe* is that the opinion only hints at the constitutional foundation for the majority opinion. As noted above, one of the reasons for this may have been the universal distaste for the *Lochner* line of decisions. As a consequence, the *Roe* decision is more a listing of cases than a reasoned discussion of the due process clause. But it is the duty of the Court to make its decision on a principled basis.[131] It is not enough to declare that the Bill of Rights and the Fourteenth Amendment are "broad enough" to include a woman's right to choose. There are sound reasons inherent in the nature of democratic government and the constitutional scheme that support prohibiting the government from entering this area of our lives. It is to be hoped that with the basic right to abortion as articulated in *Roe* now secure, the Court can begin to articulate with greater specificity its view of the full scope of the privacy right. If the Court can fully articulate a principled view of this right and apply it consistently in areas other than that of abortion, the constitutional underpinnings for the abortion decisions will become more apparent and the perception that the debate over abortion at the Supreme Court level is nothing more than a smokescreen for the moral views of the justices will diminish.

NOTES

1. Roscoe Pound, *An Introduction to the Philosophy of Law* (New Haven, Connecticut: Yale University Press, 1954), p. 49.

2. Quoted in Ronald J. Yengich and David A. Nelson, *The Law is an Ass: A Collection of Quotations About the Law* (Salt Lake City: Little Dog Publications, 1987), p. 49.

3. 5 U.S. (1 Cranch) 137 (1803).

4. Although it is an interesting question whether Marshall "set up" this case in order to make a ruling on judicial review, such an issue is beyond the scope of this chapter.

5. *See generally* Gerald Gunther, *Constitutional Law*, 11th ed. (Mineola, New York: Foundation Press, 1985), pp. 10-11.

6. 5 U.S. (1 Cranch) at 173.

7. U.S. Const. art I, §2.

8. U.S. (1 Cranch) at 175-176.

9. *Id.* at 176.

10. *Id.*

11. *Id.* at 177-178.

12. *See* Gunther, *supra* note 5, at 11.

13. Robert H. Bork, *The Tempting of America* (New York: The Free Press, 1990), p. 23.

14. Alexander M. Bickel, *The least Dangerous Branch*, 2nd ed. (New Haven: Yale University Press, 1962).

15. 17 U.S. (4 Wheaton) 316 (1819).

16. *Id.* at 432.

17. *Id.* at 407.

18. *Id.*

19. *Id.* (emphasis in the original).

20. *See* Bickel, *supra* note 14, at 36.

21. 32 U.S. (7 Pet.) 243 (1833).

22. Alexander Hamilton, James Madison, and John Jay, *The Federalist* (New York: Bantam Classic Edition 1982).

23. *Id.* at 437.

24. *Id.*

25. U.S. Const. amend. IX.

26. 83 U.S. (16 Wall.) 36 (1872).

27. *Id.* at 79.

28. *See Cleveland Bd. of Educ. v. Loudermill*, 470 U.S. 532 (1985): *Goldberg v. Kelly*, 397 U.S. 254 (1970).

29. *See Williamson v. Lee Optical Co*, 348 U.S. 483 (1955).

30. Philip K. Dick, "The Minority Report" in Philip K.Dick, ed. *The Minority Report: Collected Stories of Philip K. Dick* (New York: Carol Publishing, 1987), pp. 71-102.

31. Bork, *supra* note 13, at 32.

32. 60 U.S. (19 How.) 393 (1856).

33. *Id.* at 450.

34. Although slavery is certainly "wrong" in a moral sense, Congress did not ban slavery in the slave holding states prior to the passage of the Thirteenth Amendment. Thus, from a legal viewpoint, Dred Scott was merely personal property, like a horse or a cow. According to the Court, the morality of the species of property was not at issue.

35. 198 U.S. 45 (1905).

36. *Id.* at 57.

37. *Id.* at 64.

38. *Id.* at 75.

39. *Id.*

40. *Id.* at 76.

41. *West Coast Hotel v. Parrish*, 300 U.S. 379 (1937).

42. For the history of this era, *see generally*, Gunther *supra* note 5, at 441-475.

43. 262 U.S. 390 (1923).

44. 268 U.S. 510 (1925).

45. 302 U.S. 319 (1937).

46. *Id.* at 325.

47. Ruth Bader Ginsburg, "Some Thoughts on Autonomy and Equality in Relation to *Roe v. Wade*," 63 *N.C.L. Rev.* 375 (1985).

48. Laurence Tribe, *Abortion: The Clash of Absolutes* (New York: W. W. Norton, 1990), p. 105.

49. 83 U.S. (16 Wall.) 36 (1872).

50. *Id.* at 81.

51. 336 U.S. 106 (1949).

52. *Id.*

53. *See Cleburne v. Cleburne Living Center*, 473 U.S.432 (1985).

54. *Id.*

55. Gunther, *supra* note 5, at 788.

56. *Frontiero v. Richardson*, 411 U.S. 677 (1973). The law in question illustrates the dual nature of protective legislation. Although the law made it easier for women to qualify as *dependents*, it put women who entered the armed services at a disadvantage because their spouses did not qualify for automatic dependent coverage.

57. *Kirchberg v. Feenstra*, 450 U.S. 455 (1981).

58. *Mississippi University for Women v. Hogan*, 458 U.S. 718 (1982).

59. 381 U.S. 479.

60. *Id.* at 480.

61. *Id.* at 482.

62. *Id.*

63. *Id.* at 486.

64. Citing to *NAACP v. Alabama*, 357 U.S. 449 (1958).

65. William Morris, ed. *The American Heritage Dictionary of the English Language* (Boston: American Heritage Publsihing Co., and Houghton-Mifflin, 1975), p. 971.

66. 381 U.S. at 484.

67. *Id.* at 485.

68. *Id.* at 491.

69. *Id.* at 499; 502.

70. *Id.* at 500.

71. *Id.* at 504-507.

72. *Id.* at 514-515.

73. *Id.* at 521.

74. 405 U.S. 438 (1972).

75. *Id.* at 453 (emphasis in the original).

76. 410 U.S. 113 (1973).

77. *Id.* at 152.

78. 262 U.S. 390 (1923).

79. 268 U.S. 510 (1925).

80. 388 U.S. 1 (1967).

81. 316 U.S. 535 (1942).

82. 321 U.S. 158 (1944).

83. Bork, *supra* note 13, at 114.

84. 388 U.S. at 12.

85. 316 U.S. at 542.

86. 274 U.S. 200 (1927).

87. 410 U.S. at 153.

88. *Id.*at 155.

89. *Id.* at 159.

90. *Id.* at 162.

91. *Id.*at 212 n. 4.

92. *Id.* at 168.

93. *Id.* at 221-222.

94. *Id.* at 173.

95. *Id.*

96. 505 U.S. __, 112 S.Ct 2791, 120 L.Ed 2d 674 (1992).

97. 120 L.Ed 2d at 782.

98. 478 U.S. 186 (1986).

99. 120 L.Ed 2d at 695.

100. 367 U.S. 497 (1961).

101. *Id.* at 542.

102. 120 L.Ed 2d at 712.

103. *Id.* at 713.

104. 458 U.S. 718 (1982).

105. *Griggs v. Duke Power Co.*, 401 U.S. 424 (1971).

106. *Washington v. Davis*, 426 U.S. 229 (1976); *Arlington Heights v. Metropolitan Housing Dev. Corp.*, 429 U.S. 252 (1977).

107. 442 U.S. 256 (1979).

108. Cass Sunstein, "Neutrality in Constitutional Law (with Special Reference to Pornography, Abortion, and Surrogacy)" 92 *Colum. L. Rev.* 1, 32-33 (1992).

109.*Id.* (emphasis in original).

110. 417 U.S. 484 (1974).

111. 506 U.S. __, 113 S. Ct 753, 122 L. Ed 2d 34 (1933).

112. *Id.* at 47.

113. Sunstein, *supra* note 108, at 43.

114. *Id.*

115. Ummuhan Turgut and James Bowers, "Classical Liberalism, the Constitution, and Abortion Policy: Can Government Be Both Pro-Choice and Anti-Abortion?" 17 *U. Dayton L. Rev.* 1, (1991/1992).

116. *Id.* at 7.

117. The Declaration of Independence Para. 2 (U.S. 1776).

118. Turgut, *supra* note 115, at 18.

119. Tribe, *supra* note 48, at 111.

120. This is a paraphrase of a comment made by Neils Bohr with respect to quantum physics. Quoted in John R. Gribbin, *In Search of Schrodinger's Cat: Quantum Physics and Reality* (New York: Bantam Books, 1984).

121. 304 U.S. 144 (1938).

122. *Id.* at 152 n.4.

123.__ U.S. __, 120 L. Ed 2d 782.

124. Paul Brest, "The Misconceived Quest for the Original Understanding," 60 *B.U.L. Rev.* 204 (1980).

125. *Id.* at 216.

126. 42 U.S.C. §2000e, et seq.

127. *Henson v. City of Dundee*, 682 F. 2d 897 (11th Cir. 1982), and cases cited.

128. *Id.*

129. *Meritor Savings Bank v. Vinson*, 477 U.S. 57 (1986).

130. *McCulloch v. Maryland*, 17 U.S. (4 Wheaton) 316 at 407 (1819)

131. Bickel, *supra* note 14.

6

Conclusion: Perspectives on the Politics of Abortion

Patricia Fauser, Jeanne Lewis, Joel A. Setzen, Finian Taylor, and Ted G. Jelen

In his recent book, *Culture Wars*, James Davison Hunter[1] argues that contemporary American politics and culture are in the process of realigning along a moral axis of conflict, pitting the forces of "orthodoxy" against those of "progressivism." To the extent that Hunter's analysis is a reasonable description of the American political scene, it seems obvious that the issue of legalized abortion can be expected to be an important component of the culture war. Indeed, the assassinations of abortion providers David Gunn in March of 1993 and John Britton in July of 1994, as well as the more recent anti-abortion violence in Brookline, Massachusetts, suggests that the martial imagery may constitute an appropriate metaphor where the abortion issue is concerned.[2]

There are at least two reasons why the abortion issue has generated so much intense (and occasionally uncivil) political conflict. In the first place, the issue of legalized abortion stands at the point of intersection of two central aspects of the American political culture: Lockean individualism and a somewhat vague Judeo-Christian tradition. In the case of the former, there appears to exist a presumption that people should be allowed to do as they please, as long as they do not harm other people.[3] However, the high level of religiosity among the American people (relative to that found in other industrialized nations) suggests that many citizens have strong religious commitments, which may occasion restrictive attitudes on issues of personal morality.[4] In the case of the abortion issue, opponents of legal abortion are able to invoke the Lockean individualist tradition by arguing that, indeed, *someone* (specifically, the unborn) is in fact harmed by the act of abortion.

Although the analysis presented by Clyde Wilcox in Chapter 3 of this volume suggests that a respect for fetal life is not the only, or even the primary, source of anti-abortion attitudes, such an argument provides a warrant with which opponents of abortion may enter the public discussion.

Second, abortion is what Amy Fried has termed a "condensational symbol."[5] That is, the abortion issue derives much of its emotional force from the fact that it exists at the intersection of so many fundamental human concerns. As is shown by the chapters that constitute this volume, and the reactions to those arguments contained in this chapter, the abortion issue involves our most basic conceptions of human life, family, religion, sexuality and sex roles, law, and citizenship. The issue of whether a woman should be allowed to terminate a pregnancy intentionally is not so simple but evokes genuinely intense and complex emotions surrounding a variety of topics. With these considerations in mind, we turn to an analysis and conclusion of the preceding chapters in this collection.

THE LIMITS OF INDIVIDUALISM

In Chapter 2, Eileen McDonagh has provided an excellent analysis of the burdens on the woman of nonconsensual pregnancy and, indeed, of the burdens of pregnancy as such. McDonagh challenges the traditional patriarchal assumptions that the fetus is a sacred entity that completes a woman's identity and constitutes a woman's greatest fulfillment and happiness. In this respect her analysis is therapeutic and contributes to an informed understanding of maternity in its psychic and social complexity.

McDonagh's chapter may be situated in modern feminist debates about the representation of motherhood and female autonomy. Indeed, as early as 1949 in *The Second Sex*, Simone de Beauvoir wrote of pregnancy in graphic detail as a parasitic body proliferating within her body, bringing fear of monstrous swelling, tearing, and hemorrhage that haunted her.[6]

Postmodern feminists make two charges against this view of maternity that might speak against McDonagh's conception of fertilized ovum as a parasitical mugger inflicting battery on the victim-woman. (1) Feminists claim that this concept of maternity continues the spread of an essentially masculine horror of profoundly feminine experiences, of the female body, and female sexuality. (2) This view of fetus-woman relationships incorporates an historically masculine, enlightenment era view of human person or subjectivity-- namely, person as absolute autonomy, radically independent of other persons, untouched by social environment and intersubjective relationships. Thus in McDonagh's chapter we have both a perpetuation of masculinist language and a "walled city" concept of human person, both of which fail to provide a basis for human interaction and sensitivity to responsibility for others. Many feminist values such as caring, empathy, noncompetitiveness, and willingness to work with others in society are antithetical to McDonagh's view of the fetus-woman relationship and the individualist language she uses in her analysis.

McDonagh's reluctance to develop a stronger concept of human subjectivity and autonomy is again apparent in her treatment of the fetus. She presents the fetus as either an autonomous aggressor against the victim-mother on the one hand, or a mass of foreign parasitic cells on the other.

Chiding *Roe v. Wade* for its ruling on abortion without addressing pregnancy, McDonough herself proceeds to discuss pregnancy without going beyond what can only be called a caricature of the fetus/person. In one sense McDonagh's view of the fetus as being capable of intentionally choosing to inflict battery on the victim mother constitutes a reduction to absurdity of the argument of those on the extreme right who claim that the fetus is in every sense a person equal to the adult mother. Surely there is some concept of being that is prima facie more appropriate to the fetus, some place between this fully autonomous chooser and a blob of parasitic cells. McDonagh exploits the difference between potential person and fully actualized person, treating the person first as a completely autonomous being with no dependency and no vulnerability; and second as something comparable to a blob of cancerous cells with no potential for developing autonomy, rationality, responsibility, and personal individuality. It might quite reasonably be argued that the fetus is neither of these. Failure to grapple with what Gabriel Marcel calls "the mystery of being," which is simultaneously human being and the capability of actualizing powers to develop further human potential, contributes in part to the sterility of the abortion debate today.[7]

Since an important objective of her discussion is to interpret pregnancy as an assault upon the woman, McDonagh cannot draw a clearer distinction between consensual and nonconsensual intercourse.

But is the abortion debate really furthered by holding the fertilized ovum responsible for a woman's pregnancy? Surely this is erecting a controversial model that flies in the face of common sense and continues the tendency to treat women as passive beings lacking essential agency in the midst of one of their most critical experiences. To claim that sexual intercourse does not cause pregnancy but is only a transfer of gametes, and that only a fertilized ovum can cause pregnancy, is to exploit the ambiguity involved in the fact that the reproductive process can be separated into a variety of processes: impregnation, fertilization, implantation, and so on. In the vast majority of cases the act of intercourse performed by human persons must be considered a primary cause of the resulting pregnancy. To deny this effective agency to women is simply counterintuitive and results in the controversial notion of agency on the part of the fertilized ovum on the one hand and the victim adult mother on the other, deprived of autonomy and the ability to effect consequences by her actions.

Thus, McDonagh's claim that in every moral situation one can separate consent to engage in a risk from responsibility for the consequences to the risk might be regarded as problematic. In cases where voluntarily engaging in a risk is inseparable from a certain consequence--where, for example, the risk of pregnancy is an inseparable consequence of the choice of intercourse--and is clearly foreknown as such, both moral theorists and the law recognize some degree of responsibility for the consequence. The classic case is, of course, the choice to get drunk, coupled with foreknowledge that consequences of drunken behavior will occur. The relationships between choice and responsibility need to be further explored in McDonagh's analysis. It will not do to merely insist on separating the choice to take a risk from the responsibility for the consequences of the risk--all in the name of autonomy. McDonagh's concept of autonomy is itself diminished by this separation, thereby reinforcing the view of woman as victim, an inevitable outcome of an impoverished account of subjectivity and its relationship to autonomy in her discussion.

Today modern reproductive technologies make it increasingly possible to separate each state of the reproductive process. To the extent that McDonagh makes the argument that women can separate choice, action, and responsibility, she applies the same sort of reasoning that is sometimes used in moral debates surrounding the separating of intercourse from conception, conception from implantation, and childbearing from motherhood.

However, one of the central questions raised by the new reproduction technologies is precisely how the new freedoms of both men and women will enable us to address the complex individual and social/moral problems involved in the conception, care, and development of future generations of Americans. McDonagh's chapter is effective in linking furtherance of State interest in protection of potential life with child care benefits, assistance to child caretakers, educational benefits, and pensions. But her decoupling of choice and responsibility throughout her discussion of pregnancy exacerbates the trend toward breaking human reproduction and parenting into discrete processes for which no one bears ultimate moral responsibility.

It might be argued that McDonagh lacks an adequate philosophical concept of fetus and feminine subjectivity with corresponding notions of freedom and responsibility. Her attempt to separate choice of action and responsibility for consequences, dividing reproduction into morally unrelated segments is problematic and, for many, counterintuitive. At the same time, her paper is eminently successful in focusing debate on cultural myths surrounding female sexuality, childbearing, and family.

Perhaps more fundamentally, McDonagh has shown the complex and perhaps perverse consequences of a discourse based on the notion of "rights." Rights, if understood as unqualified prerogatives,[8] suggest precisely the illegitimacy of certain forms of political interaction. The assertion of a "right" (be it a "right to choose" or a "right to life") suggests that the prerogative in question "trumps" and that other competing or mitigating considerations are not only irrelevant but illegitimate as well.[9] McDonagh's analysis shows that even if we could settle the question of the humanity of the fetus, such a determination would not solve the abortion controversy. The question of when the fetus becomes a person is not definitive and can only serve as the starting point for discussions of the legitimacy of legalized abortion. McDonagh has recast the normative debate over legal abortion in a fundamental manner.

ABORTION AS A CULTURAL SYMBOL

One of the most interesting points that emerges from Clyde Wilcox's analysis (see Chapter 3) of the sources and consequences of public attitudes toward abortion is the apparent disparity between what seems to be the weight of public opinion on this issue and the positions taken by the national parties. Thus, although a narrow majority of Americans have favored legalized abortion with some restrictions since 1972, ever since 1980 the two parties have established increasingly extreme, polarized positions that are supported by only a minority of American voters.

As Wilcox points out, following Downs, not only do the parties' positions not reflect majority public opinion on abortion, they also contradict the dynamic characteristic of a two-party system with a moderate public, a dynamic in which both parties tend toward moderate positions on contested issues and in which issues are themselves relatively unimportant in voting decisions. Further, the extreme positions of the two parties are at odds with their more moderate positions on other contested issues such as national health care and the economy, on which, in keeping with Downs' model, they do not provide clearly divergent choices to the American public.

In explaining this apparent anomaly, Wilcox suggests that candidates may take extreme positions on the abortion issue despite the more moderate positions of contributors, party delegates, and voters because these positions in fact attract money, delegates, and votes. Using data from recent presidential elections as well as a number of senatorial and gubernatorial contests, Wilcox then goes on to argue that in those cases in which candidates took clearly divergent positions on abortion and the issue was emphasized, it did indeed influence voting behavior.

In making this argument, Wilcox characterizes the abortion issue, like other issues that appear to influence voting behavior, as an easy issue. That is, it is an issue that (1) has been on the political agenda for some time, (2) focuses is ends rather than means, (3) contains a heavy symbolic component that ties it to wider discussions and controversies. We wish to explore this latter feature of the issue in somewhat greater depth by considering abortion as a symbolic or cultural construct that is systematically related to other cultural constructs such as gender and sexuality. In doing so, it might be suggested that abortion has come to serve as a core symbol for other contested cultural constructs and that as a political issue it has come to represent an attempt to resolve a much wider broader about the nature and meaning of American culture.

As a cultural construct, abortion is not so much an act or any specific set of medical procedures as a more or less coherent set of ideas, meanings, and valuations that inform or give meaning to the acts or procedures to which it is taken to refer.[10] As is the case with other cultural symbols or constructs, the meanings embodied in abortion are multiple, ambiguous, and frequently paradoxical.[11] Thus, among other things, abortion as an American cultural construct can mean any or all procedures for terminating pregnancy, a right, murder, a woman's control over her own body, a choice, an unnatural act, a necessity, a humane act, an effective means of birth control, a legal but immoral act, a legal and morally neutral act, and so forth. Not all of these or any of the additional meanings that may constitute abortion as a cultural construct are necessarily available to or held by all members of American society, although they are intelligible to most. Which of these meanings an individual selects to interpret his/her own and others' behavior in light of is probably influenced by life experiences and expectations that can be summarized in the kinds of demographic profiles that Wilcox characterizes as pro-life and pro-choice and that are more fully developed in Cook, Jelen, and Wilcox's book *Between Two Absolutes*.[12]

Regardless of what abortion is, what it means to the individual is always a matter of belief rather than a product of formal empirical or logical operations. Although one can certainly make a logical argument about what abortion is or is not and can even marshall empirically based scientific statements to buttress these arguments, as is the case with other cultural constructs, any meaning of abortion is ultimately symbolic in nature, true only to the extent that it is believed and acted upon.[13] That such meanings on the individual level are under no greater constraints of internal consistency than they are on the cultural level is evident in the findings of the 1989 *CBS News/New York Times* poll cited by Wilcox, which showed that one-fourth of the American public simultaneously believes that abortion is murder and sometimes the best choice.

As a cultural construct, the symbol of abortion and the meanings that constitute it do not stand alone but are embedded in a system of other symbols with which it shares some elements or meanings. It is this system as a whole that mediates between the cultural construct of abortion and its social grounding. Its varied meanings are as much a function of its place within this wider symbolic system as they are of its relevance or reference to any particular social reality.[14] It is the entire system of symbols from which individuals draw their separate but never wholly unique understandings of the meaning of abortion in the context of contemporary American life and that is invoked with varying degrees of consciousness in any abortion debate.

Given this, it might be suggested that as a cultural construct abortion appears to participate in, share meanings with, or perhaps even connect two larger sets of opposed cultural constructs or domains that include as members all the other symbols or constructs to which abortion is connected and with which it shares a number of meanings. The first set is the opposition between culture and nature into which abortion is subsumed by its connections to other significant American cultural constructs such as those concerning gender, kinship and sexuality. The second set of core oppositions in which abortion appears to participate is that between self and society or self-interest versus the public good, with which it is connected through a number of constructs, many of which are understood as relevant to American political thought and processes--that is, individualism, choice or freedom, and rights.

While any exhaustive treatment of this wider system of meanings and the connections among them is outside the scope of this chapter, we suggest the direction that such a treatment might take and will do so by choosing as a somewhat arbitrary starting point the cultural construct of gender. In the traditional and still dominant understanding of gender in American culture, women's relational, kinship, and thus reproductive roles remain crucial to the meanings of femininity in ways that analogous male roles are not critical for masculinity. The most critical of these roles for the understanding of femininity has been and remains that of mother, understandings of which not only dominate the cultural symbol "feminine" but serve to anchor it firmly within the domain of nature.[15] Like other American kinship constructs, woman as mother (or mother as woman), is taken to entail both (1) a physical relationship of shared or common substance, a natural substance brought into being by a natural act, and (2) a code of conduct, acts, and attitudes of love and nurturance considered not only appropriate to but a necessary outcome of the sharing of substance by mother and child.[16]

Although fatherhood is less crucial to understandings of the gender category "male" or "masculine" than is motherhood to "feminine", motherhood as shared substance and code of conduct is nonetheless the means through which much of the opposition between the two gender categories is both maintained and mediated, insofar as it is only in the shared physical substance of a child that the link between masculine and feminine, between male and female, can be more than code of conduct clearly contingent on social conventions and can participate in the solidity and inevitability of the natural.

It is, then, not simply the relationship between mother and child that is disrupted and nullified by abortion. Abortion, not merely as an act but as an established cultural reality, simultaneously nullifies as constitutive of woman both the physical substance and the code of conduct that is motherhood. But in doing so it also disrupts what is perhaps the central distinction that maintains "feminine" in opposition to "masculine" and the major mode of mediation between the two. Thus, abortion simultaneously destabilizes the meanings of gender, sexuality, and kinship and the balance of nature and culture they express by threatening to push them wholly into the domain of culture, the realm of contingency and choice where purely human ends must provide their order and constraints.

Woman, of course, is not only mother but also a member or type of the construct "individual," the construct generally understood to be that in which choice or freedom inhere as well as that to which rights do or do not belong and by, for, or through whom they are exercised. In this system of meanings the pregnant woman is an anomaly, an individual enclosing a separate individual, or a single but fragmented individual, or merely a single individual that stands in some relationship to a not-as-yet- realized, never-necessarily realized individual, each or any of which might have separate, identical, overlapping, or contradictory rights and freedoms. The multiple, often divergent meanings generated by these symbols remain debatable and unclear. What is clear, as Wilcox has argued, is that the *Roe* decision activiated the connections among these symbols for most Americans and made them relevant to the abortion debate in public consciousness.

While this treatment of abortion as part of a system of cultural symbols is of necessity sketchy and speculative, insofar as it is not grounded in the kind of field research that would be necessary to establish it as an authentic American cultural rhetoric, it is plausible and, in some sense, informative. Certainly it helps make sense of claims that legalized abortion is destructive of the family, the natural organization of gender and sexuality, human rights, and constitutional guarantees--in short, destructive of the American way of life. But it equally enlightens claims to the contrary that abortion is a necessary part of an appropriate structuring of gender, sexuality, the family, constitutional and human rights, and the inviolable status of the individual--in short, of the American way of life.

Further, it seems clear that the split within the situationalist position described by Wilcox as one between (1) those who favor abortion only in circumstances involving physical traumas that women do not choose freely or inflict upon themselves and (2) those who regard so-called social rationales as equally convincing is, in the cultural sense, a split between those whose understandings of abortion are drawn primarily from the nature versus culture opposition and those who understandings derive primarily from the self versus society domains.

In the absence of any social entity or institution wtih authority to limit and define this welter of interconnected meanings in terms of social imperatives that are clear and can be accepted by all Americans, and, indeed, in the absence of any neutral public forum more extensive than the sound-bite to engage in the dialogue needed to disentangle and explore them, the task has fallen by virtue of both *Roe* and tradition on the political process. By posing the debate over abortion in its most extreme form, the two parties may be--however unwittingly--framing the boundaries of this dialogue, which in fact may be less about abortion as such than about the still emergent content of American culture.

CITIZENSHIP, DISCIPLESHIP, AND THE POLITICS OF ABORTION

From the outset, Mary Segers states in Chapter 4 that the Catholic Church's participation in this country's political process requires no lengthy justification (although she does question during the course of her discussion the *means* by which the church participates).

In 1984, Joseph Cardinal Bernardin, Archbishop of Chicago, stood on the campus of Illinois Benedictine College and said:

> Examining the proper place of the Church in the public arena was a continuous task. Most often it was done in response to charges that we were violating the separation of Church and State. Usually when people make that accusation, their intent is to tell religious bodies to be quiet; thatthey have no business talking about such issues. However,my reading of the constitutional principle is that the separation of Church and State is designed to provide religious organizations space to speak. The separation of Church and State means that religious communities should expect neither favoritism nor discrimination in the exercise of their religious and civic functions. They are free to participate in any aspect of the public debate, but they must earn the right to be heard by the quality of their arguments. Accordingly, we assumed a posture which was designed to keep our role both ecclesial and public. The challenge was how to

speak *as* a church *to* a public issue; how to speak *from* a tradition of faith in a language which was *open* to public acceptance by citizens of several faiths and no faith.[17]

The Cardinal's remarks here on the role of the church in a democracy were made not in the context of abortion but in the context of the bishops' then recent pastoral letter on war and peace.[18] However, he used those same remarks at other times in regard to other issues as well. This is because Bernardin argues issues on the basis of his "consistent ethic of life" notion, often referred to as the "seamless garment" approach in which he claims that the garment of life is all of one piece, whether the issue be abortion, nuclear war, capital punishment, pornography, euthanasia, hunger, or poverty.

This consistent life ethic has now become the policy of all the U.S. bishops, even though some bishops, like Cardinal O'Connor of New York, have emphasized the single issue of abortion.

Also, Bernardin lays great stock in the necessity for the Church to influence public opinion. In the same speech quoted above, he went on to say:

In a democratic society, the Church's role in the public life of the nation is directly related to, though not exhausted by, the theme of public opinion. Public opinion plays both a positive and a restraining role. At times it should provide support for necessary but perhaps unpopular initiatives; atother times public opinion should place limits on the direction of policy.

My conviction is that public opinion has an important but not guaranteed effect on major policy decisions. If we fail to cultivate an active, engaged public opinion on key questions,we lose an important moral as well as political resource. But even a carefully nurtured public opinion will not guarantee specific results.[19]

Segers describes in detail how the U.S. Catholic Church operates as an interest group. Interestingly, in the 1992 U.S. Catholic Conference's (hereafter, USCC) statement on *Political Responsibility*, which has been issued before every general election since 1976, the bishops said:

...there is often confusion and controversy over theparticipation of religious groups in public life. The religious community has important responsibilities in political life. Our constitution protects the rights of religious bodies to speak out without governmental interference, endorsement or sanction. What we seek is not a religious interest group, but a community of conscience within the larger society, testing public life on these central values. Our call to political responsibility is neither a partisan or a sectarian appeal. This kind of political responsibility does not involve religious leaders telling people how to vote or religious tests for candidates. These would be, in our view, pastorally inappropriate, theologically unsound and politically unwise. We bishops specifically do not seek the formation of a religious voting bloc; nor do we wish to instruct persons on how they should vote by endorsing oropposing candidates."[20]

Many wish that the U.S. bishops would follow their own advice. Segers has provided some specific examples of how the bishops have singled out specific politicians for criticism regarding abortion during election campaigns, even threatening some with excommunication. Her colleague, Timothy Byrnes, provides more examples in their jointly edited book, *The Catholic Church and the Politics of Abortion*.[21]

One should never underestimate the rancor that such public condemnations of individuals by the bishops has caused among both Catholics and non-Catholics.

Catholic laity today go to great lengths to observe the Bishops' *Voter Education Guidlines* which are widely distributed before every general election and are jointly prepared by the USCC and the IRS. The *Guidelines* state that:

> ...a tax exempt organization may not support or oppose a particular candidate or party....or take action that could be construed as an endorsement....the effectiveness of these guidelines demands that they be impartially applied to all candidates or parties, *whether an individual candidate or party supports the Church's position on a specific issue or not* [emphasis added][22]

Besides these guidelines, the USCC has issued a memorandum entitled, "Memorandum on Political Activion Prohibition for Tax Exempt Organizations", in which it reminds Catholic organizations that as 501 (c) (3) tax-exempt groups they

> ...may not make oral or written statements supporting or opposing any candidate for public office, whether in a sermon or parish bulletin, through an editorial position in a Catholic newspaper, or through distribution of fill-in sample ballots . . . . labeling a candidate as . . . . pro-abortion or anti-peace.[23]

Although Catholic parishioners around the country might carefully avoid the slightest breach of these guidelines, they need only turn on the nightly news and watch Cardinal "X" in heated battle with politician "Y," thereby violating if not the letter at least the very spirit, of these guidelines.

Segers also addresses the lobbying role of the U.S. Catholic Church. She should avail herself of the recent statement (August 1992) by the USCC's general counsel on the political conduct of Catholic organizations as tax-exempt 501 (c) (3) organizations. Such detailed descriptions of permissible and prohibited election activities, as mandated by the IRS, are extremely unusual.

If nothing else, the statement attempts to distinguish the nuances between lobbying and political activity:

> unlike lobbying, which is merely limited, political campaign activity is strictly prohibited. . . . Lobbying includes contacting or urging the public to contact members of a legislative body . . . . for the purpose of proposing, supporting or opposing legislation or advocating adoption or rejection of legislation.
>
> The code permits exempt organizations to engage in lobbying activity provided it does not constitute a substantial part of their total activities. Unfortunately, neither the code nor the regulations define what is "substantial" in this context.
>
> *Any* political campaign activity can jeopardize an organization's exempt status.[24]

The statement then points out the monetary penalties imposed by the IRS for violations of the 501 (c) (3) code. Some have argued that the Catholic bishops are more concerned about losing their tax-exempt status than they are about maintaining a proper political decorum.

Finally, Segers evaluates the effectiveness of the Church's political lobbying. Relevant to this topic are some figures from a recent study of abortion and public opinion.[25] Among U.S. Catholics only 11% are decidedly pro-life (compared to 10% of the U.S. population), 34% identify themselves as pro-choice, and 55% claim to be situationalists (i.e., their views depend on the circumstances). Fully 89% are open to the possibility of abortion.

But these statistics are deceptive. Perhaps the comments of Notre Dame theologian Richard McBrien can elucidate the nuances of these figures. According to McBrien, the overwhelming majority of Catholics are opposed to abortion (on moral grounds), but that same majority, according to polls, is uneasy about the criminalization of abortion and the militancy of the pro-life movement. Thus, these Catholics take the position of being *legally* pro-choice or situationalist, while remaining *morally* against abortion. McBrien concludes that so much time has been spent arguing about abortion at the public policy level that Catholics run the risk of describing themselves as pro-choice while forgetting why they are anti-abortion.[26]

When one looks at statistics on other "life" issues (e.g., capital punishment, euthanasia), one again finds a deep gap between the U.S. bishops' stated position on an issue and the positions held by the Catholic faithful, who are 55 million strong.

Government officials and politicians are aware of this gap, but interestingly they seem to be more influenced by the Church's policy on abortion than by its policy on any other issue.

What does all this suggest? It should be noted that one of the underlying themes of this volume is the challenge of being Catholic and a U.S. citizen, simultaneously, within the context of the abortion debate. While some Catholics find this relationship between believer and citizen antagonistic, other Catholics feel very little tension at all. Why is there a spectrum of reactions among members of the same denomination? Why is there a difference in styles of political activism?

In 1951 H. Richard Niebuhr (a Protestant theologian) wrote a classic study on the various typologies or schemata that Christians have used to explain to themselves how they relate to the state, society, and the culture. Niebuhr delineates 5 topologies.[27] In 1974 Catholic theologian Avery Dulles proposed 5 models of church-state relationships.[28] Most recently, in 1985 Catholic historian David O'Brien propounded 4 distinctively Catholic models of "options."[29]

The typologies of all three authors can be reduced to three essential positions: (1) church as counter-cultural movement; (2) church as accommodating itself to the prevailing cultural values; and (3) church as transformer and converter of society.

To understand these models or typologies is to understand the discrepancy between the bishops and their faithful, as well as to comprehend the differences among all Catholics on how they respond to public policy.

Each model or paradigm brings its own set of images, rhetoric, values, certitudes, commitments, and priorities.[30] For example, according to Dulles' models, the most outspoken bishops (e.g., Cardinal O'Connor of New York) appear to be in the first category, called the institutional model. Here the Church is a visible, hierarchical, authoritarian structure, that is willing to stand over and against and take on any other structure, even the State. Here the cardinals and archbishops are the church's prize-fighters on moral issues, in the ring with any other prominent public figure.

A second model, called the communion model, typifies those Catholics who are, in a sense, apolitical. They recognize that the church and state are divided and that never the twain shall meet. They go about their business, living in the quiet and comforting knowledge that they are invisibly connected to other Catholics who share their convictions about moral issues, regardless of what the rest of the public thinks.

A third model, the sacramental model, encompasses those Catholics who resort to rosary crusades, candlelight marches, and civil disobedience. Their mission is to convert the world primarily through their prayerful witness and example, which is to be seen and experienced by others. These people ritualize their convictions.

A fourth model, the herald model, reflects those Catholics who equate their media crusade against abortion with the proclamation of the Gospel. They employ every available technology to communicate their message. A prime example is Mother Angelica's "Eternal Word" television station, which broadcasts to millions. Hers is a spiritual, not a political, agenda.

A fifth model, the servant model, is the most overtly political of all. Here Catholics pursue the quest for a better world of peace and justice for the sake of human dignity, the most fundamental value. Catholics are prepared to work for or against the state in this pursuit. Catholic lawmakers and elected officials typify this win-some, lose-some approach to the public forum. Some Catholic officials distinguish between public and private morality, while others conflate the two.

Interestingly, it might be argued that individuals as diverse as Mario Cuomo and Henry Hyde are two sides of the same coin: Cuomo (the servant) wanting to help seek a public consensus about values in a pluralistic society, and Hyde (the servant) wanting to help educate the public to a designated set of humanitarian values.

It is apparent that there exists a wide spectrum from institutional Catholic to servant Catholic. But the range makes intelligible the conflict among Catholics themselves as to how the Church might be a political actor on one particular issue.

Mary Segers points out the difference in method as to how the bishops approach moral issues. In terms of their statements on war and peace, and on the economy, they have engaged in a consultative approach--especially Archbishop Rembert Weakland, whose approach was exceptionally collegial. But when it comes to sexual matters, there is no consultative approach. Witness the bishops' recent attempt to write a pastoral letter on women. After 9 years of work and 4 increasingly restrictive revisions, the bishops finally abandoned the project.

In other words, as Segers suggests, there is an absolutism about sexual matters that does not admit of discussion. What would happen if it did? The bishops may have a sense that their authority is most directly threatened by dissent on issues that are of most immediate importance to the laity, and that the teaching authority of the Church may well depend on holding the line on these issues.

Segers points out that it has been precisely the "elitist, undemocratic, hierarchical, and monied" nature of the Church's interest group lobbying that explains its ability to win at least some victories on the state and federal levels in the abortion battle. But what has been the cost of these victories? Not only have they reinforced undemocratic tendencies in the political process (the object of attention of Ross Perot's campaign), but they may also explain why there exists an organizational gap in the contemporary U.S. Catholic Church.

Once upon a time everybody thought they knew where the Catholic Church stood on every possible issue. We may still know where the institutional church stands, but how shall we pinpoint where the "other" church stands--the self-reforming church of rank and file U.S. Catholics? In other words, there are two churches. Most of Segers' analysis has addressed only one of these two.

The Pope and the U.S. Bishops may well be in trouble. After all, there is a rising tide of dissent to issues ranging from birth control to a celibate clergy in the Western Church. How will the Vatican command agreement and respect? Among Americans, its credibility is languishing.[31] Many Catholics seem unaffected by the positions of Church leaders, remaining in the Church but paying little attention to what their leaders say. The statistics cited earlier on U.S. Catholics' attitudes toward abortion are a testament to this.

What lies ahead and is currently underway is a democratization of the Church. As this democratization progresses, we may see some of the

Church's present styles of political activism disappear and new ones appear. One is left to wonder what these new styles will be.

ALTERNATIVE LEGAL BASES FOR ABORTION RIGHTS

In discussing whether there is a constitutional basis for a woman's right to choose an abortion (see Chapter 5), Kent Sezer argues that such a right exists as a corollary of citizenship under democratic government. In a democracy each individual has a share of the total sovereignty and, thus, forms a political will in tandem with all other people. The liberty that is assured to all under this political will has been interpreted by the U.S. Supreme Court as incorporating all choices as to who we are and what we will become. This must surely include freedom over all aspects of reproduction.

On the way to reaching this conclusion, Sezer evaluates and then rejects the following doctrines in support of the right to an abortion: substantive due process, natural law, and original intent of the framers. He also analyzes *Roe v. Wade*[32] in some detail, concluding that the liberty interest upheld in such precedents as *Pierce v. Society of Sisters*[33] and *Meyer v. Nebraska*[34] has a closer relationship to First Amendment rights than to Fourteenth Amendment due process predictions referred to in *Roe*. Because of the volatility of the abortion issue, it may be useful to set forth the contemporary constitutional standards governing the right to abortion and then to examine whether such a right may be implicit in the equal protection clause of the Fourteenth Amendment.

Until the 1992 case of *Planned Parenthood of Southeastern Pennsylvania v. Casey*,[35] the trimester scheme of *Roe* remained the major precedent for analysis of states' restrictive abortion laws. Due to the change of personnel on the Court, there was support for modification of the trimester scheme on the grounds that a state's compelling interest in preserving the life of a fetus does not vary according to the gestational age. This was the major criticism of the trimester approach, which had recognized that a state's compelling interest in protecting potential life was triggered only at the point of viability of the fetus. Justice Sandra O'Connor had been associated with the above criticism since 1983 and, fittingly, wrote for the plurality in *Planned Parenthood*. The new standard was summarized as follows:

> To protect the central right recognized by *Roe v. Wade* while at the same time accommodating the State's profound interest in potential life we will employ the undue burden analysis . . . . An undue burden exists, and therefore a provision of a law is invalid, if its purpose or effect is to place substantial obstacle in the path of a woman seeking an abortion before the fetus attains viability . . . . As with any medical procedure, the State may enact regulations to further the health or safety of a woman seeking an abortion. Unnecessary health regulations that have the purpose or effect ofpresenting a substantial obstacle to a woman seeking an abortion impose an undue burden on the right.[36]

In the context of the provisions of the Pennsylvania statute under review, it was not considered an undue burden to require a minor to obtain parental consent for an abortion. Nor was it conisdered an undue burden upon any woman to be informed at least 24 hours before the procedure of the probable gestational age of the fetus. The signed statement of the married woman seeking an abortion attesting to the fact that she had notified her spouse of the procedure was, however, held to constitute an undue burden.

The current status of a woman's right to seek an abortion has been somewhat narrowed, pursuant to *Planned Parenthood*. It is a question of judges evaluating state restrictions and disincentives for an abortion, determining whether they pose "substantial obstacles." The formula itself, however, is "so diaphanous and elastic as to invite subjective judicial preferences or prejudices relating to particular types of legislation, masquerading as judgments."[37] Hence, a woman of childbearing age is deprived of a measure of liberty, in Sezer's formulation, because she is no longer the ultimate arbiter in deciding what she will become. In sum, *Planned Parenthood* constitutes a subtle restriction of a right conferred by *Roe*, although falling short of overruling that landmark decision.

As Sezer notes, the equal protection clause of the Fourteenth Amendment was at issue in some of the cases cited as precedent in *Roe*. It might well be argued that if a woman's right to an abortion can be categorized as fundamental, then a state may not impose any burden upon such a right without demonstrating that the burden would advance a compelling interest. Otherwise, the state would have abridged the woman's guarantee of equal protection under the law.

A major objection to such a viewpoint is that this would amount to judicial activism, that is, judges substituting their own judgment for the decisions of legislators and overriding the original intent of the Constitution's framers. But 20 years ago, it was stated:

> I would like to know where the Constitution guarantees the right to procreate . . . . or the right to vote in state elections, ... or the right to appeal from a criminal conviction . . . . These are instances in which, due to the importance of the interests at stake, the Court has displayed a strong concern with the existence of discriminatory state treatment . . . . [I]t cannot be denied that interests such as procreation, the exercise of the state franchise, and access to criminal appellate processes are not fully guaranteed to the citizen by our Constitution. But these interests have nonetheless been afforded special judicial consideration in the face of discrimination because they are, to some extent,interrelated with constitutional guarantees. Procreation is now understood to be important because of its interaction with the established constitutional right of privacy. The exercise of the state franchise is closely tied to basic civil and political rights inherent in the First Amendment. And access to criminal appellate processes enhances the integrity of the range of rights implicit in the Fourteenth Amendment guarantee of due process of law. Only if we closely protectthe related interests from state discrimination do we ultimately ensure the integrity of the constitutional guarantee itself.[38]

By analogy with the right of procreation, the woman's right to terminate her pregnancy is an integral aspect of her right to privacy. Hence, such a right is fundamental and entitled to the same heightened protection as the other rights referred to here. This could well satisfy the plea raised in Sezer's conclusion for a more specific articulation of the constitutional basis for abortion rights. As a fundamental right under the equal protection clause, the burden would fall on the state to justify abortion restrictions by proving that compelling governmental interest are being furthered. This would relegate the current undue burdens test to the dust bin of history.

CONCLUDING THOUGHTS

The abortion issue seems destined to occupy a position near center stage in American politics for some time to come. As the chapters that constitute volume make abundantly clear, the question of legal abortion touches on a number of different facets of the American political culture: at a minimum, law, medicine, family life, religion, psychology, and public opinion.

In sociological terms, the abortion issue raises a number of "boundary maintenance" issues concerning the relative authority of various forms of discourse. For example, to what extent are the status of various "rights" invoked in the debate contingent on the state of the medical arts? Does the extent of "intrusiveness" of the fetus on the pregnant woman to which Eileen McDonagh alludes depend on a particular set of medical research findings? Similarly, Mary Segers raises the issue of the hierarchy of obligations. Does the authority of the Roman Catholic Church supersede temporal political authority, or is the Catholic Church obligated, in some sense, to adapt to the political culture in which it finds itself? Does the use of religious insights violate an epistemological requirement of democratic discourse?[39] In sum, it seems clear that the abortion issue will continue to derive much of its power from the fact that different actors will continue to regard different forms of discourse authoritative. We cannot agree whether the issue is primarily about privacy, gender roles, sexual morality, human life, or the authority of the Courts over the elected branches of government.

The fact that the abortion question touches so many central aspects of our common public life suggests that the issue will have remarkable staying power and will affect political competition at a variety of levels and in a number of diverse settings. It is our hope that the chapters in this volume will reduce, to some extent, the polemical rhetoric that surrounds this issue and will help provide a common language with which the question of abortion can be calmly and civilly debated. A respect for the benign motives and good intentions of one's opponents is an important aspect of civil democratic discourse. This volume will contribute, we hope, to a public conversation well begun.

NOTES

1. James Davison Hunter, *Culture Wars: The Struggle to Define America* (New York: Basic Books, 1992).

2. See Paul Gray, "Thou Shalt Not Kill," *Time* 141 (March 22, 1993): 44-46; Richard Lacayo, "One Doctor Down, How Many More?" *Time* 141 (March 22, 1993): 46-47; Eloise Salholz, Peter Kater, Spencer Reiss, Daniel Glick, and John McCormick, "The Death of Dr. Gunn," *Newsweek* (March 22, 1993): 34-

35; and Ronald Smothers, "Abortion Doctor and Bodyguard Slain in Florida," *New York Times* July 30, 1994:1:1,7. For an analysis of war imagery as utilized by pro-life direct activists, see Carol J. C. Maxwell and Ted G. Jelen, "Commandos for Christ: Narratives of Male Pro-Life Activists," *Review of Religious Research* (forthcoming).

3. See especially John Stuart Mill, *On Liberty* (New York: Bobbs-Merrill, 1956); and Brian Barry, "How Not to Defend Liberal Institutions," *British Journal of Political Science* 20 (1990): 1-14.

4. Kenneth D. Wald, *Religion and Politics in the United States* (Washington, D. C.: CQ Press, 1991); and Elizabeth Adell Cook, Ted G. Jelen, and Clyde Wilcox, *Between Two Absolutes: Public Opinion and the Politics of Abortion* (Boulder, CO: Westview Press, 1992), pp. 4-5.

5. Amy Fried, "Abortion Politics as Symbolic Politics: An Investigation into Belief Systems," *Social Science Quarterly* 69 (1988): 137-154.

6. Simone de Beauvoir, *The Second Sex*, trans. and ed. H. M. Parshley. (New York: Vintage Press, 1974), pp. 540-588.

7. See Gabriel Marcel, *Mystery of Being*. (Chicago: Gateway, 1970).

8. See especially Mary Ann Glendon, *Abortion and Divorce in Western Law* (Cambridge, MA: Harvard University Press, 1987); and Glendon, *Rights Talk (New York: The Free Press, 1991).*

9. For fuller explication of this, see Cook et al *Between Two Absolutes*, 193-196.

10. David M. Schneider, *American Kinship: A Cultural Account* (Englewood Cliffs, N. J.: Prentice-Hall, 1968), pp. 2-4.

11. Clifford Geertz, *Local Knowledge: Further Essays in Interpretive Anthropology* (New York: Basic Books, 1983), p. 161.

12. Cook, Jelen, and Wilcox, *Between Two Absolutes*.

13. Clifford Geertz, "Religion as a Cultural System," in Michael Banton, ed. *Conference on New Approaches in Social Anthropology: Anthropological Approaches to the Study of Religion* (London: Tavistock, 1965).

14. Sherry B. Ortner and Harriet Whitehead, "Introduction: Accounting for Sexual Meanings," in Sherry B. Ortner and Harriet Whitehead, eds. *Sexual Meanings: The Cultural Construction of Gender and Sexuality* (Cambridge: Cambridge University Press, 1981), pp. 3-4.

15. Ortner and Whitehead, "Introduction": 21-22.

16. Schneider, *American Kinship*, pp. 23-24; 37-38.

17. Joseph Cardinal Bernardin, "The Church and Public Policy," Illinois Benedictine College, February 8, 1984.

18. National Conference of Catholic Bishops, *The Challenge of Peace: God's Promise and Our Response* (Washington, D. C.: United States Catholic Conference, 1983).

19. Bernardin, "The Church and Public Policy."

20. United States Catholic Conference Administrative Board, "Political Responsibility: Revitalizing American Democracy," *Origins* 21, no. 20 (October 24, 1991): 316-318.

21. Timothy Byrnes and Mary C. Segers, eds. *The Catholic Church and the Politics of Abortion* (Boulder, CO: Westview Press, 1992), pp. 16-17.

22. United States Catholic Conference, *Voter Education Guidelines*, August 1992.

23. "Memorandum on Political Action Prohibition for Tax-Exempt Organizations," July, 1992.

24. USCC, "Election-Year Actions of Tax-Exempt Organizations," *Origins* 22, no.10 (August 6, 1992): 180.

25. Cook, Jelen, and Wilcox, *Between Two Absolutes*.

26. Richard P. McBrien, "Abortion: The Moral Issue," syndicated column, week of July 13, 1992.

27. H. Richard Niebuhr, *Christ and Culture* (New York: Harper and Row, 1951).

28. Avery Dulles, *Models of the Church* (Garden City: Doubleday, 1974).

29. David J. O'Brien, "The Future of Ministry: Historical Context," in *The Future of Ministry* (New York: Sadlier, 1985), pp. 34-35.

30. Dulles, *Models*, p. 29

31. See especially Patrick H. McNamara, *Conscience First, Tradition Second: A Study of Young Catholics* (Albany, NY: SUNY Press, 1992).

32. 410 U.S. 113 (1973).

33. 268 U.S. 510 (1925).

34. 262 U.S. 390 (1923).

35. 505 U.S. ____, 112 S. Ct. 2791, 120 L. Ed. 2d 674 (1992).

36. *Id.*, 120 L. Ed. 2d at 715-716.

37. Justice Rehnquist, dissenting, *Craig v. Boren*, 429 U.S. 190, 221 (1976).

38. Justice Marshall, dissenting, *San Antonio Independent School District v. Rodriguez*, 411 U.S. 1, 100-103 (1973).

39. See Kent Greenawalt, *Religious Convictions and Political Choice* (New York: Oxford University Press, 1988), for a superlative discussion of this issue.

Index

About the Contributors

About the Contributors

PATRICIA FAUSER is Professor of Philosophy at Illinois Benedictine College in Lisle, Illinois. In 1978-79 she was a Fellow at the National Humanities Institute at the University of Chicago, where her research focused on humanistic approaches to aging. She teaches and has published papers in modern philosophy and biomedical ethics. She directs workshops in medical ethics and serves as a consultant to academic and community projects in applied ethics. She has served as a member of the Board of Trustees of the Illinois Humanities Council, DuPage Family Services, and Hospice of DuPage. She serves on the ethics committee of Central DuPage Hospital and Community Nursing Service of DuPage County.

TED G. JELEN is Professor of Political Science at Illinois Benedictine College. He has written and edited numerous books and articles on religion and politics, feminism, and the politics of abortion. He is the coauthor (with Elizabeth Adell Cook and Clyde Wilcox) of *Between Two Absolutes: Public Opinion and the Politics of Abortion*, and the coeditor (with Marthe A. Chandler) of *Abortion Politics in the United States and Canada: Studies in Public Opinion* (Praeger, 1994).

JEANNE LEWIS is Associate Professor of Anthropology at Illinois Benedictine College. Her research interests include contemporary religious movements, the anthropology of gender, and applications of culture theory to international business and economics.

CAROL J. C. MAXWELL is currently the St. Louis Project Coordinator for the National Cooperative Inner-City Asthma Study. Her research interests include ethnicity and class, self-identity, decision-making, religious experience, activism, and oral history.

EILEEN L. McDONAGH is Associate Professor of Political Science at Northeastern University and a Visiting Scholar at the Murray Research Center at Radcliffe College. She has published widely in the area of public policy and gender issues in *American Political Science Review*, *Journal of Politics*, and *Studies in American Political Development*. She is completing a book on abortion rights.

MARY C. SEGERS is Professor of Political Science at Rutgers University in Newark, New Jersey, where she teaches political theory, women and politics, and religion and politics. She has written books and articles on equality and affirmative action policy, on abortion politics, and on the political role of the Catholic Church. Her latest volume, co-edited with Timothy A. Byrnes, is *Abortion Politics in American States*.

JOEL A. SETZEN is Professor of Political Science at Illinois Benedictine College, with a special interest in the American legal system. As a collateral activity, he has a part-time law practice in Westmont, Illinois.

L. KENT SEZER is General Counsel for the Illinois Human Rights Commission, a position he has held since 1983. The Commission is an agency that decides cases of alleged discrimination. Prior to this, he served as a Deputy Divisions chief with the Illinois Attorney General.

FINIAN TAYLOR is Professor of Religious Studies at Illinois Benedictine College. With Jean Laporte, he coauthored *Understanding Our Biblical and Early Christian Tradition*.

CLYDE WILCOX is Associate Professor of Government at Georgetown University. He the author of numerous scholarly publications, including *God's Warriors: The Christian Right in Twentieth Century America*. He is the coauthor, with Ted G. Jelen and Elizabeth Adell Cook, of *Between Two Absolutes: Public Opinion and the Politics of Abortion*.

ISBN 0-275-95225-8
90000>
EAN
9 780275 952259
HARDCOVER BAR CODE